IMAGES
of America

ROME

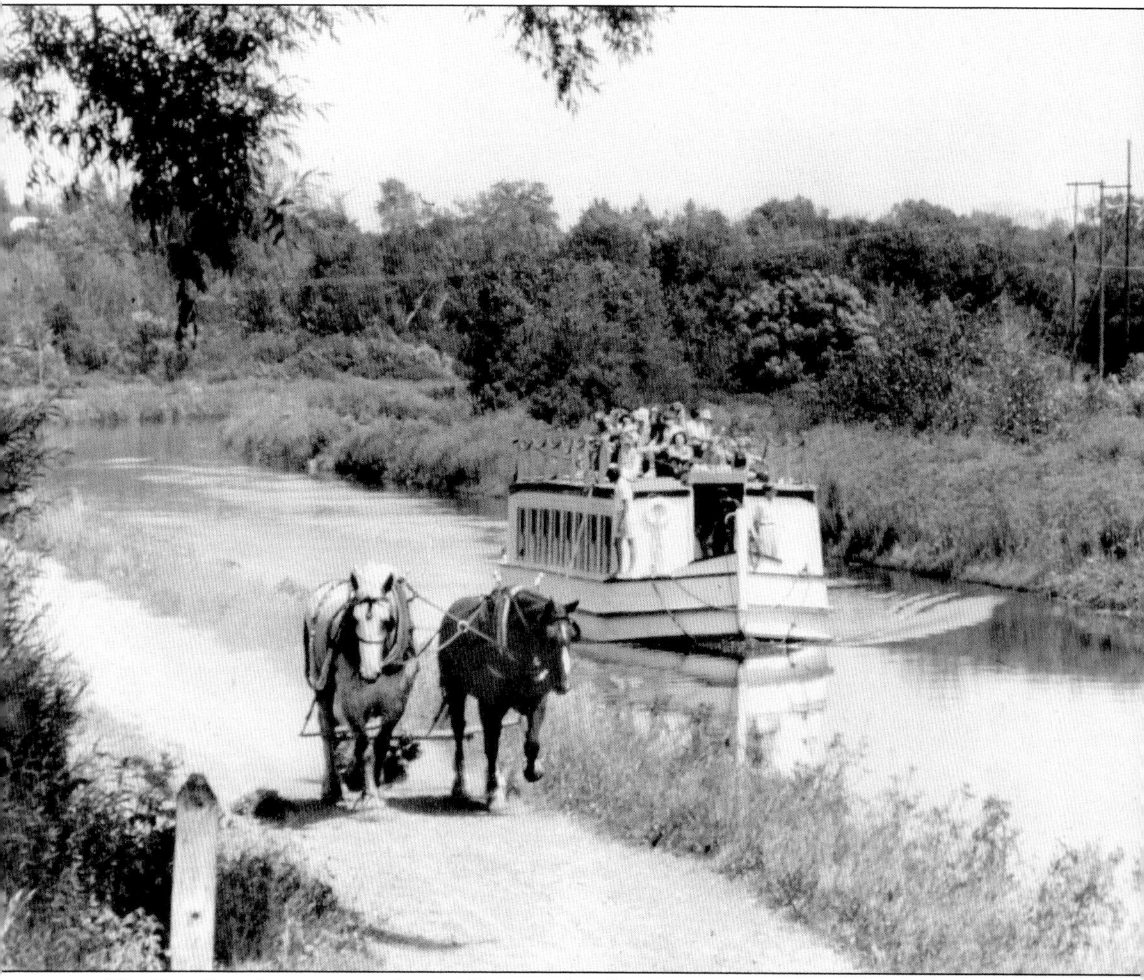

The Erie Canal was a critical part of Rome's development as a city, bringing industry and people to Rome. The original canal actually ran south of the city, but when the canal was improved and enlarged in 1844, the route was altered to run through the city. (RHS.)

IMAGES
of America

ROME

Portia Vescio
and the Rome Historical Society

ARCADIA
PUBLISHING

ISBN 978-0-7385-3499-2

Published by Arcadia Publishing
Charleston, South Carolina

Printed in the United States of America

Library of Congress Catalog Card Number: 2003115049

For all general information contact Arcadia Publishing at:
Telephone 843-853-2070
Fax 843-853-0044
E-mail sales@arcadiapublishing.com
For customer service and orders:
Toll-Free 1-888-313-2665

Visit us on the Internet at www.arcadiapublishing.com

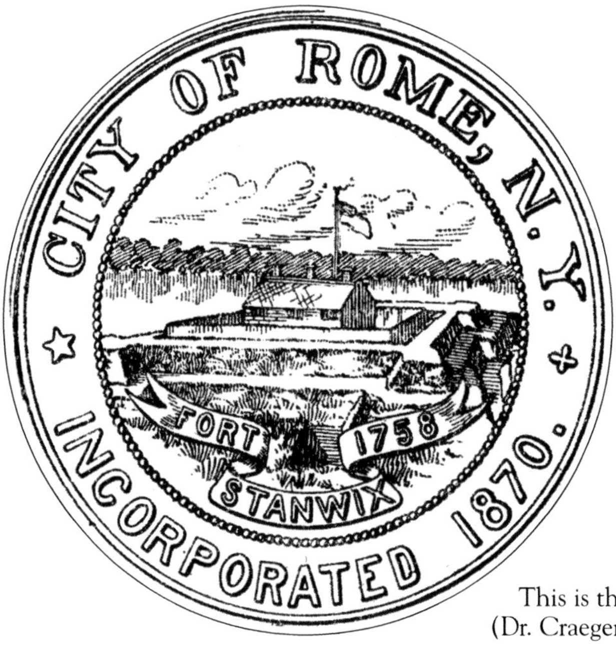

This is the seal of Rome from 1893. (Dr. Craeger Boardman.)

Contents

Acknowledgments

The images in this history come from a variety of sources. The Rome Historical Society is the biggest single donor of images, but contributions from individual members of the community helped enrich the book. Several staff members from the Rome Historical Society assisted with the research process of this book. I would like to thank all staff members involved, and give a special note of thanks to Merry Speicher, Jeni Rizio, and especially Ann Swanson, without whom there would be no book.

The following individual people or businesses donated images to this history: Tony and Val Mario of Margo Studio, Phil and Carol Vescio, Patty Hudak, Sophie Taubert, Dr. Craeger Boardman, Richard Wilson, Bill Guglielmo and the Rome Area Chamber of Commerce, and Steven Beach. Joseph Vescio and Melody Kiepert Milewski deserve extra thanks for the lengths they took to find images and information to make this a better history.

The following people also helped with research, publicity, and encouragement: Rosemary Maio, Carl and Sue Eilenberg, the staff of the Jervis Public Library, Matthew Fidler of the Rome City School District, Alyssa Brown, Kathy Perez, Terri Geitgey, and Deborah and Hugh Grounds.

Credits have been placed at the end of each caption image to identify the image donor. The Rome Historical Society has been abbreviated as RHS for these identifications. A digital copy of all images used in this book has been placed in the Rome Historical Society. The historical portion of the introduction was provided by the Rome Historical Society.

INTRODUCTION

The first people to live in the area now known as Rome were the Oneidas. Part of the Six Nations, which included the Mohawk, Onondaga, Seneca, Cayuga, and Tuscarora, they called this area *De-O-Wain-Sta* or the "Great Carrying Place." The name referred to the two-mile trek between the Mohawk River and Wood Creek that required boats to be portaged. Part of an important route that linked the Atlantic Ocean with the Great Lakes, Rome became attractive to the English and the French who were involved in the fur trade by the 1600s.

The English began building forts in the 1750s to protect themselves from French attack. They built seven defensive structures including Fort Stanwix and Fort Bull. In 1756, Fort Bull was destroyed and its inhabitants massacred by the French. Following the French and Indian War, the forts lacked further strategic importance and were abandoned.

After the Declaration of Independence in 1776, the American colonists rebuilt Fort Stanwix and renamed it Fort Schuyler after one of their generals. One of the great battles of the Revolutionary War took place at this fort. Under Col. Peter Gansevoort, the American troops and their Oneida allies fought off a 21-day British siege in August 1777. After this defeat and that of the Battle of Oriskany, Gen. Barry St. Leger retreated with his British troops and Native American allies. However, Fort Schuyler's glory days were short-lived; following the Revolutionary War, the fort was once again abandoned.

In 1786, Dominick Lynch purchased 697 acres known as the Expense Lot of the Oriskany Patent. By 1800, he had amassed 2,000 acres. Calling the town in the middle of the lot Lynchville, he even had a grid map laid out by English engineer William Weston. Lynch's policy of leasing the land rather than selling it inhibited the city's growth in the early years. Initially a market town to supply local farmers, the town was incorporated in 1819 as the village of Rome, following the trend of naming settlements after classical places. Rome became a city in 1870.

For the community to grow, it was necessary that it be located on a transportation route to major markets. On July 4, 1817, Gov. DeWitt Clinton of New York turned the first shovelful of dirt for the Erie Canal at Rome. Unfortunately, the canal ran half a mile south of Rome, so the town did not reap immediate benefits like other communities. Not until 1839, with the coming of the railway through Rome, and the 1844 relocation of the Erie Canal through the center of town, did the city truly being to prosper. In 1851, the Black River Canal opened, linking Lyon Falls in the north with Rome and the Erie Canal, which made the major markets accessible to area farmers.

Good transportation opened Rome to new industries including knitting mills, canning factories, soap manufacturers, a locomotive works, ironworks, and later, copper mills and wire manufacturers. Rome Iron Works, founded in 1863, converted to brass manufacturing in 1878, when railroad tracks began to be made from steel instead of iron. Gradually beginning to produce copper, Rome Iron Works changed its name in 1890 to Rome Brass and Copper Company. It was this company and Rome Manufacturing Company, established in 1892, that later joined other companies in 1929 to form Revere Copper and Brass, which became headquartered in Rome. This large corporation, famous for Revere Ware pots and pans and its Art Deco pieces of the 1930s, helped make Rome known as "the Copper City." In its heyday before World War II, one-tenth of copper in this country was produced in Rome, resulting in spin-off companies such as the Rome-Turney Radiator Company.

English immigrant Nicholas Spargo brought wire making to Rome and to this country in 1883, when he founded the Electric Wire Works. With the addition of such companies as Spargo Wire, General Cable, and Rome Cable, Rome became one of the main manufacturing sectors in this industry. Like many other communities in the Northeast, Rome was hit during the 1950s through the 1970s with the migration of the manufacturing sector to the South because of lower operating costs. Today, only a few industries remain.

Another economic-shaping force for this community came in February 1942, when the Rome Air Depot opened under the U.S. Army Air Force as an aircraft supply, repair, and training base. At its peak during World War II, it employed more than 9,000 civilians. Following the war, like other wartime bases, the Rome Air Depot downsized dramatically and became a storage facility. Scheduled to close, it received a reprieve in 1948, when Watson Laboratories moved to Rome from New Jersey. Renamed Rome Air Development Center (RADC), the former Watson Laboratories became one of the major research facilities of the U.S. Air Force. Also in September 1948, the base was renamed Griffiss Air Force Base after Buffalo native Lt. Col. Townsend Griffiss, who was the first U.S. airman killed in the European theater of World War II. In September 1995, Griffiss became one of the military bases realigned with a loss of almost 5,000 personnel.

Today, Rome is focused on revitalization, using the new Griffiss Business and Technology Park, with several military units at its core including the Research Information Directorate (former Rome Laboratory), the Northeast Air Defense Sector (NEADS), and Defense Finance and Accounting Services (DFAS). Rome made history by hosting at the former base the Woodstock '99, attended by more than 250,000 people from around the world.

This book tells the chronological history of Rome. While there are many historical facts and persons presented in the book, it is by no means a comprehensive history. The book is divided into four chapters to represent different periods of Rome's development. The first chapter, "A Rich History," looks at Rome before 1870. Some topics included in this chapter are Rome's involvement in the Revolutionary War, the early canals, the development of the railroad, and some of the early industries in Rome.

The second chapter, "A City Emerges," deals with period from 1870, when Rome became a city, up to the 1930s. Photographs in this chapter spotlight the early city buildings and fire department, new industries, local businesses, and the building of the Delta Dam and the Barge Canal.

Chapter Three, "The Copper Age," examines the development and growth of Rome as a city and as an industrial center. This chapter includes several photographs of downtown Rome, the Griffiss Air Force Base, and major industries such as Revere Copper and Brass. This chapter also includes images of a number of new schools and hospitals and the growing shopping and recreational areas.

Chapter Four, "Looking Forward, Looking Back," opens with the urban renewal program of the late 1960s and goes to the present time. This chapter looks at the buildings torn down for the creation of Fort Stanwix National Park and the new buildings that were created. Other main points of the chapter include major events such as Woodstock '99 and the closing of Griffiss Air Force Base. The chapter ends by looking at Rome's efforts at bringing in new industry.

One

A Rich History

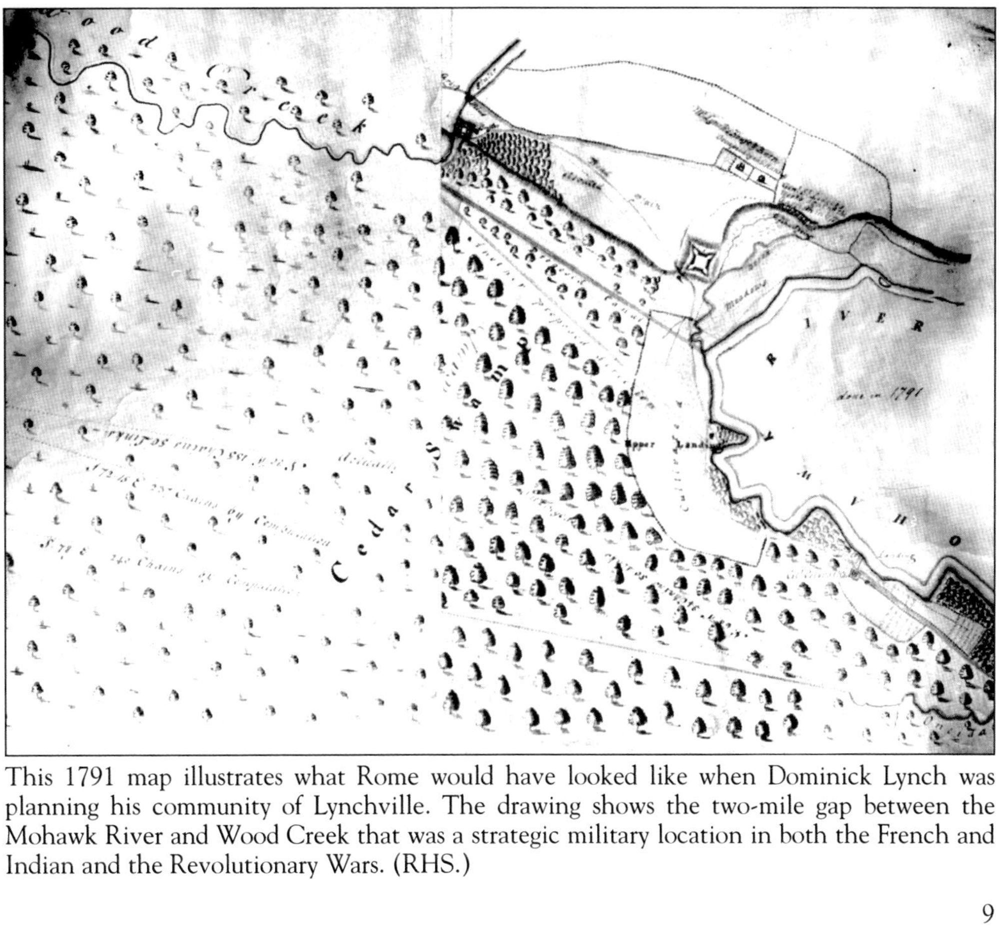

This 1791 map illustrates what Rome would have looked like when Dominick Lynch was planning his community of Lynchville. The drawing shows the two-mile gap between the Mohawk River and Wood Creek that was a strategic military location in both the French and Indian and the Revolutionary Wars. (RHS.)

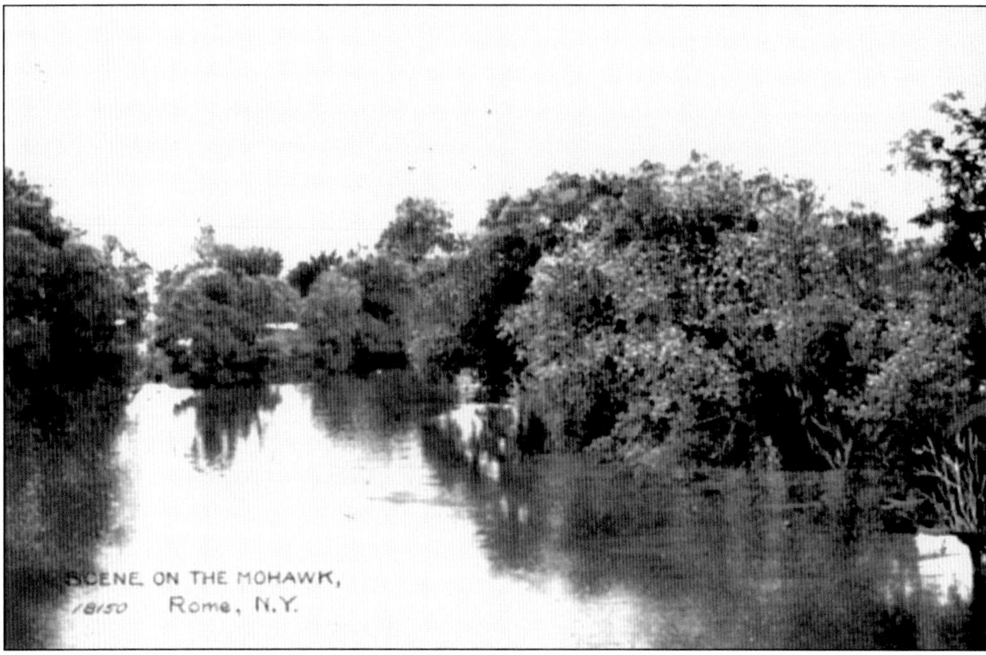

The city of Rome was built over an ancient route used by travelers and traders. It was here, in the two-mile gap between the Mohawk River and Wood Creek, that travelers between the Great Lakes and the Atlantic Ocean had to carry their belongings over land. (Richard Wilson.)

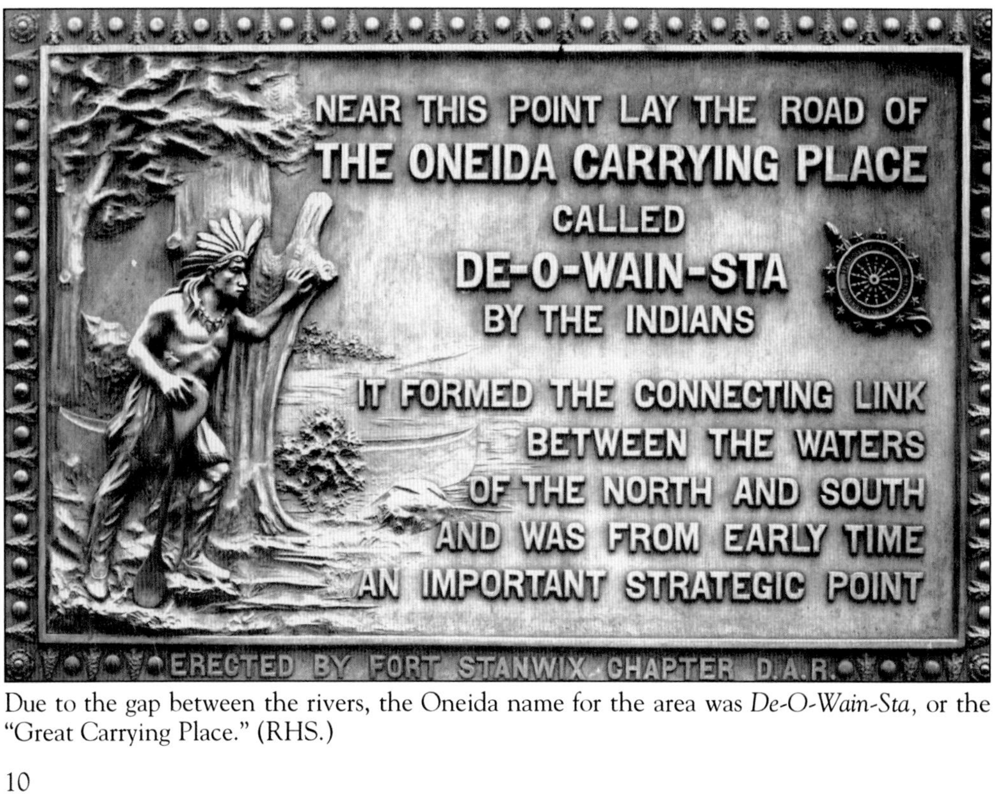

Due to the gap between the rivers, the Oneida name for the area was *De-O-Wain-Sta*, or the "Great Carrying Place." (RHS.)

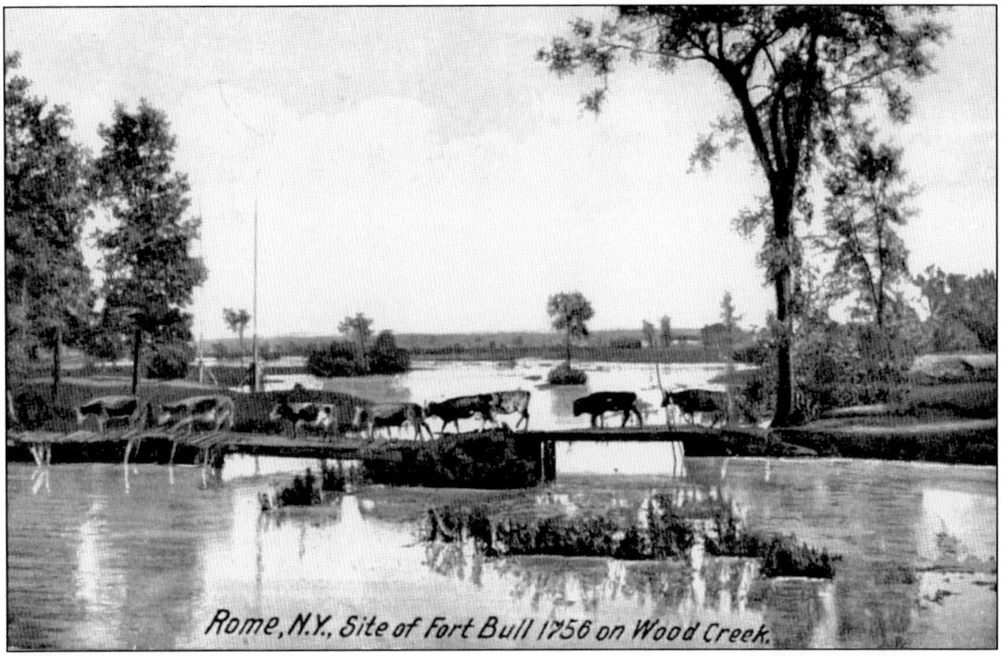

The English built Fort Bull on the Lower Landing Place on Wood Creek during the French and Indian War. Shortly after its creation, the French destroyed the fort. (Richard Wilson.)

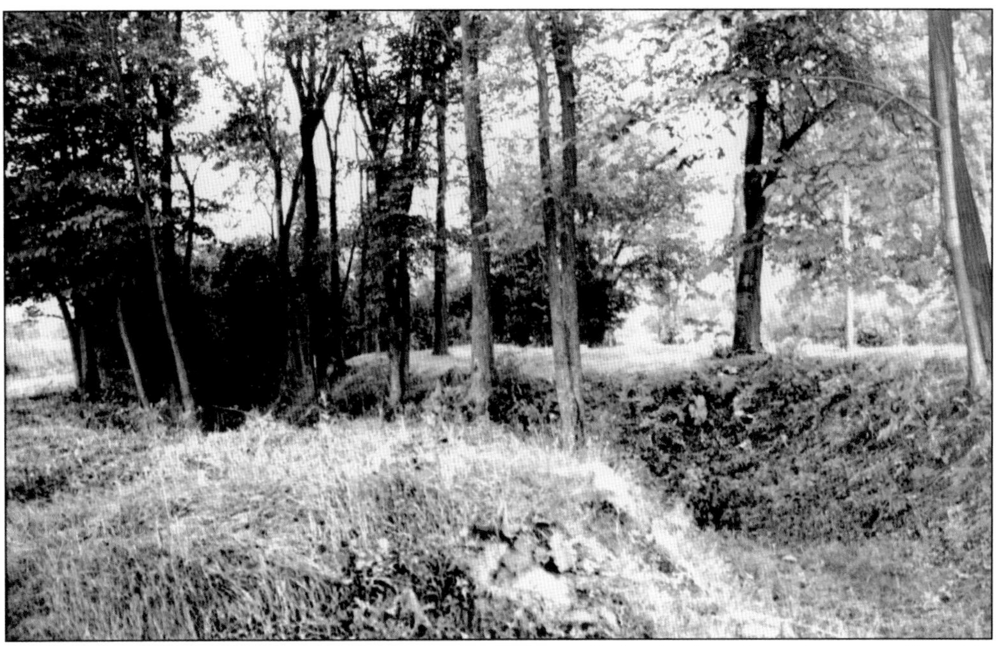

This photograph, taken in 1960, shows the moat of Fort Bull, which is the only trace still visible today. This site is currently under the management of the Rome Historical Society. (RHS.)

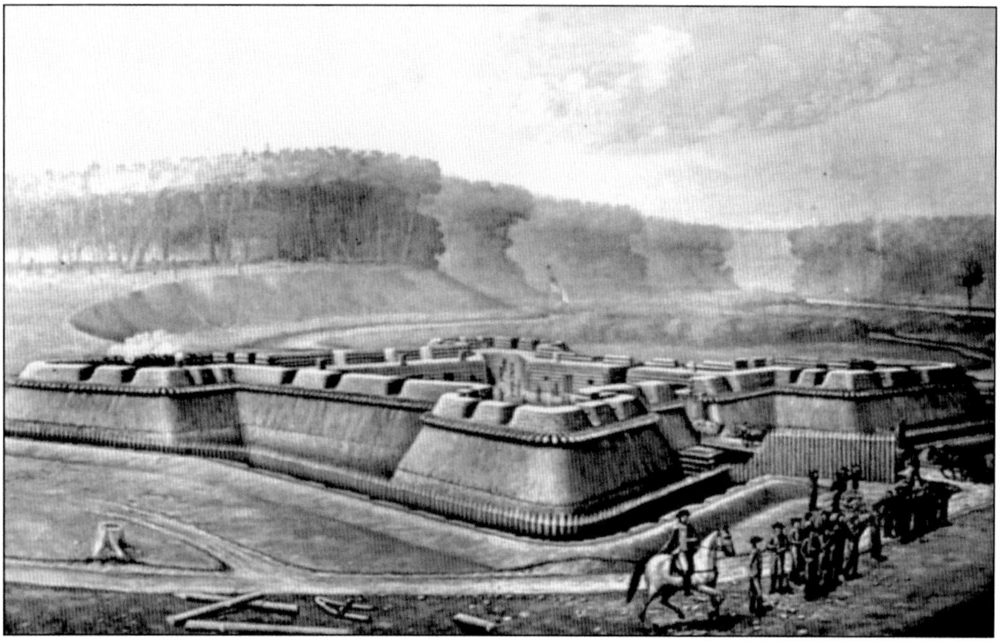

This 1897 painting by Peter F. Hugunine and commissioned by the Destito family shows Fort Stanwix as it was in 1777, at the time it was under siege by the British. Under the command of Col. Peter Gansevoort, the fort withstood the siege for 21 days before reinforcements arrived and British forces retreated. (Margo Studio.)

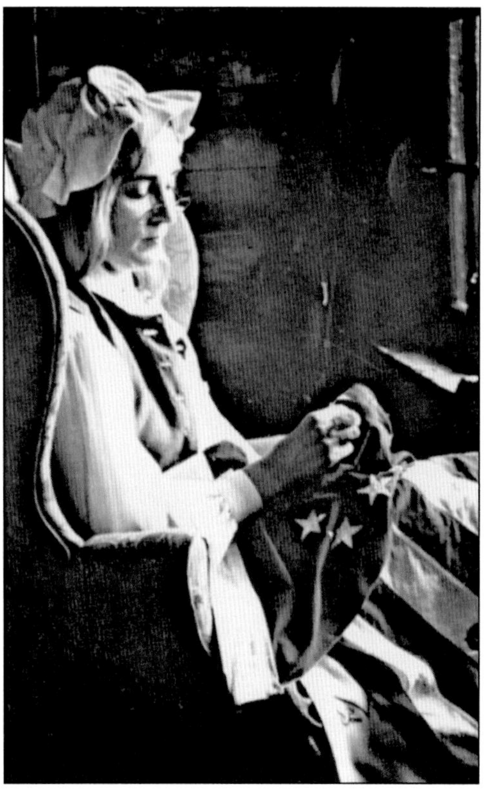

It is believed that the siege of Fort Stanwix was the first time the new American flag was flown in battle. A camlet cloak taken from a British officer was used for the union blue, regulation army shirts were used for the white stripes, and it is believed that a woman's flannel petticoat was used for the red stripes. A reenactor portrays a Revolutionary era housewife sewing her flag. (Margo Studio.)

The battle of Oriskany is considered the bloodiest battle of the Revolutionary War. Gen. Barry St. Leger and his British forces ambushed Gen. Nicholas Herkimer, his militiamen, and their Oneida allies on their way to provide reinforcement to the colonists at the siege at Fort Stanwix. Herkimer's troops were cut down, and Herkimer, himself, died a few days after the battle from a leg wound. This monument was erected on the battlefield and dedicated in 1884. (Richard Wilson.)

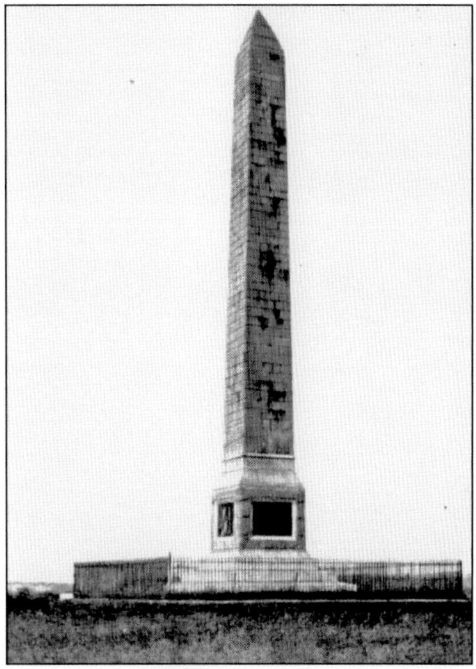

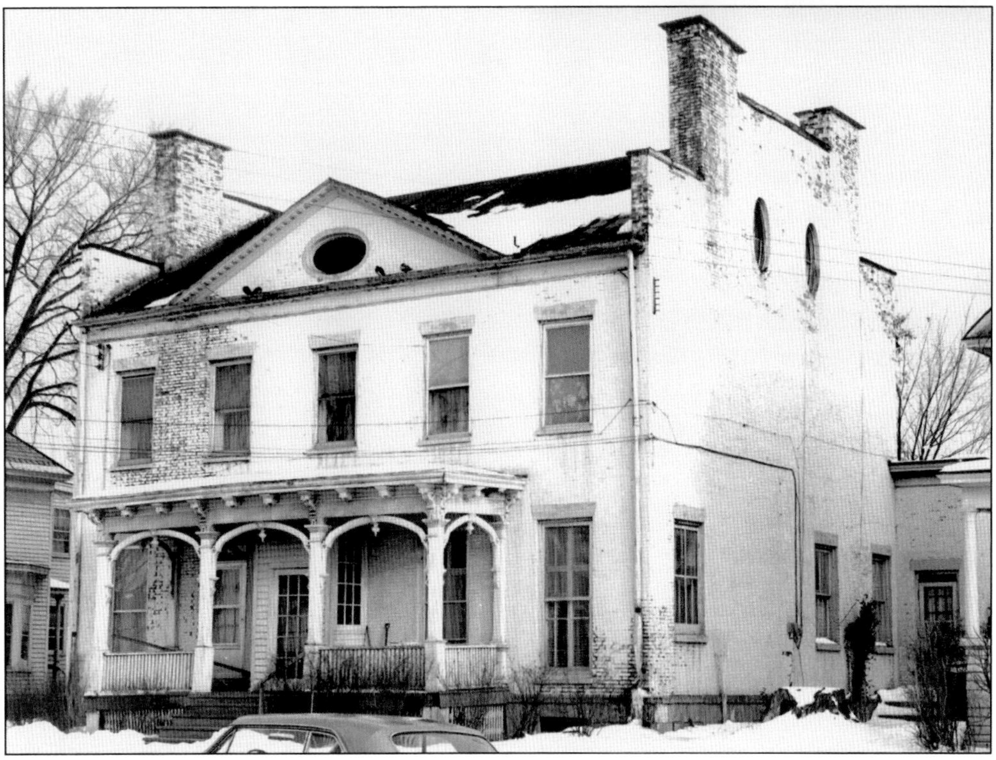

Prior to the War of 1812, the U.S. government began building arsenals in various states. Two were built in New York: one in Rome and one in Watervliet. The arsenal was maintained until 1873, when the properties were sold. The above building, which housed the officers, still stands today on the north side of Dominick Street. (RHS.)

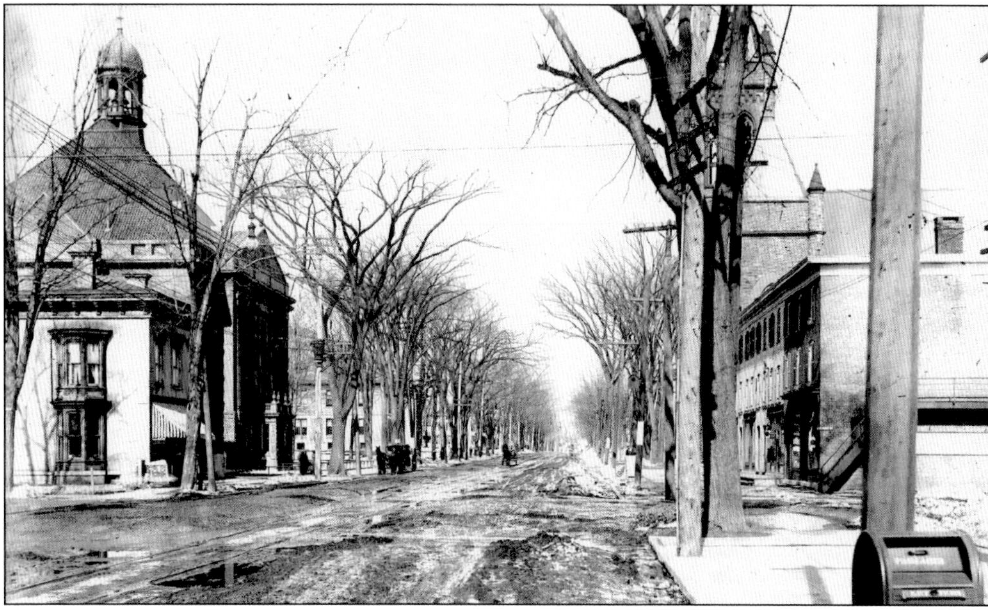

In 1786, New York City merchant Liberty Lynch purchased land in upstate New York with the plan of developing a community. Lynch wanted the name of the town to be Lynchville, but citizens voted on the classical name Rome, after the fashion of the time. Lynch left a lasting mark on the city, naming the first two streets after himself and his son, James. Shown is the corner of James and Dominick Streets. (RHS.)

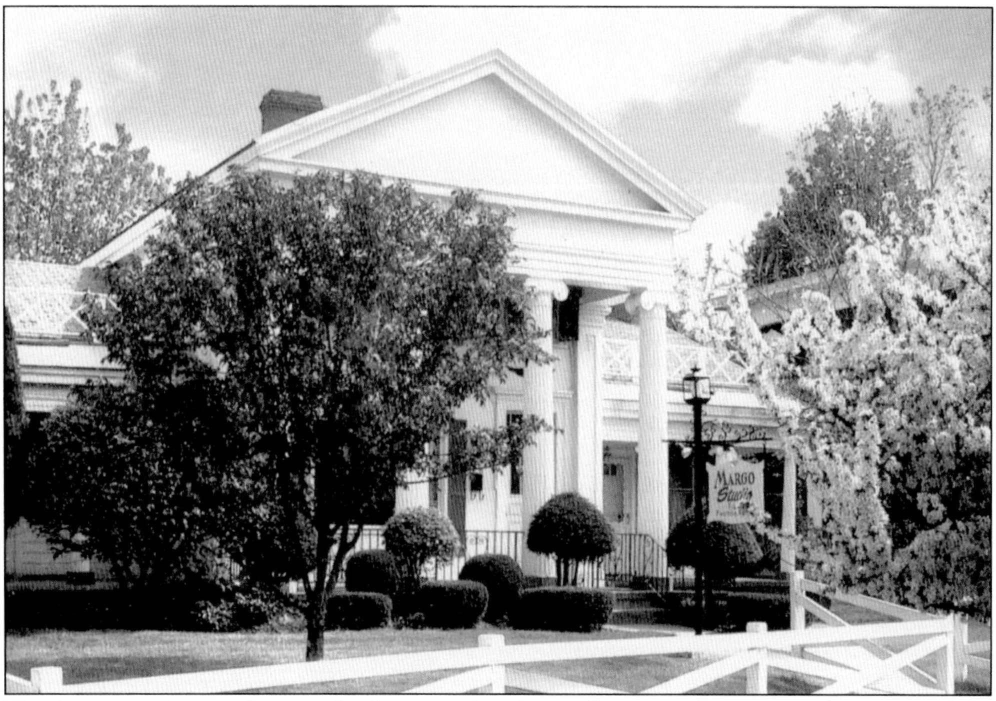

This house on Stanwix Street, which is now the place of business of Margo Studio, is one of the last remaining authentic Colonial structures in the area. Dating back to 1789, the building was already considered a landmark when early log roads were built. (Margo Studio.)

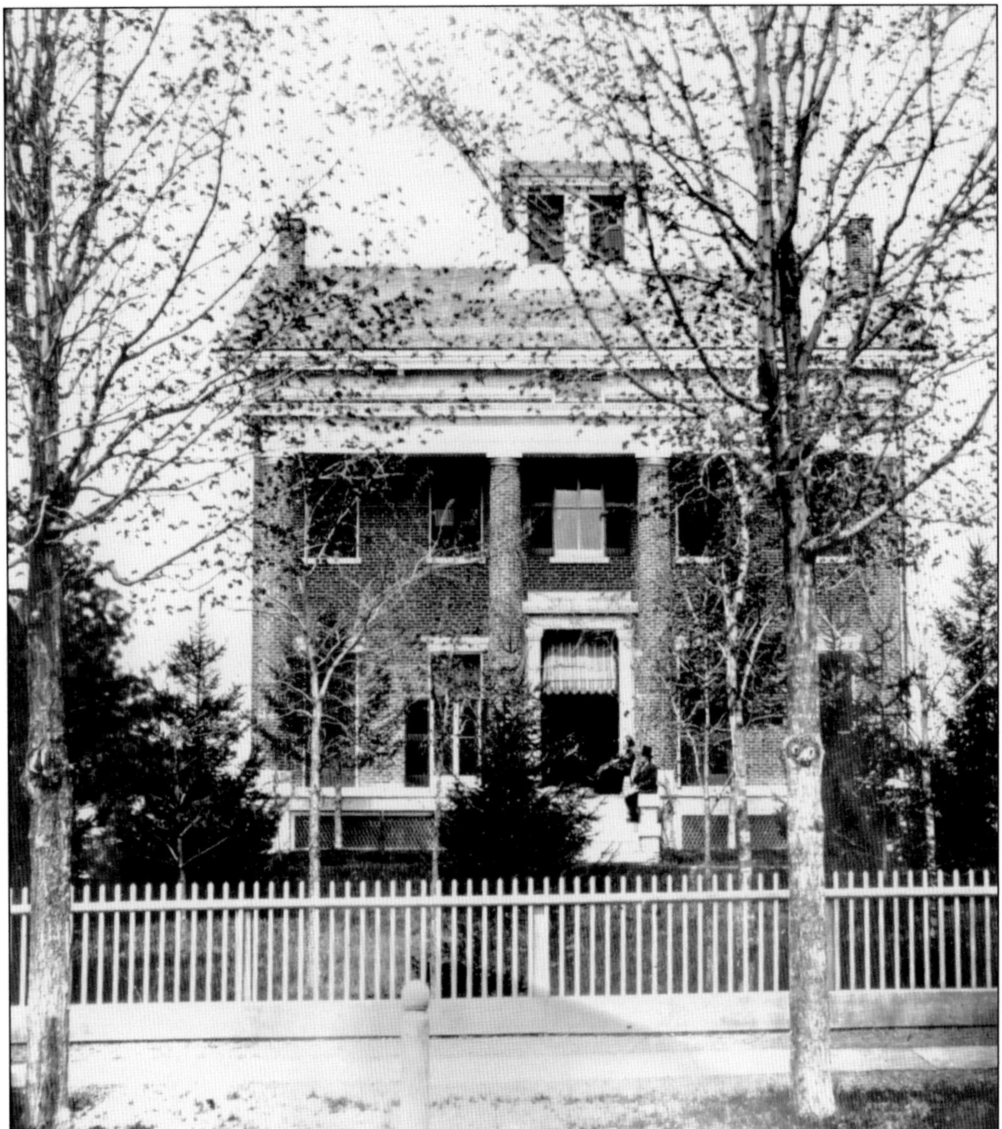

John B. Jervis and his wife are seen sitting on their front porch. During his life, Jervis was one of Rome's leading citizens. He was an engineer on the Erie Canal and built the Utica and Schenectady Railroad. Upon his death in 1885, Jervis bequeathed his house to be used as the public library, which opened in 1895 and is still open today. (RHS.)

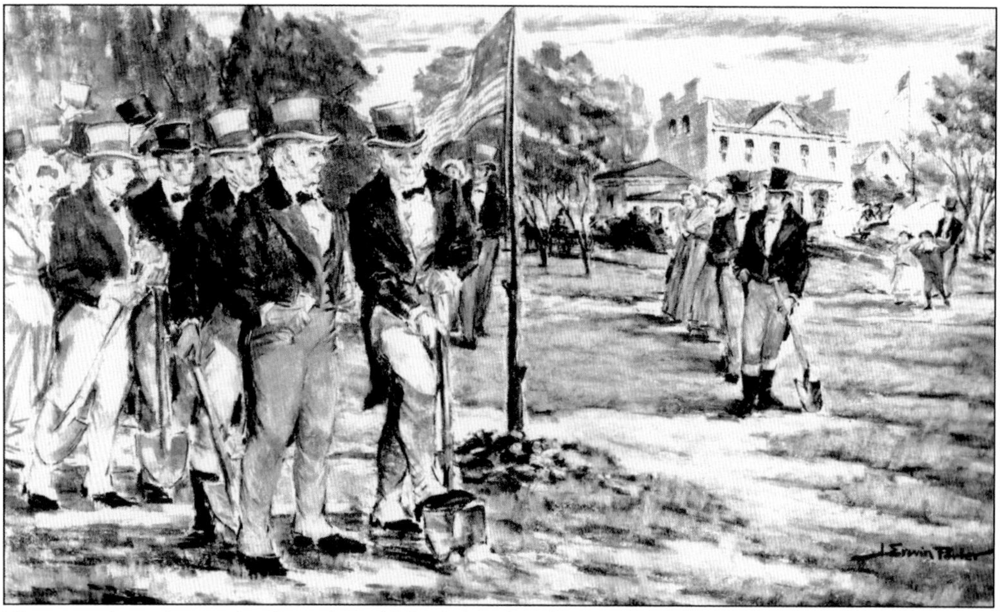

This woodcut shows the first shovelful of dirt for the Erie Canal being dug by Gov. DeWitt Clinton of New York on July 4, 1817, in Rome. As the geographic center of New York State, Rome was an ideal location for the start of the engineering marvel, which was to connect Albany and Buffalo by waterway. (RHS.)

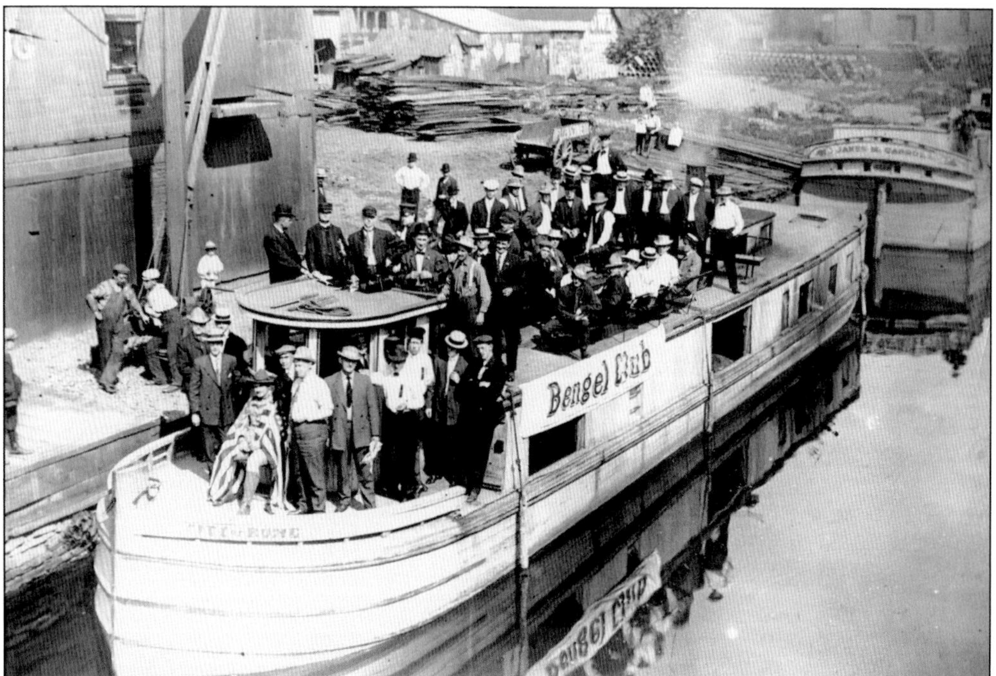

The *City of Rome* was one of the many excursion boats on the Erie Canal. Shown here, the Bengel Club goes on an outing on August 4, 1907.(RHS.)

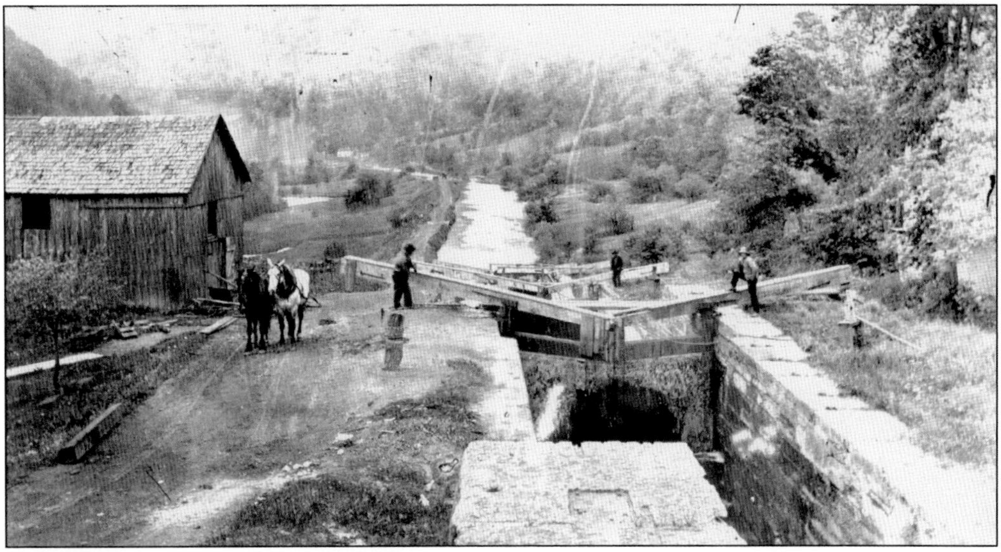

The Black River Canal, completed in 1851, was constructed through the Rome-Boonville Gorge between Rome and Port Leydon where it connected with the Black River. Men can be seen operating the locks. (RHS.)

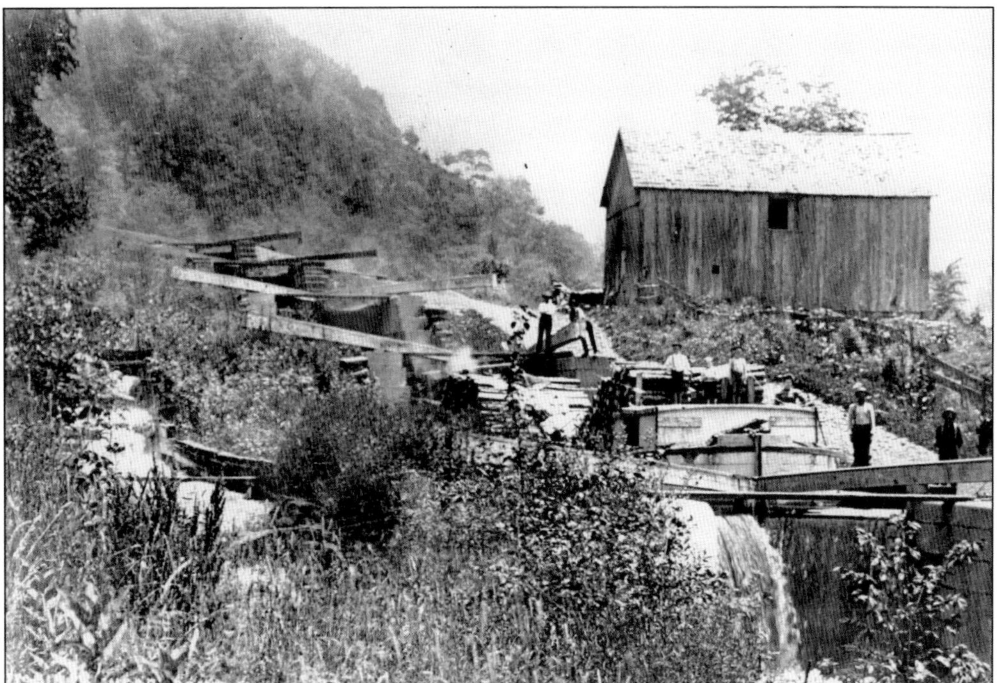

Due to the rapid rise in elevation from Rome to Boonville, the number of locks was both unusual and spectacular for the 25-mile canal as it wound through the gorge. This photograph shows the Five Combines section of the Black River Canal. (RHS.)

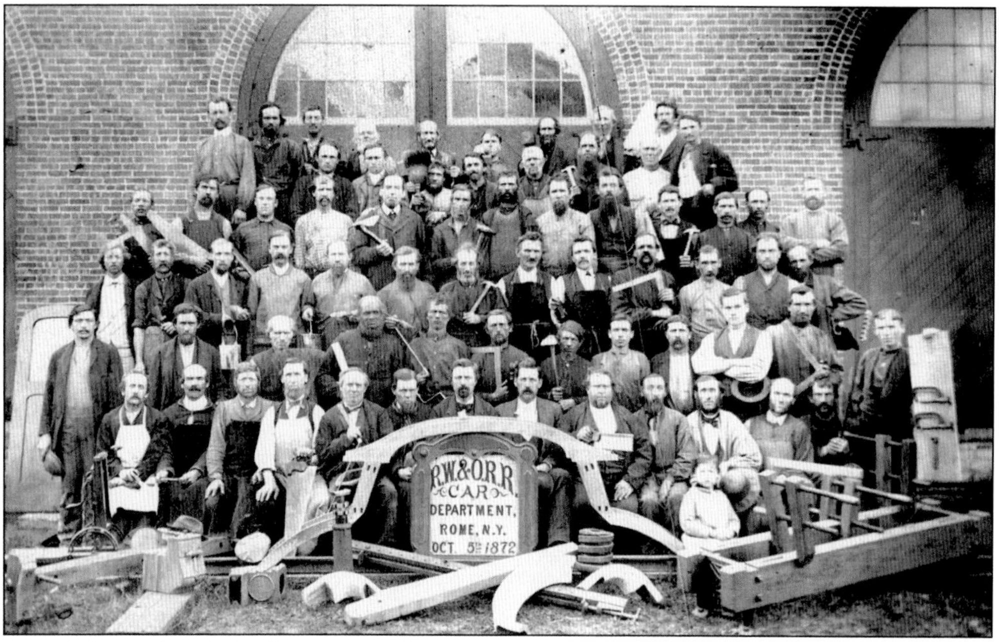

Rome's first railroad, the Syracuse and Utica, ran across the Great Rome Swamp on a trestle. Rome's second railroad started under the name Watertown and Rome Railroad. The line continued little by little until it reached Ogdensburg. The name was eventually changed to the Rome, Watertown, and Ogdensburg Railroad. Workers pose in October 1872. (RHS.)

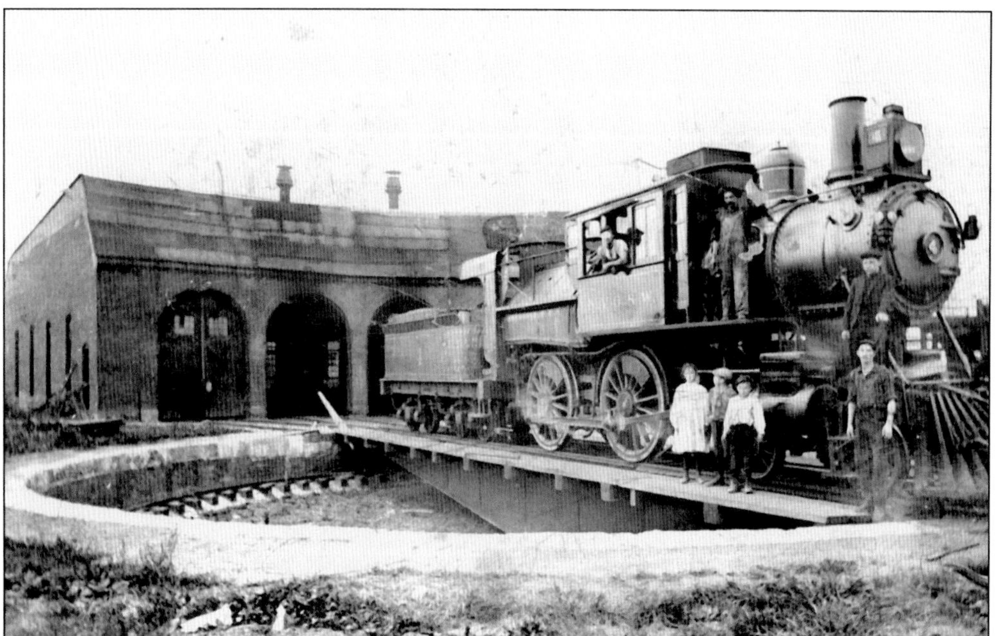

This photograph shows the New York, Ontario, and Western Railroad coming out of the old roundhouse. (RHS.)

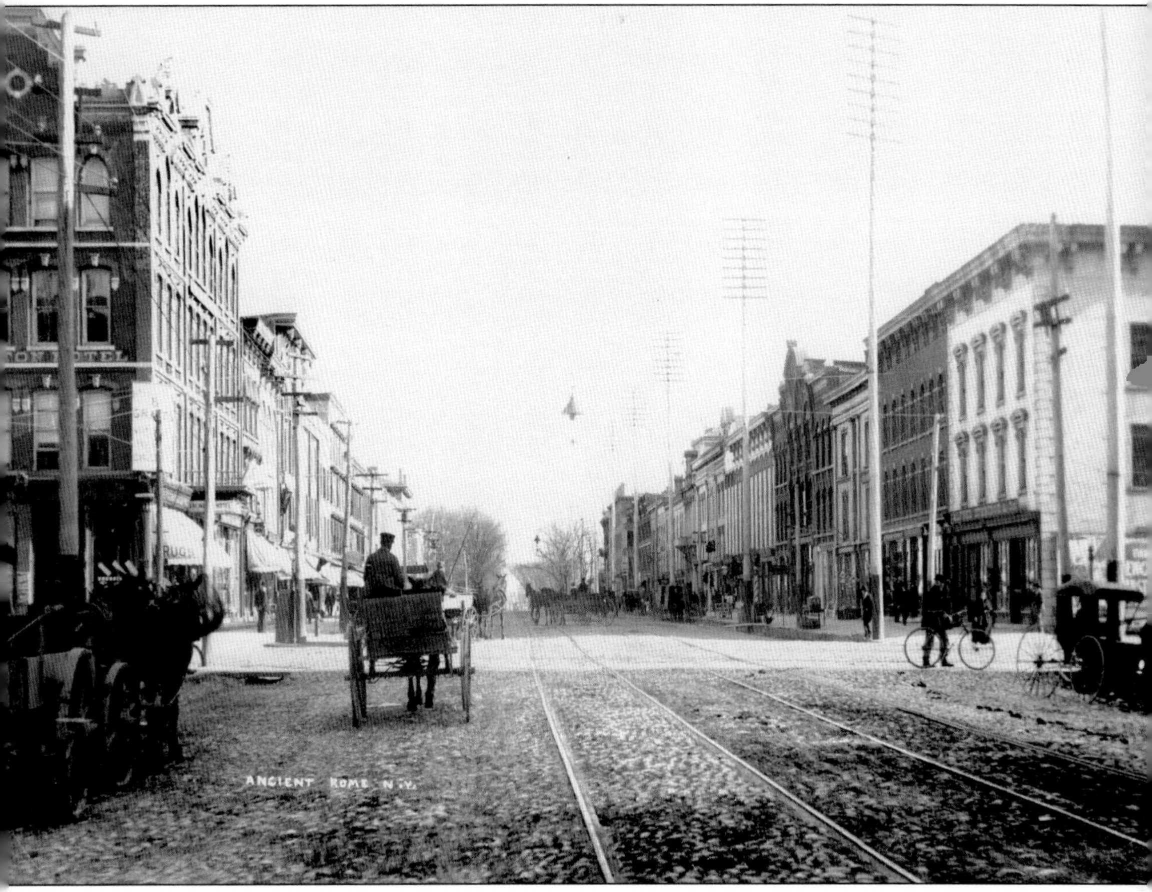

Canals and railways were developed in Rome long before good roads. Here, cobblestones are used to pave a major street. The uneven cobblestone roads were better than muddy trails but still caused damage and injury to carriages and horses. (RHS.)

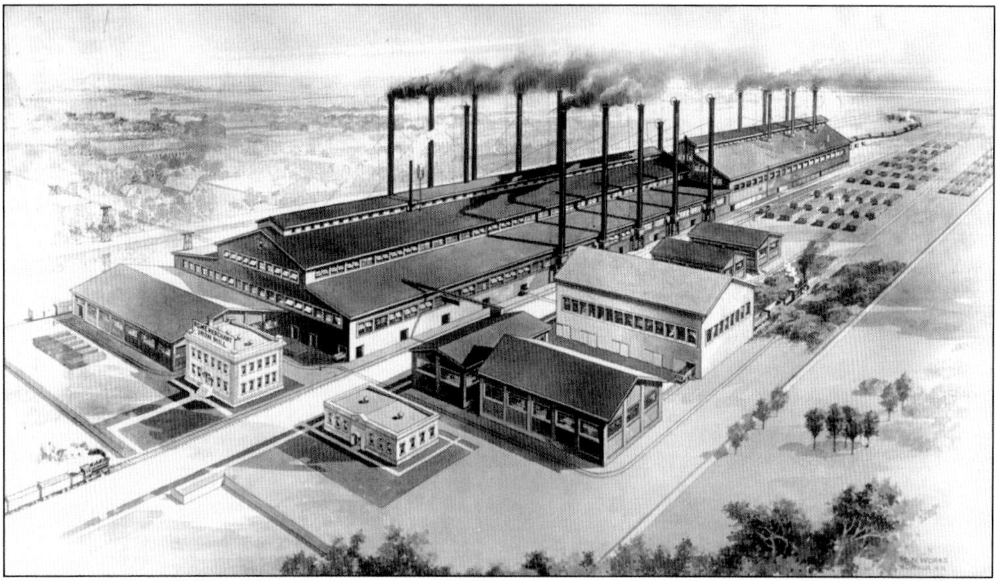

With good transportation and plenty of water for power, industry soon found Rome. Following the success of the Rome Iron Works, the Rome Merchant Iron Mills, above, came into being. The Iron Works focused on the rerolling of iron rails, while the Merchant Mills produced commercial iron, such as rods, bars, and beams. One of the leading forces behind the Merchant Mills was Rome's own John B. Jervis. Below is the building for the Adams Foundry and Machine Shop, located at 108 South George Street, on the Erie Canal. (RHS.)

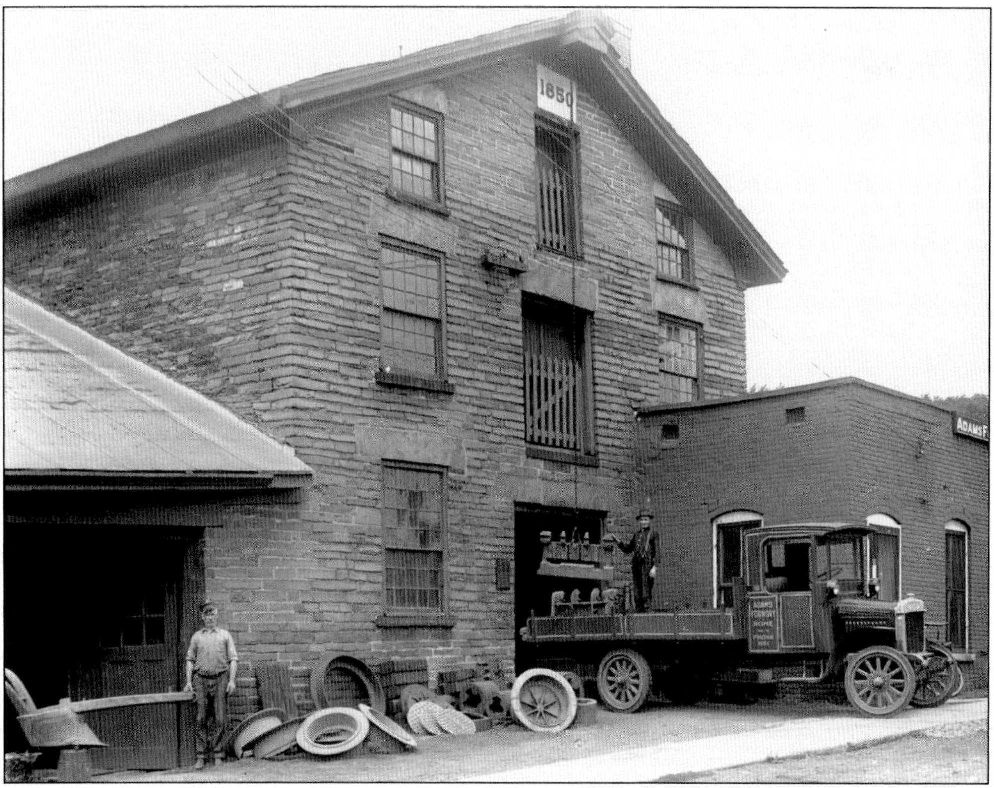

Jesse Williams established the first commercial cheese factory in the United States on May 10, 1851. Until Williams's factory, which took milk from the cow and converted it directly to cheese, factories would buy curd from farmhouses and then convert the curd to cheese. (RHS.)

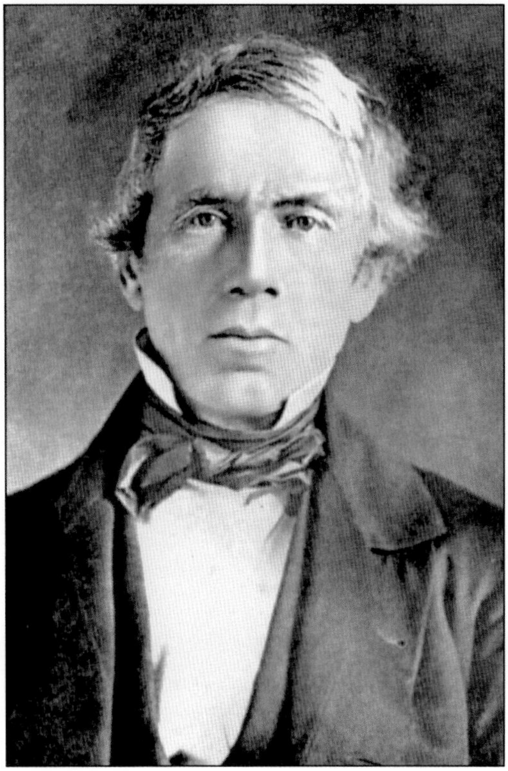

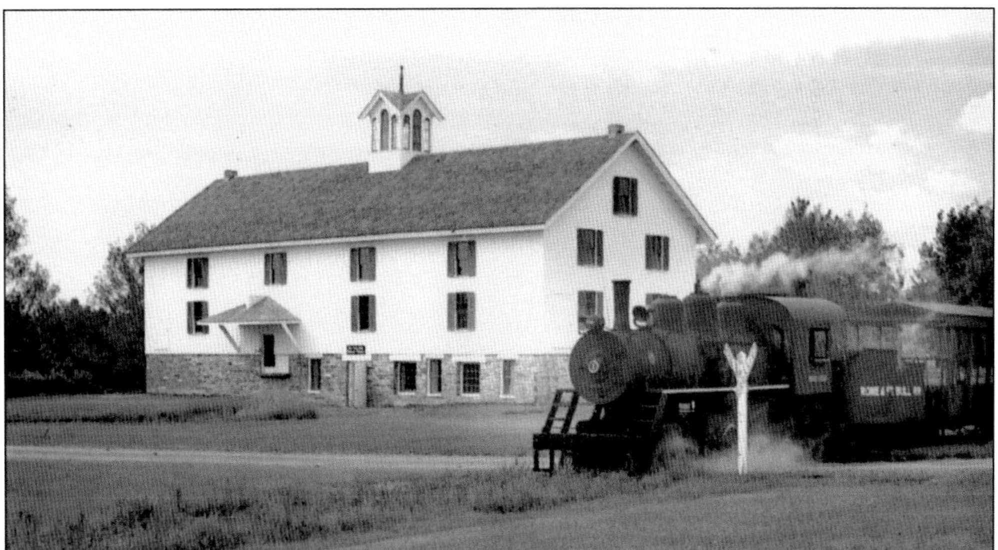

The New York State Museum of Cheese at the Erie Canal Village is seen in the background as the locomotive *Edward J. Nolan* goes past. Tourists can visit the museum and learn the history of cheesemaking as it was in Rome in 1851. (Margo Studio.)

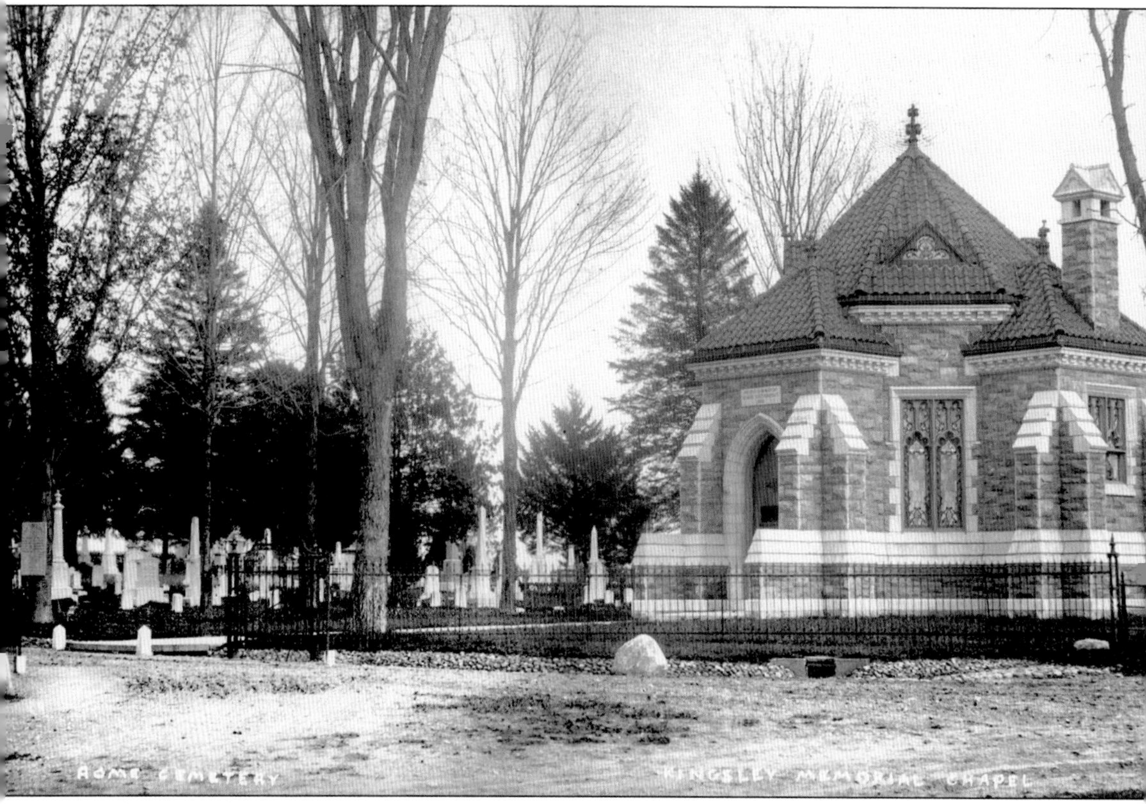

The original Rome Cemetery was located where Stanwix Park is today, at the corner of North James and Turin Streets. By 1870, the cemetery was full, and it officially closed in 1872. A new cemetery was dedicated and consecrated on July 19, 1853. Known as the Rome Cemetery, this burial ground is still in use today and is located on Jervis Avenue. The above photograph shows the Kingsley Memorial Chapel in the Rome Cemetery. Dr. W.J.P. Kingsley gave the chapel to the cemetery in memory of his son, Dr. G. Lyle Kingsley. The architecture is Third Period English Gothic and was designed by J.B. Snook and Sons, the same company that designed New York's Grand Central Depot in 1871. (RHS.)

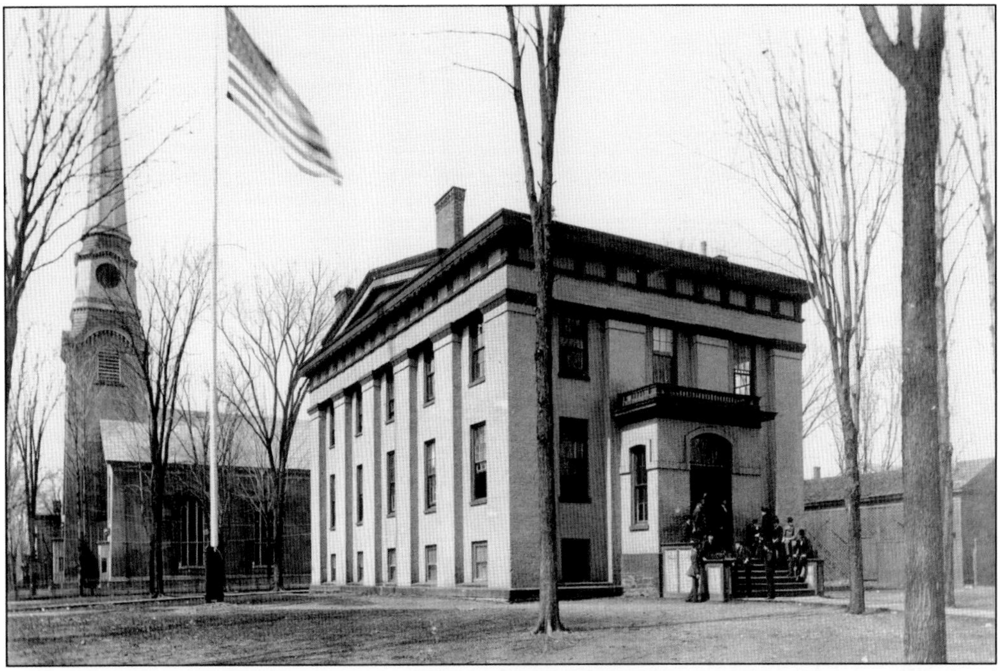

The old academy building was built in 1840 on the west side of James Street between Court and Huntington Streets. In the background is the First Presbyterian Church. In 1869, the Rome free school system began and the Rome Academy became Rome Free Academy. (RHS.)

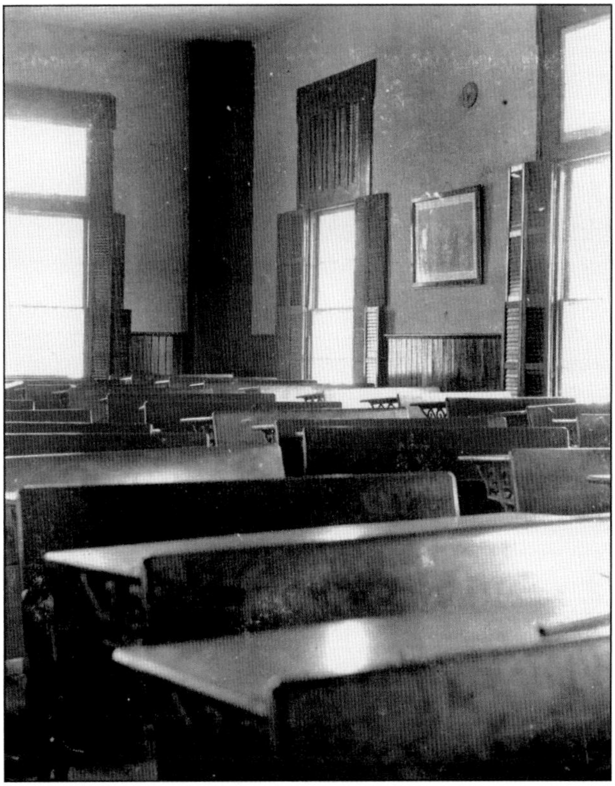

This is an early study room in the old Rome Academy. (RHS.)

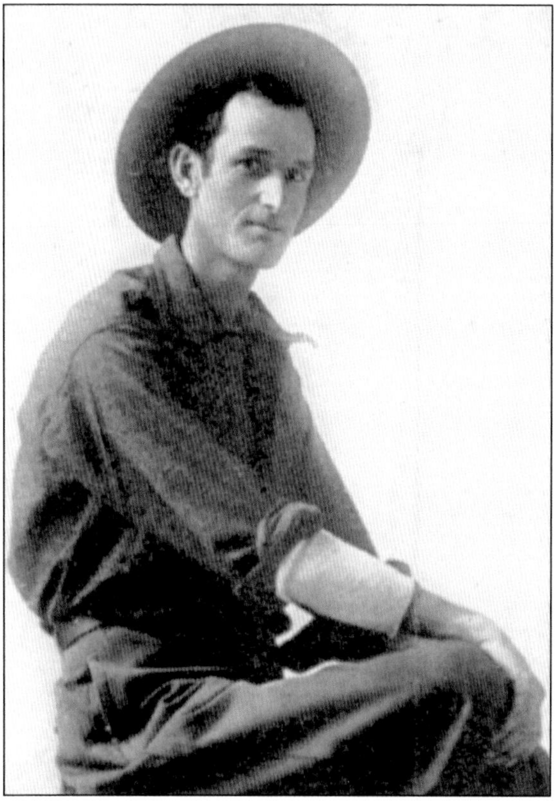

Western author Harold Bell Wright was born in Rome on May 4, 1872. During the first quarter of the 20th century, Wright outsold other American authors and was one of the first people, if not the first person, to become a millionaire by writing novels. (Dr. Craeger Boardman.)

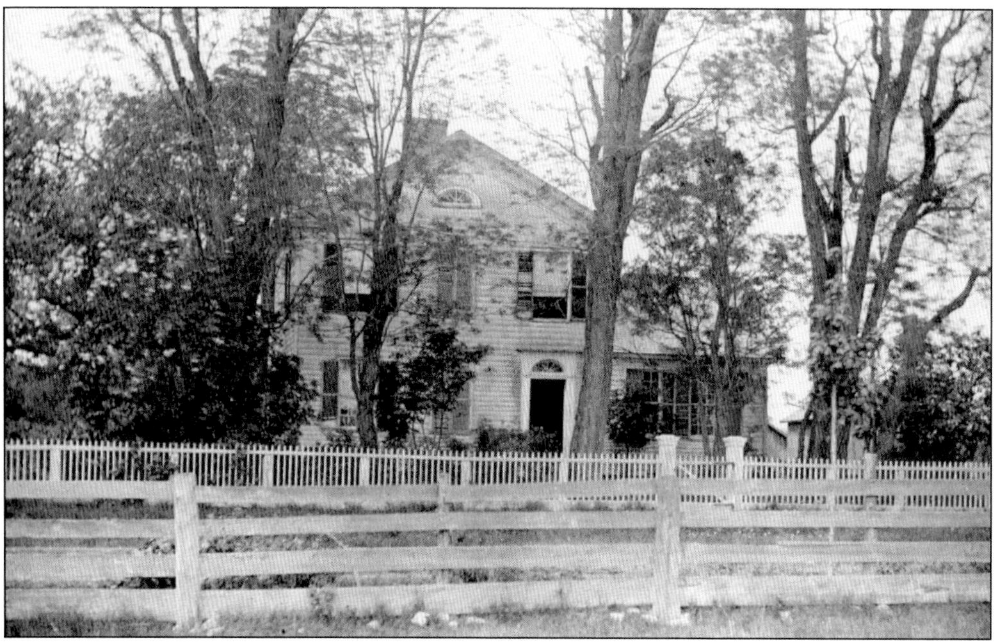

This house was the birthplace of author Harold Bell Wright. (RHS.)

Two

A City Emerges

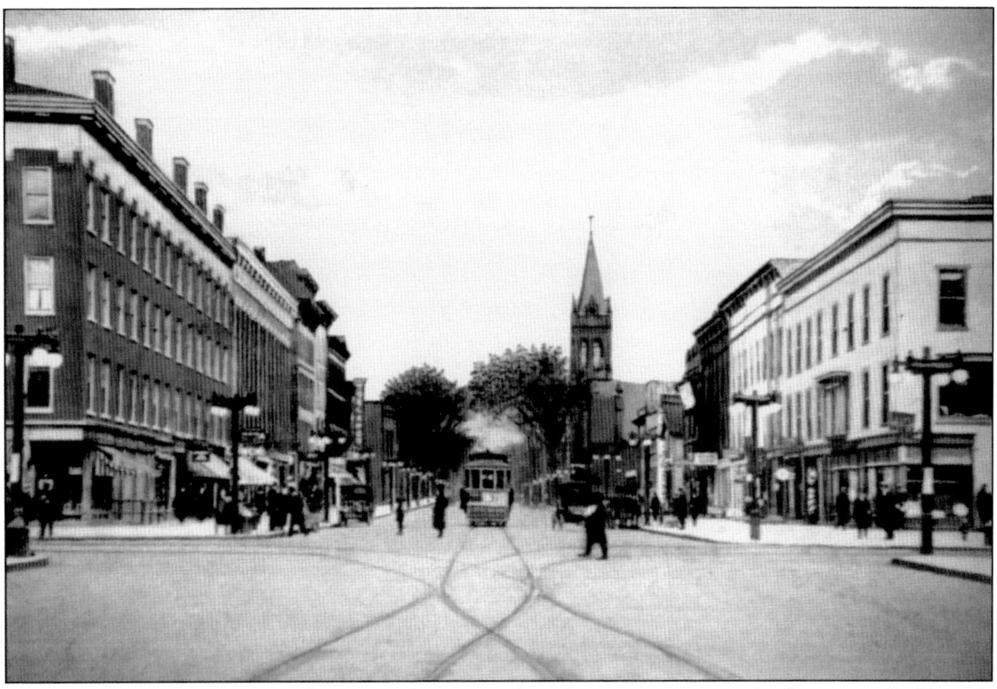

This 1916 view shows North James Street at the American corner, looking north. Rome's population nearly doubled in the decade leading up to 1870, the year Rome became a city. As the city grew, so did the number of local businesses and schools. With canals and railroads running past the city, Rome attracted many industries. By the end of the 1920s, Rome's population more than doubled and the city was a thriving community of 30,000. (RHS.)

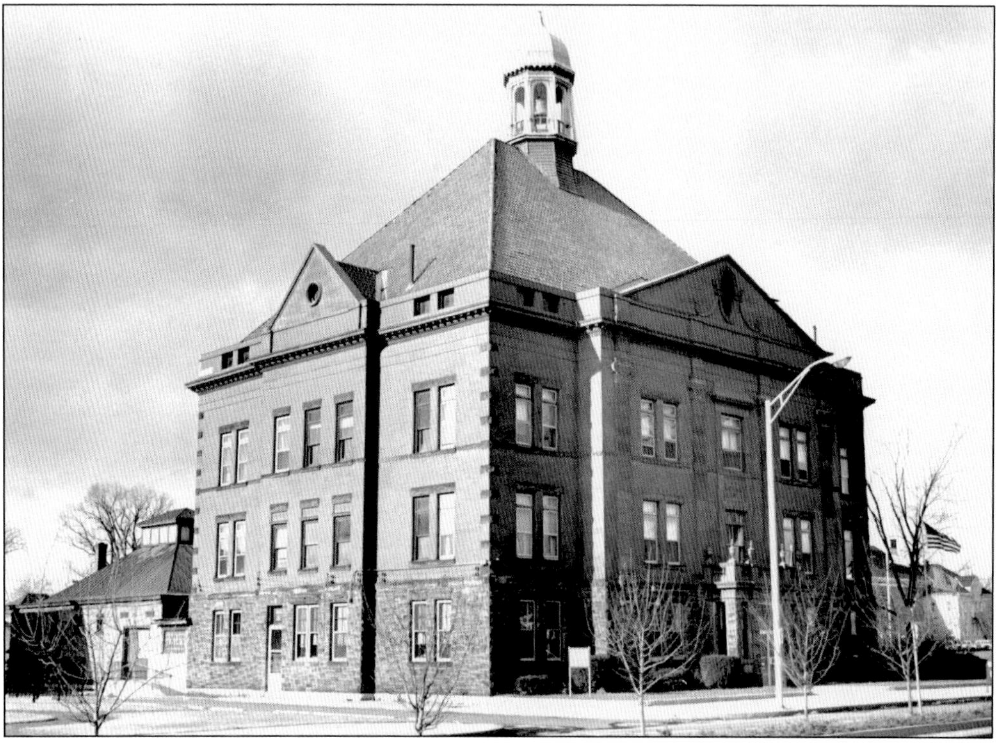

The old city hall building was built at 207 North James Street in 1894 in Dutch Revival–style architecture. Though it is no longer used as the city hall today, it still stands as the headquarters for the Mohawk Valley Community Action Agency. (RHS.)

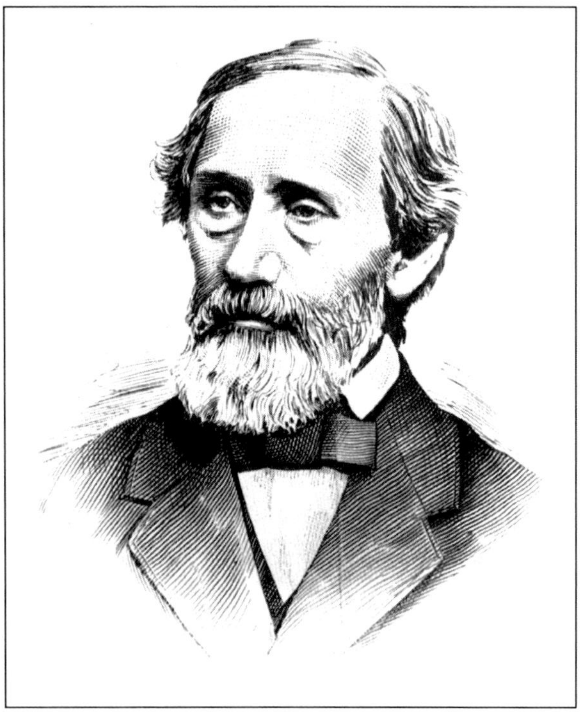

When Rome was incorporated as a city in 1870, it was divided into five wards and Calvert Comstock was elected the first mayor. Comstock was born in 1812 and came to Rome in 1838 to practice law. He moved to Albany for many years but returned to Rome in 1866 to retire. Comstock was one of the individuals instrumental in helping to secure the city charter. (RHS.)

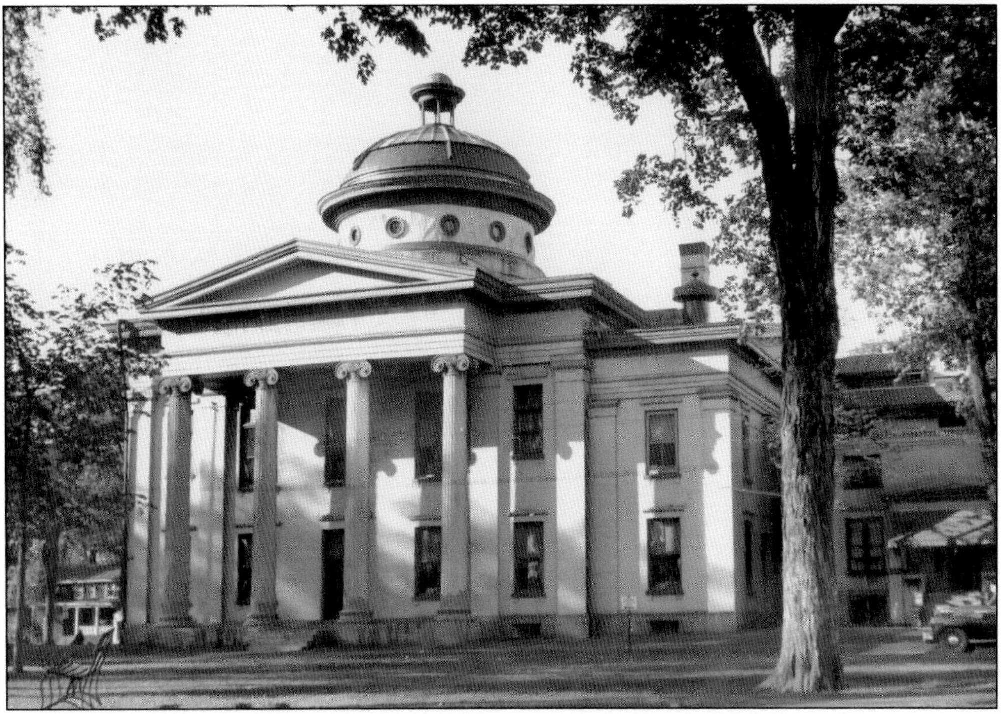

The courthouse was completed in 1851 and is an example of Greek Revival architecture. This building replaced the original courthouse, which was built in 1807 and burned in 1848. The dome was added in 1902. (RHS.)

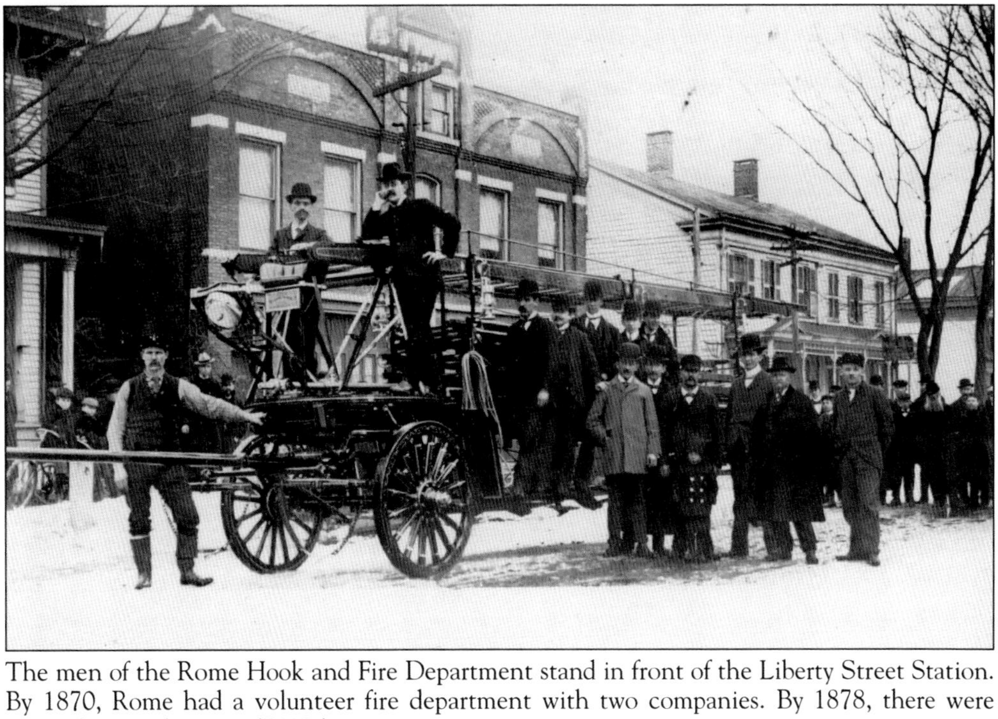

The men of the Rome Hook and Fire Department stand in front of the Liberty Street Station. By 1870, Rome had a volunteer fire department with two companies. By 1878, there were 240 volunteer firemen. (RHS.)

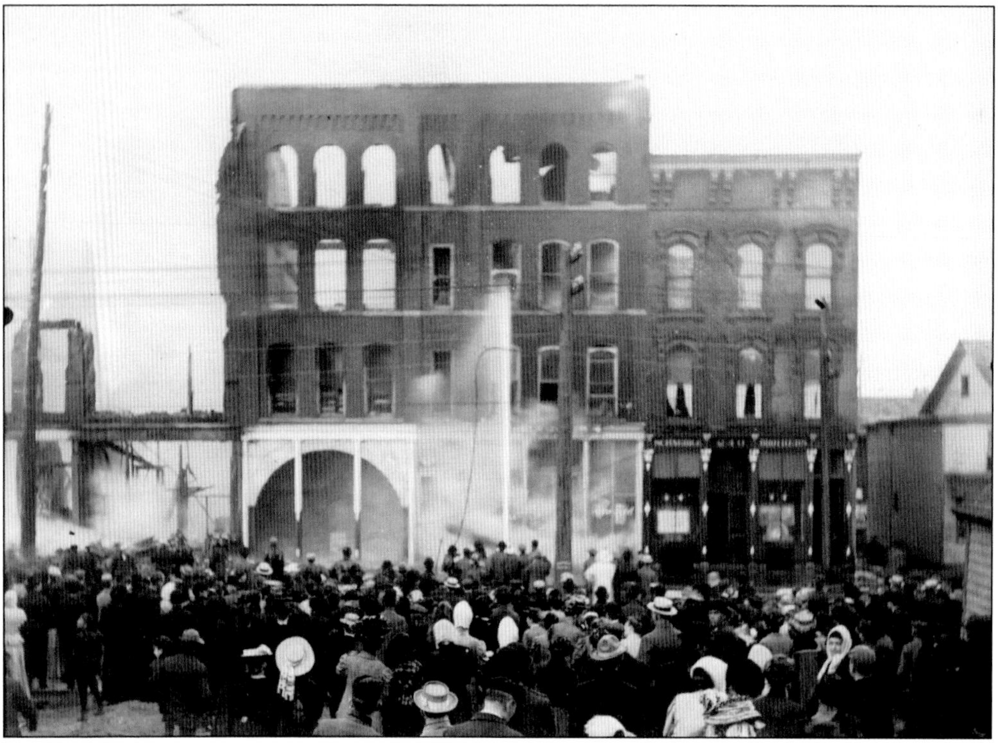

There was quite a need for a fire department in Rome's early years. Here, the department puts out a fire at the corner of Washington and Dominick Streets. (RHS.)

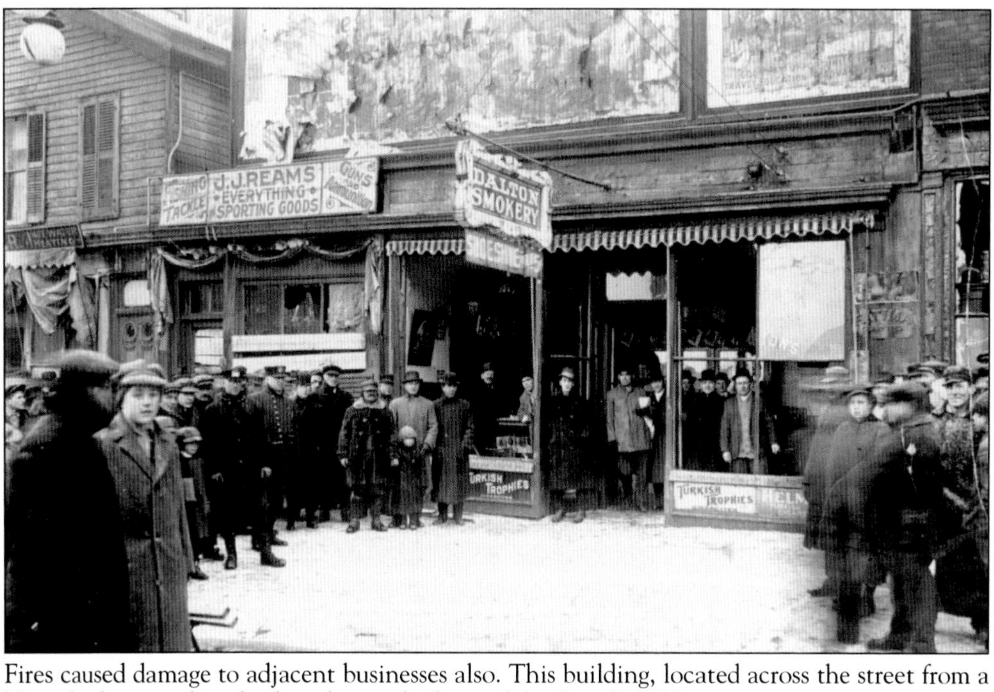

Fires caused damage to adjacent businesses also. This building, located across the street from a blaze, had its windows broken due to the heat of the fire. (RHS.)

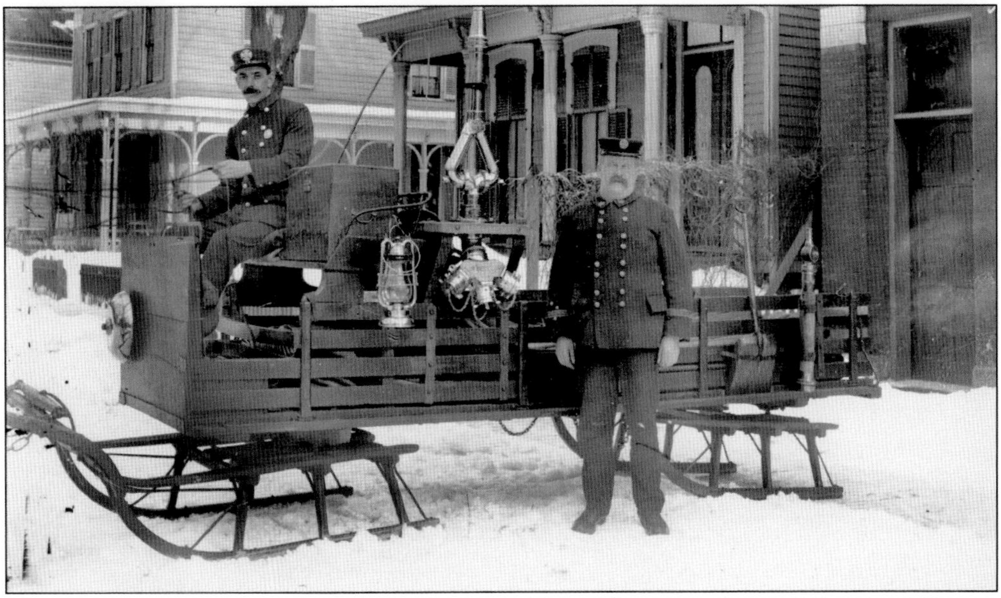

Fire Chief Briggs (standing) with Chief Bowers (driving) pose in front of the No. 2 Engine House, located on the 100 block of East Liberty Street. Notice the transport is modified for the winter. (RHS.)

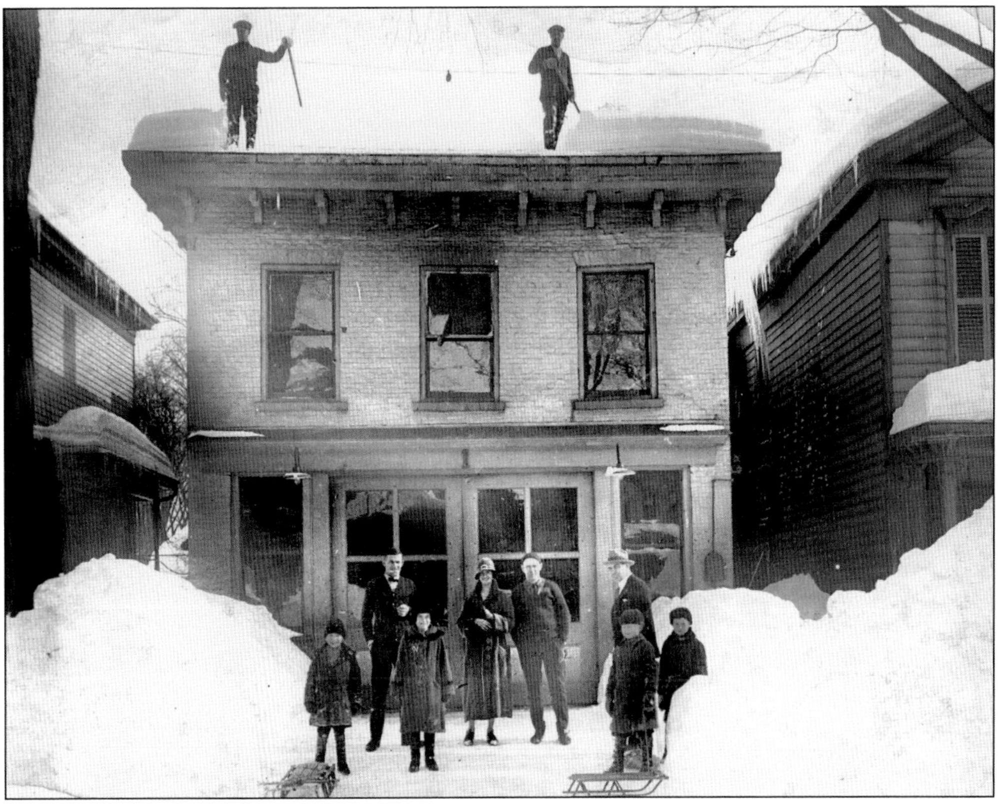

The No. 1 Fire Company, on Washington Street, tries to dig out the building after a large snowfall. (RHS.)

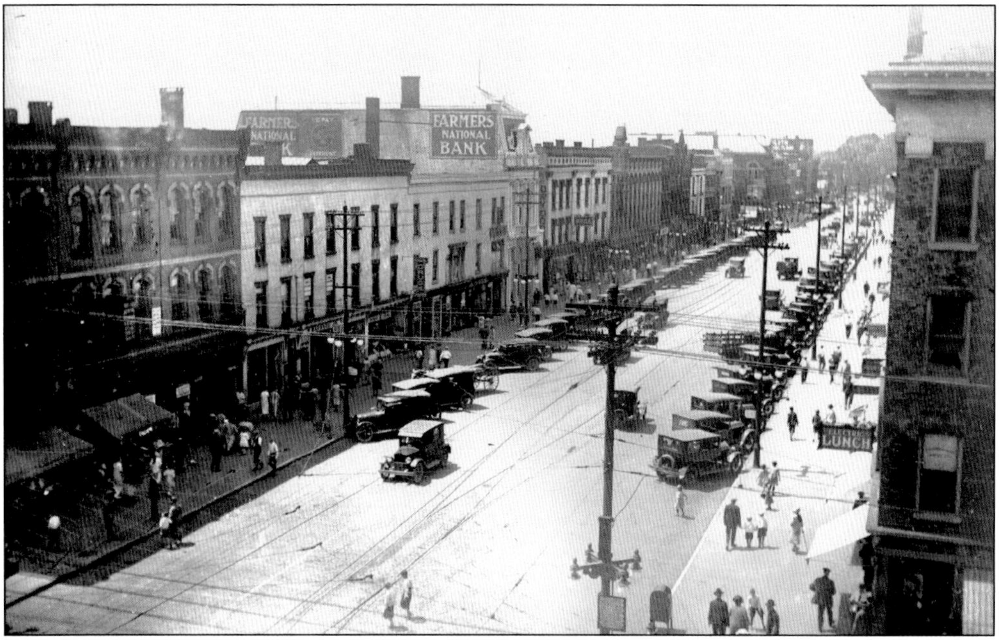

This is a view of West Dominick Street in 1925. Some of the visible signs on the businesses are for Farmers National Bank and the Electric Lunch. (RHS.)

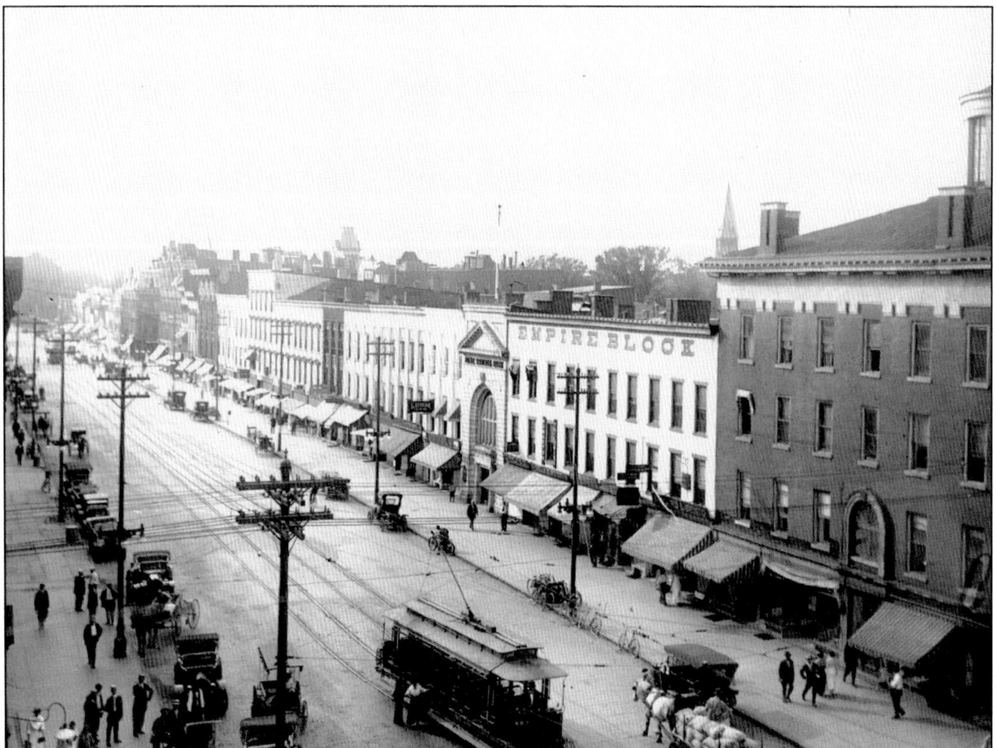

The Empire Block was located on the 100 block of West Dominick Street. This view was obtained by looking west from James Street. (RHS.)

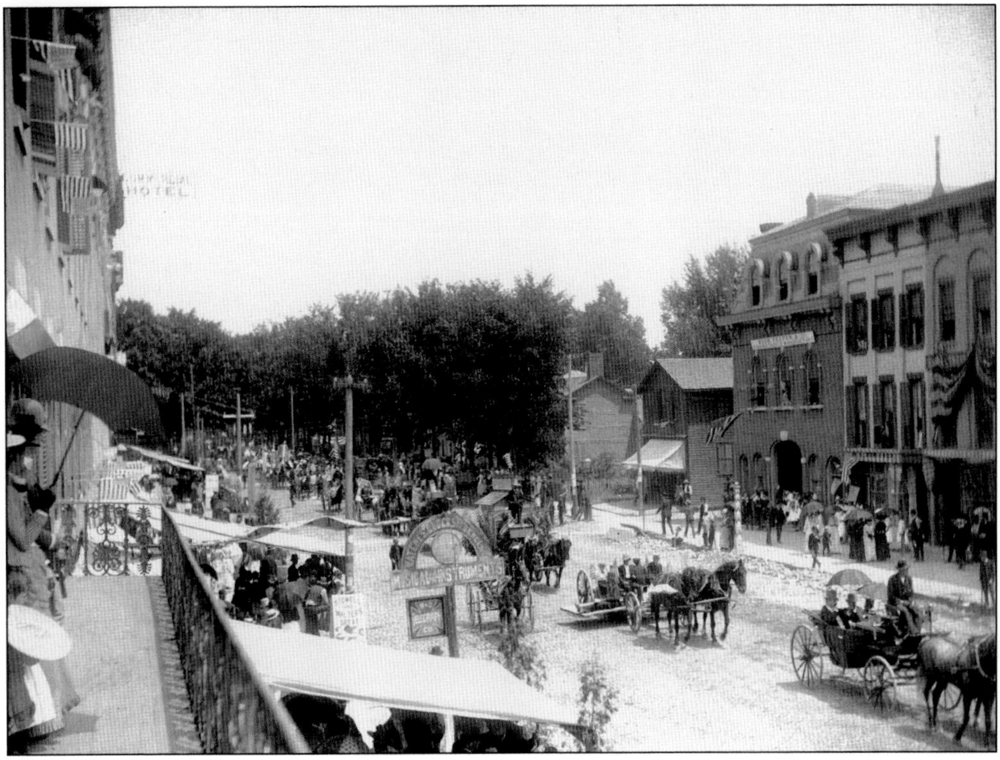

This James Street parade celebrates the opening of the Rome City Street Railroad on July 4, 1887. The railroad was an early streetcar system that had 6.75 miles of track. (RHS.)

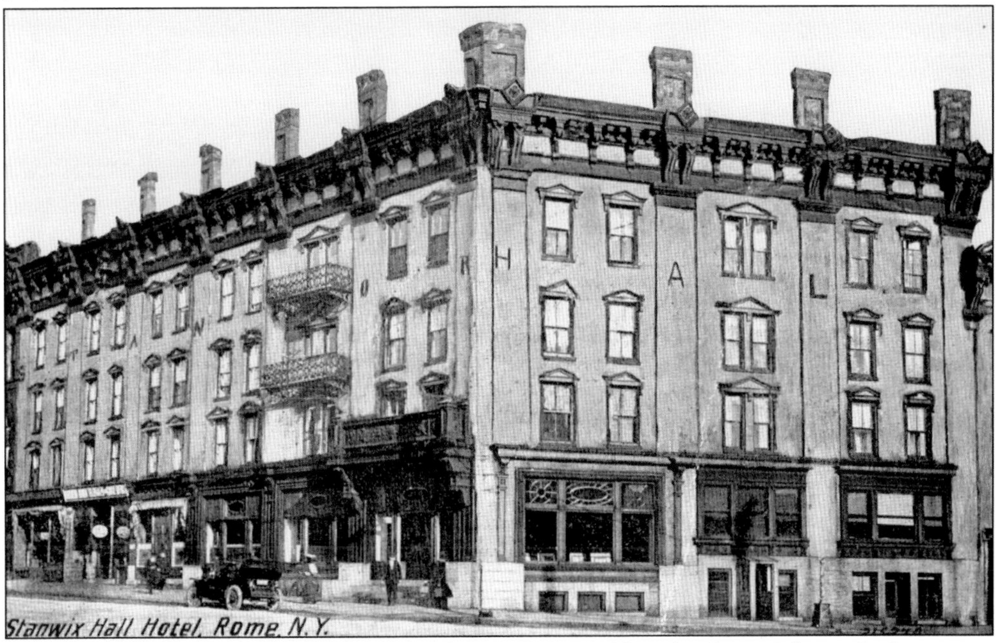

Rome was once a center for travelers, with as many as 16 hotels. One of the early downtown businesses to thrive because of the Erie Canal was the Stanwix Hall Hotel, located on the Erie Canal. (Dr. Craeger Boardman.)

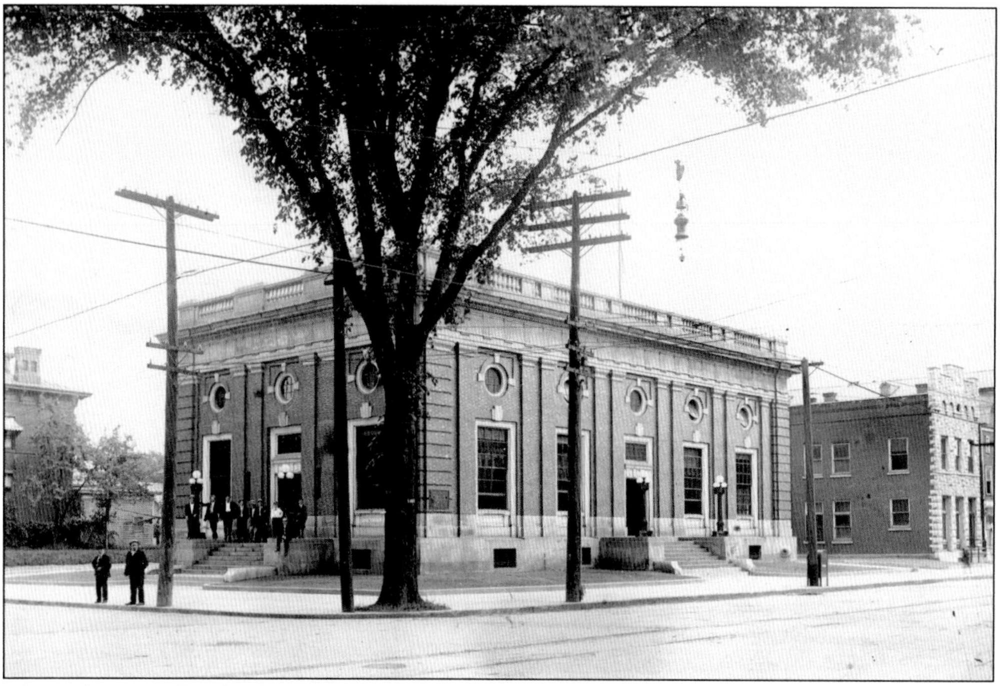

The early post office building was located on the corner of James and Liberty Streets. The post office moved to Church Street in 1937. (RHS.)

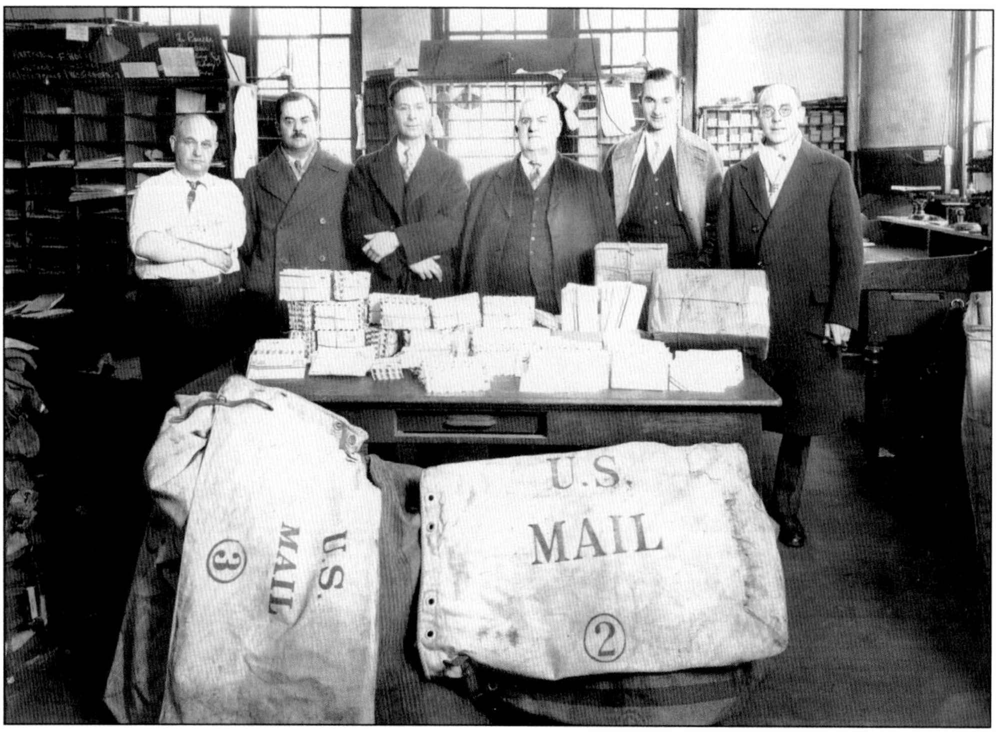

Shown is the first airmail received in Rome, on January 7, 1929. The room is the interior of the post office that is pictured above. (RHS.)

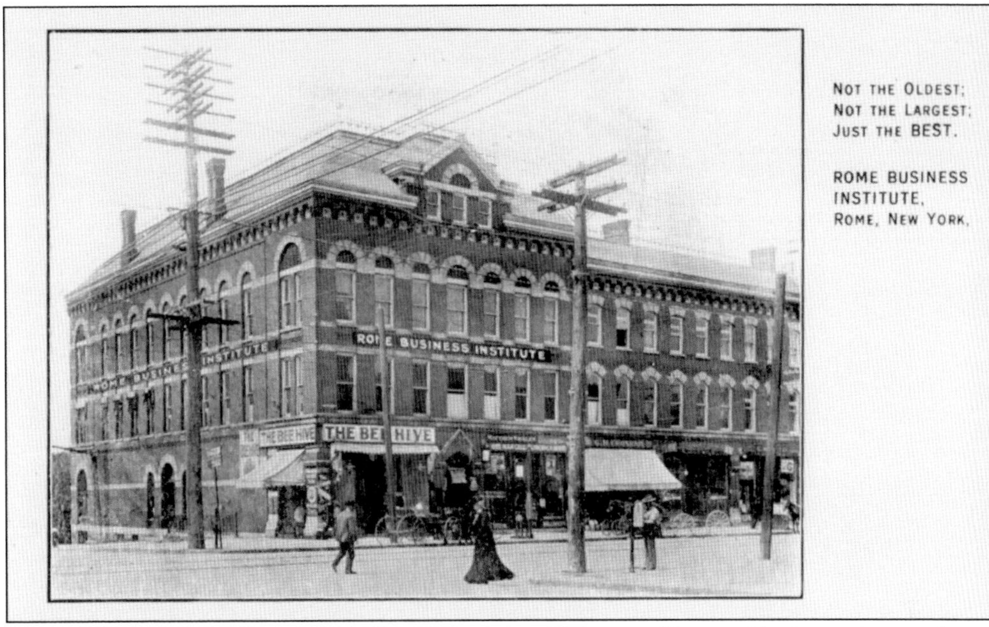

The Rome Business Institute was located at the Glesmann-Hower Block on the southwest corner of Dominick and Washington Streets. This postcard advertising the school is from 1906. (Dr. Craeger Boardman.)

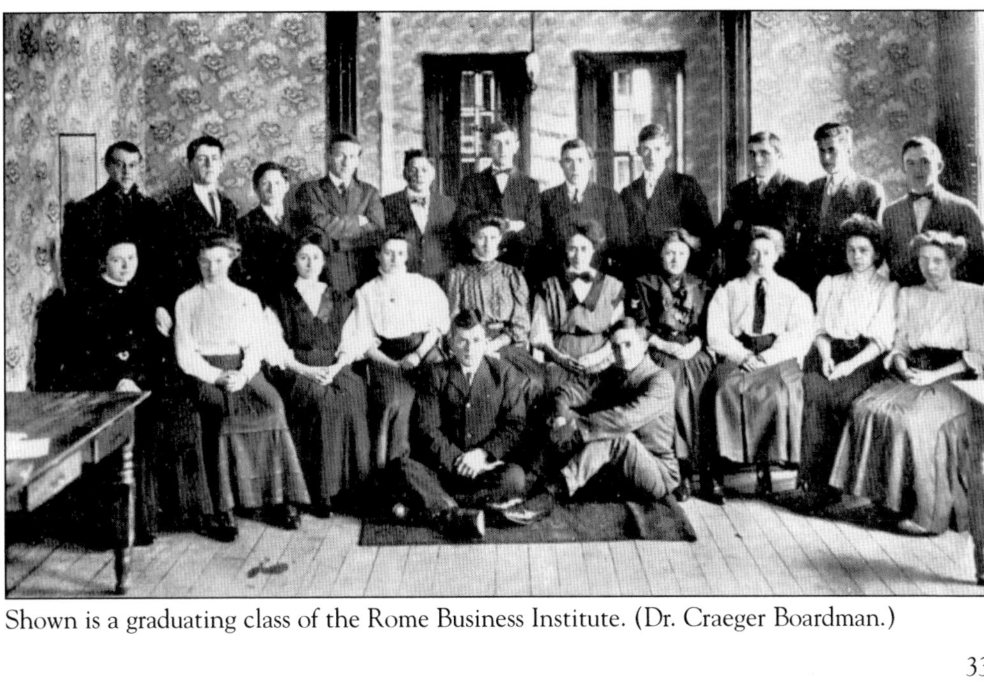

Shown is a graduating class of the Rome Business Institute. (Dr. Craeger Boardman.)

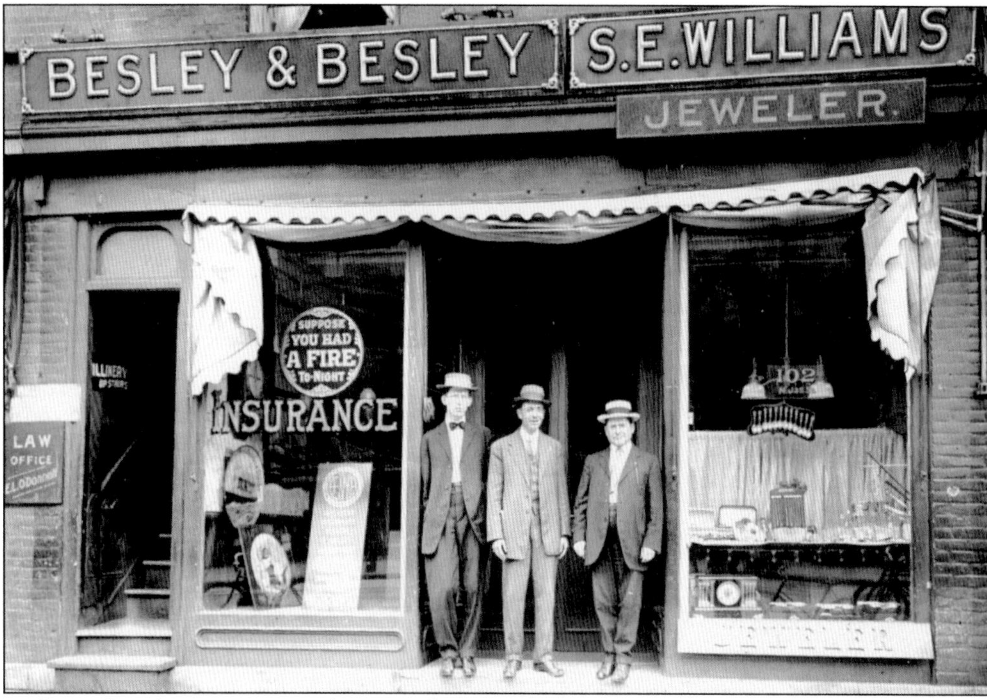

Besley and Besley Insurance and S.E. Williams Jeweler were located at 102 North James Street. The sign in the window reads, "Suppose you had a fire tonight." (RHS.)

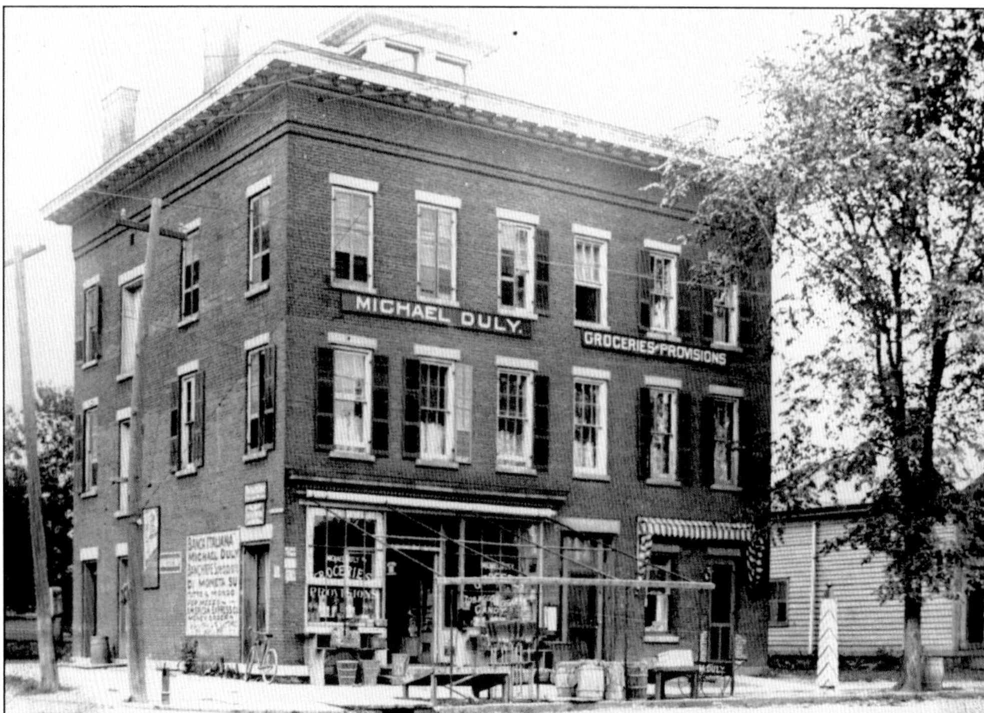

This photograph shows Duly's Grocery in 1900. Notice the building has signs in Italian, evidence of Rome's mixed ethnic background. (RHS.)

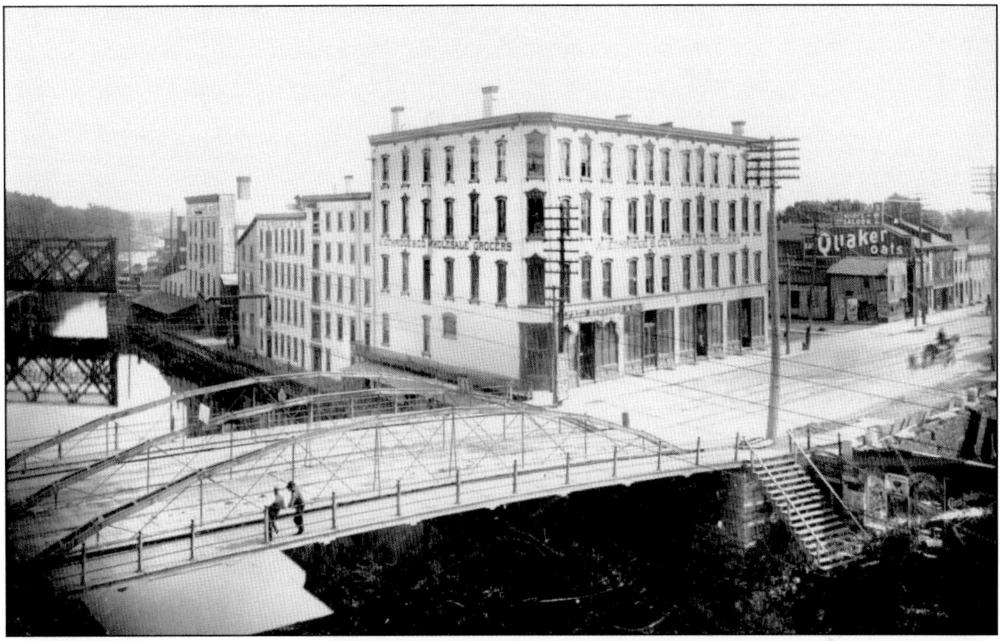

Grocery stores were a popular business in early Rome. This 1885 view shows the A. Ethridge and Company Wholesale Grocers and the James Street Bridge over the Erie Canal. The company had started as a general goods store, but became exclusively a wholesale grocery by 1875. (RHS.)

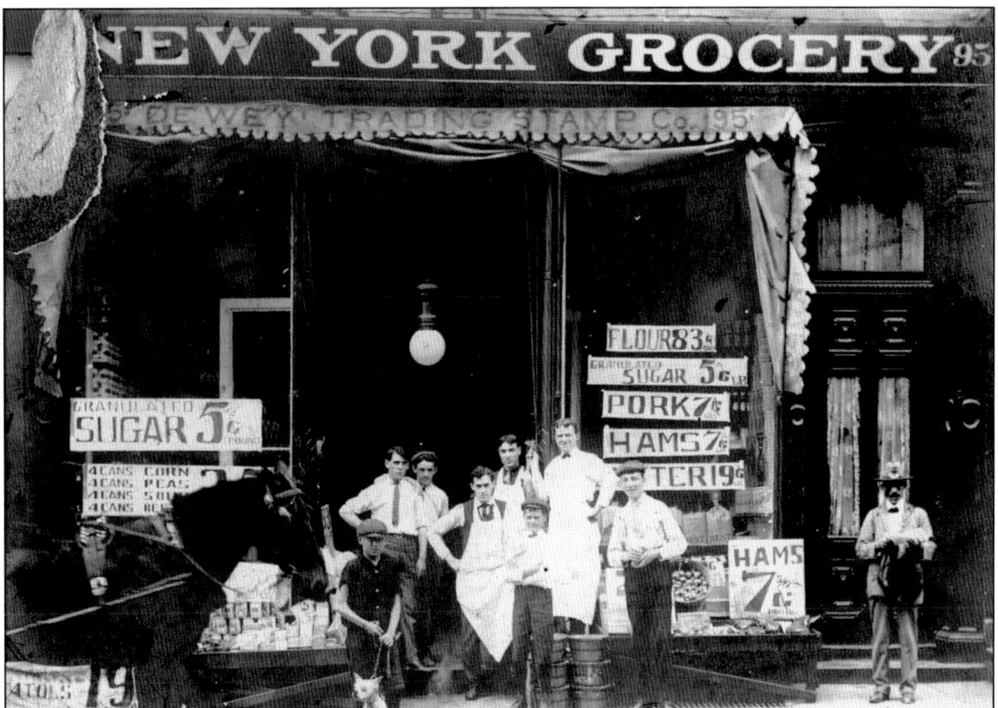

The workers of the New York Grocery stand outside for a photograph. The signs in the window advertise granulated sugar at 5¢ per pound and ham and pork at 7¢ per pound. (RHS.)

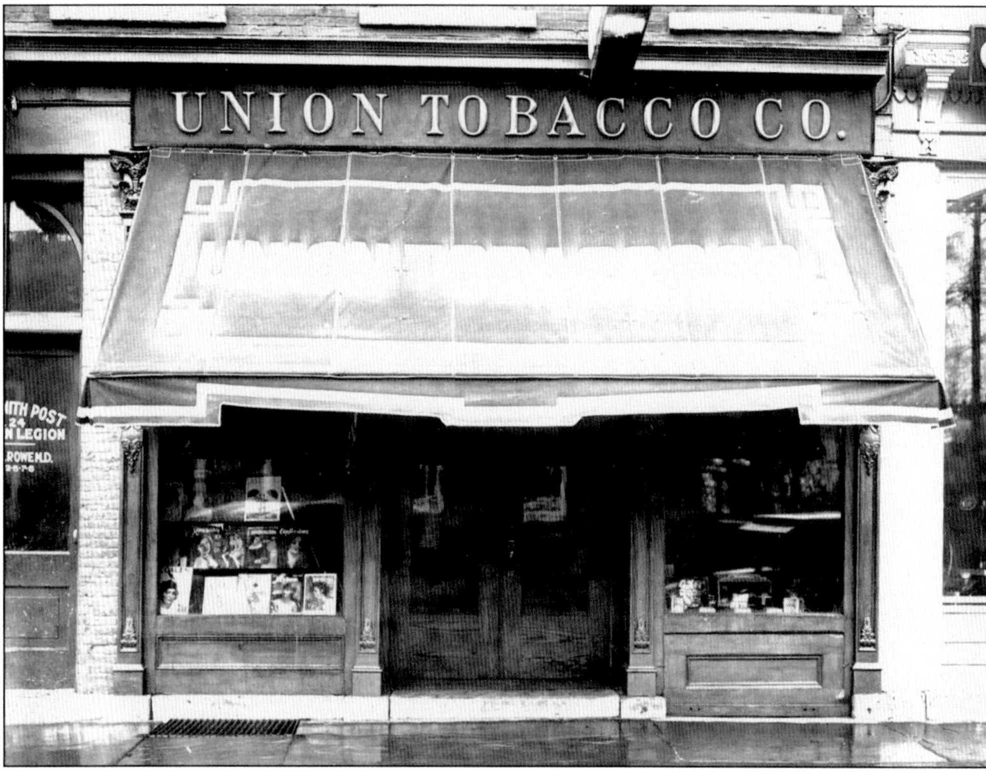

Another popular early type of store in Rome was the tobacconist. Above, a rainy day slows down business at the Union Tobacco Company, located at 147 North James Street. Below, "Seifert's Bunch" celebrates Armistice Day at 204 North James Street. (RHS.)

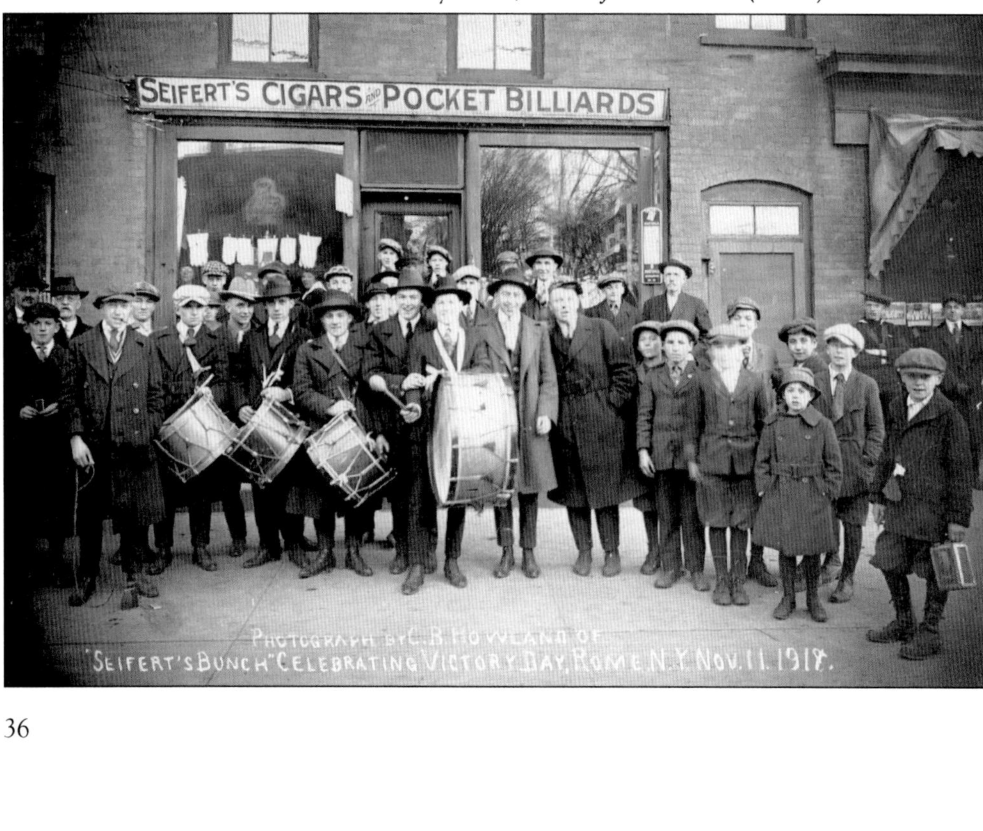

Rome Savings Bank was organized in 1851. The bank originally operated out of the offices of the Fort Stanwix Bank. Here, the bank, located in its own building, encourages citizens to buy war bonds in 1918. (RHS.)

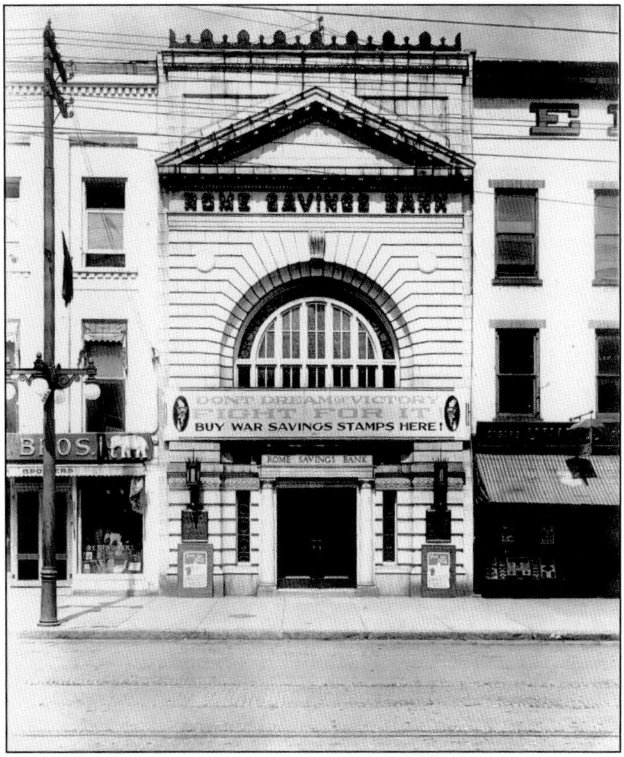

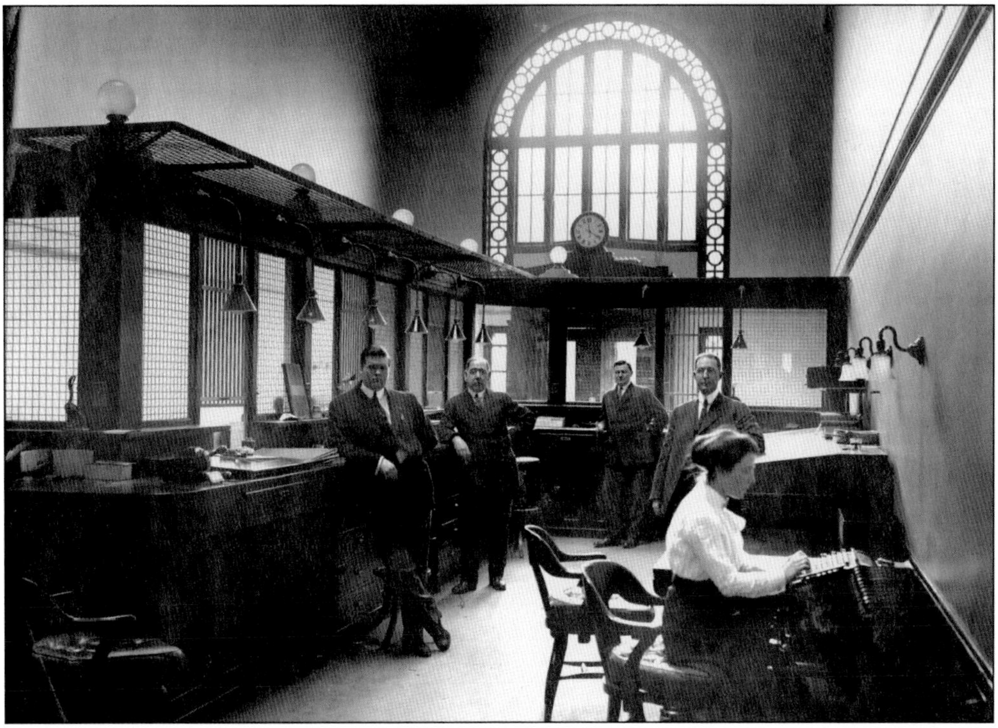

This is what the interior of the Rome Savings Bank looked like in 1918. The man standing on the right is bank president Samuel H. Beach. (RHS.)

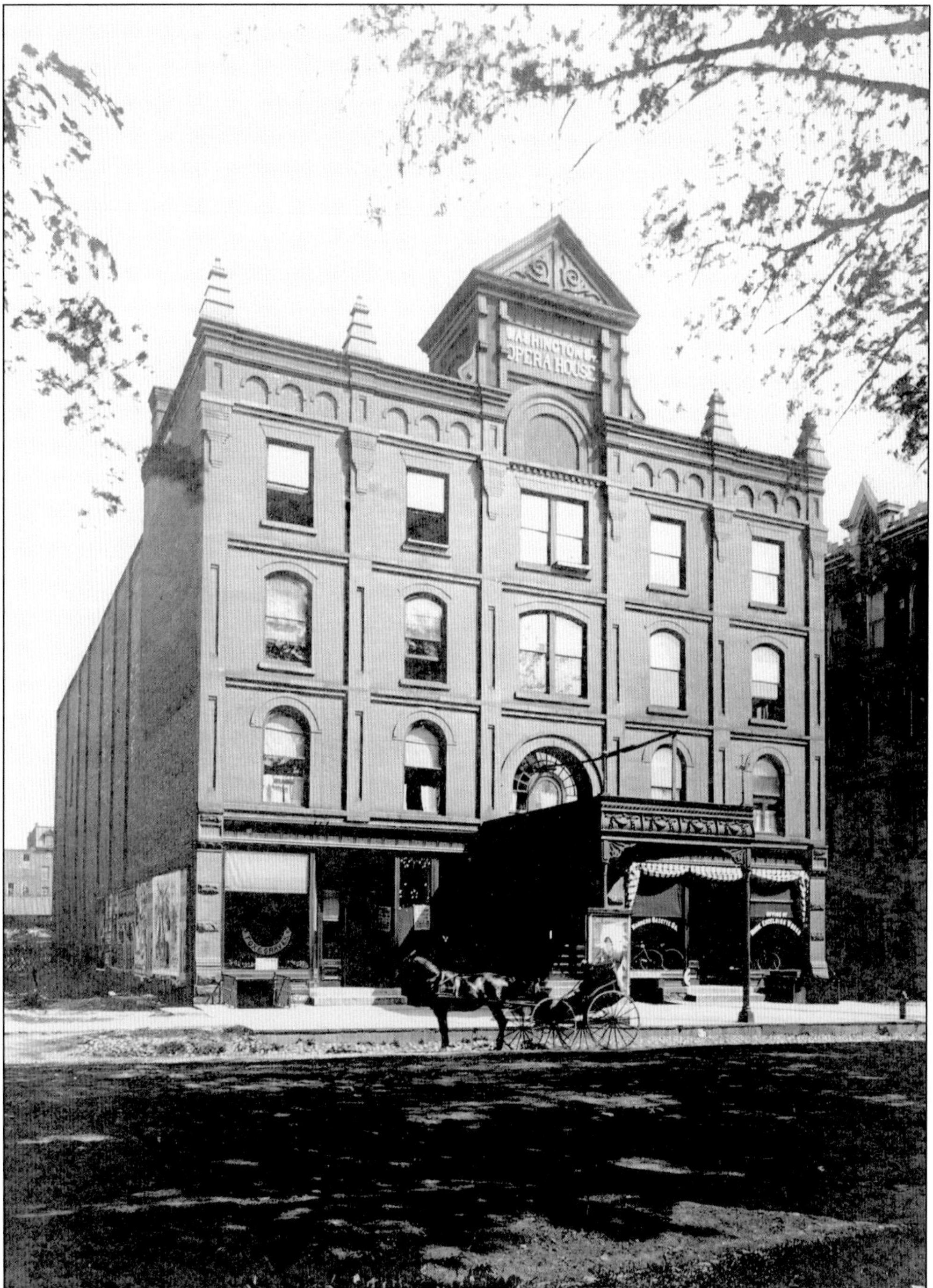

The Washington Street Opera House opened in 1889 with a performance of *The Wife*, by Daniel Frohman's Company. The theater burned down in 1903. (RHS.)

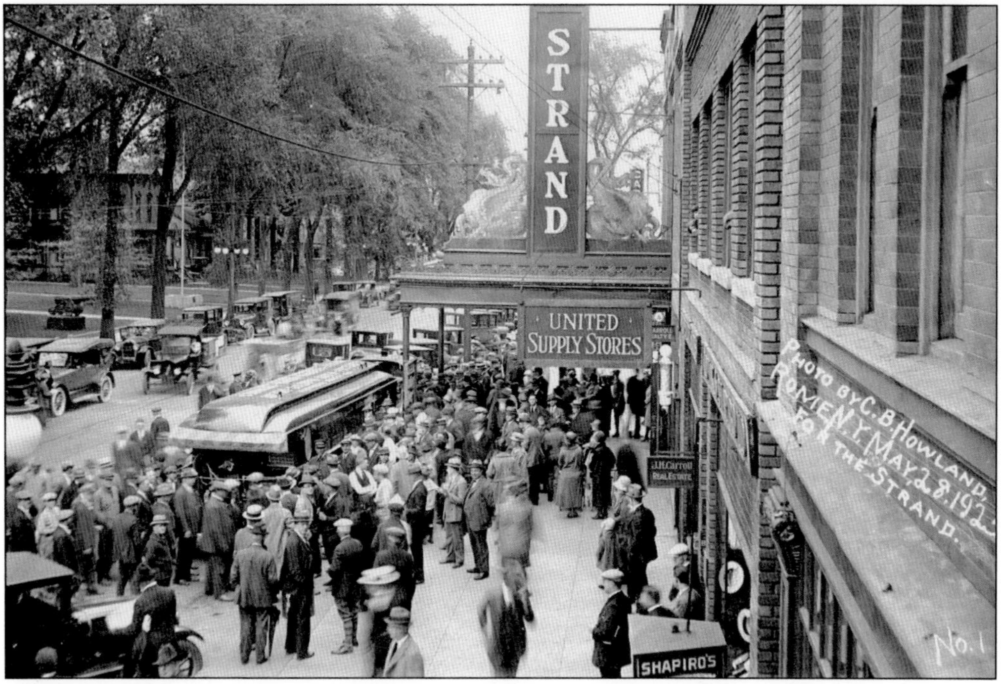

America's first automotive-powered transcontinental train stands in front of the Strand Theater on Dominick Street on May 28, 1925. The train was a great advertising vehicle for MGM. It traveled from Los Angeles to New York City and then toured Europe. The man in the foreground with his hands in his pockets, turning to face the camera, is H.C. Midlam, mayor of Rome. (RHS.)

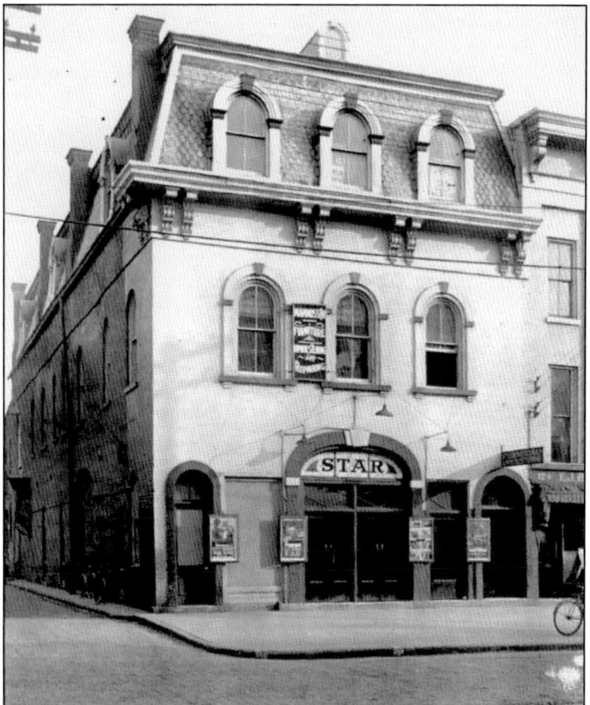

Rome's last small movie house was the Star Theater, located at 128 North James Street. Famous for its 5¢ matinee, the Star showed movies with piano accompaniment. (RHS.)

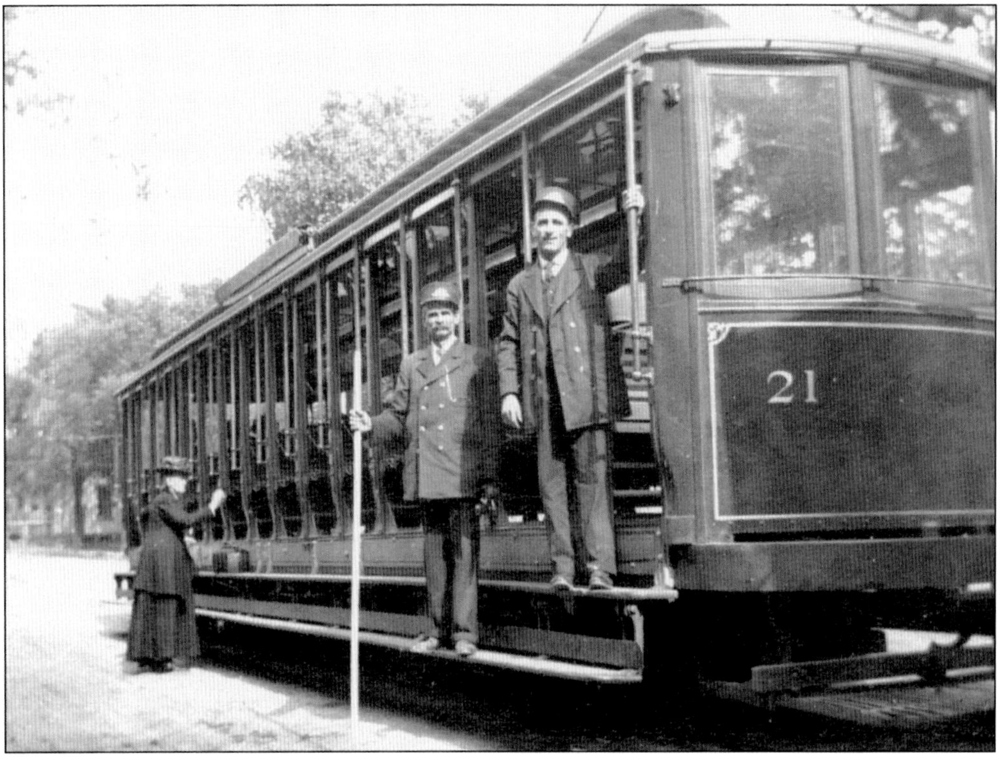

Trolley cars, with overhead electric wires, succeeded the Rome City Street Railroad as Rome's public transportation. The route ran along Dominick Street between Charles Street and St. Peter's Cemetery, up James Street to Linden Street, over to Madison Street, to Thomas, to Expense, and back to Dominick Street. (RHS.)

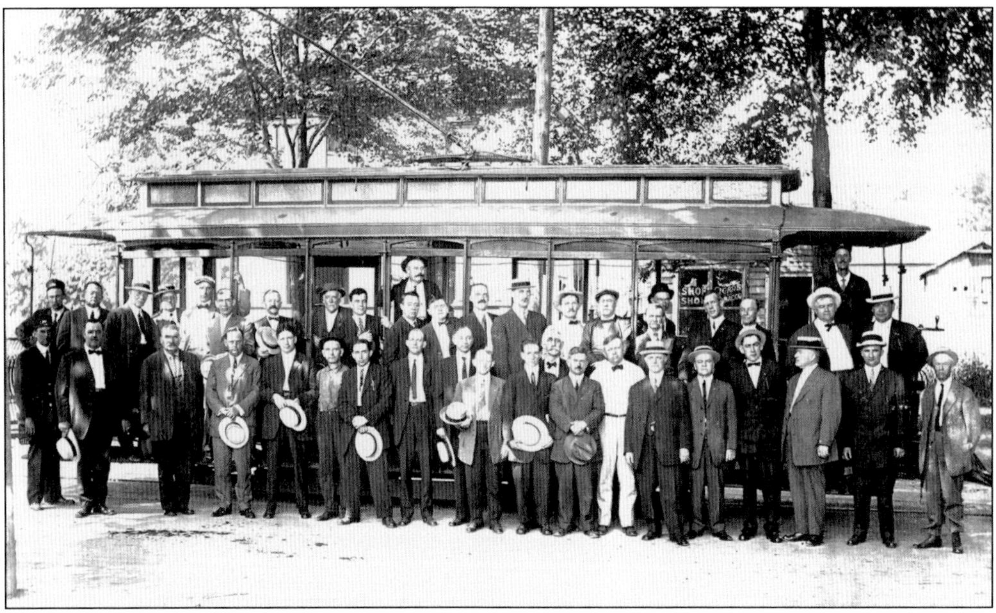

The opening of the Charles Street Trolley Line extension in 1913 was a great event. More than 40 well-known citizens of Rome gathered for the first trip over the new line. (RHS.)

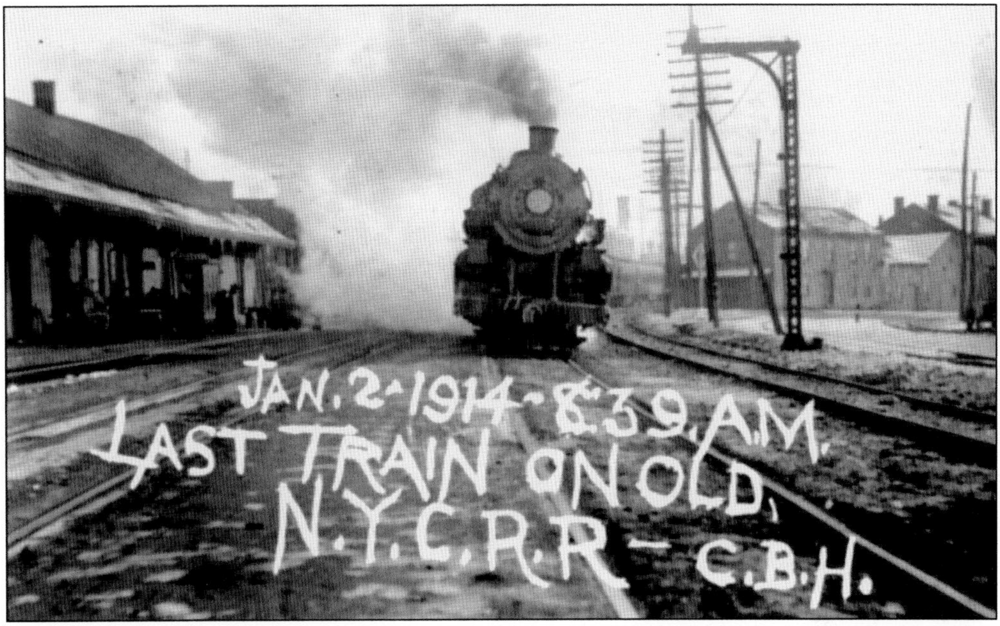

The New York Central Railroad was a consolidation of other smaller, local railroad companies. The railroad lines were moved outside the heart of the city to run near the Barge Canal. The last train on the old New York Central lines went through Rome to the James Street station on January 2, 1914. (Richard Wilson.)

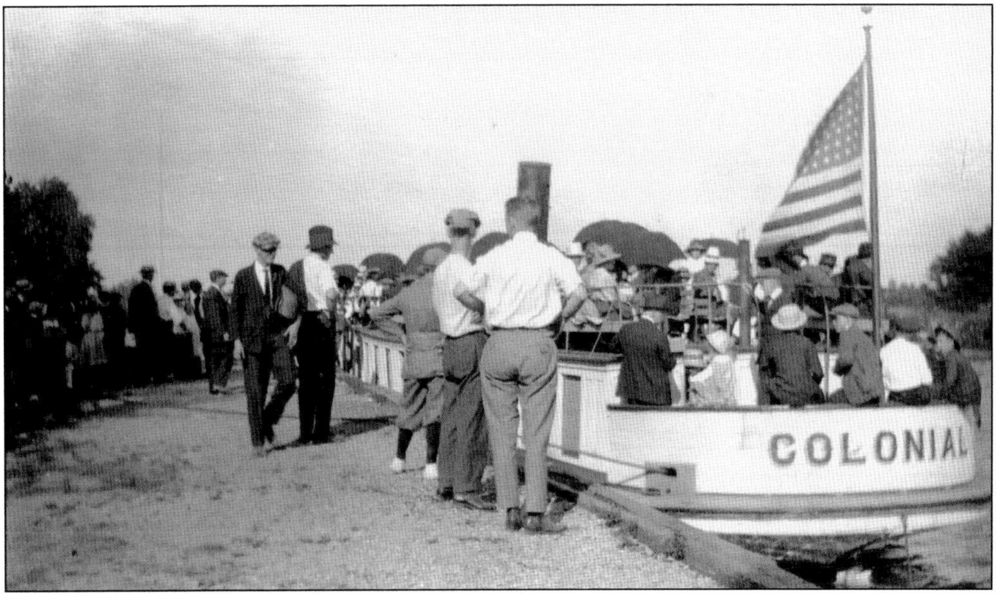

Work began on the Barge Canal in 1905. The eastern division, including the Delta Reservoir, was completed in 1915. The rest of the work was completed in 1918. Seen here is the *Colonial*, a popular excursion boat, which could carry up to 500 passengers and frequently took people from Rome to Sylvan Beach. (RHS.)

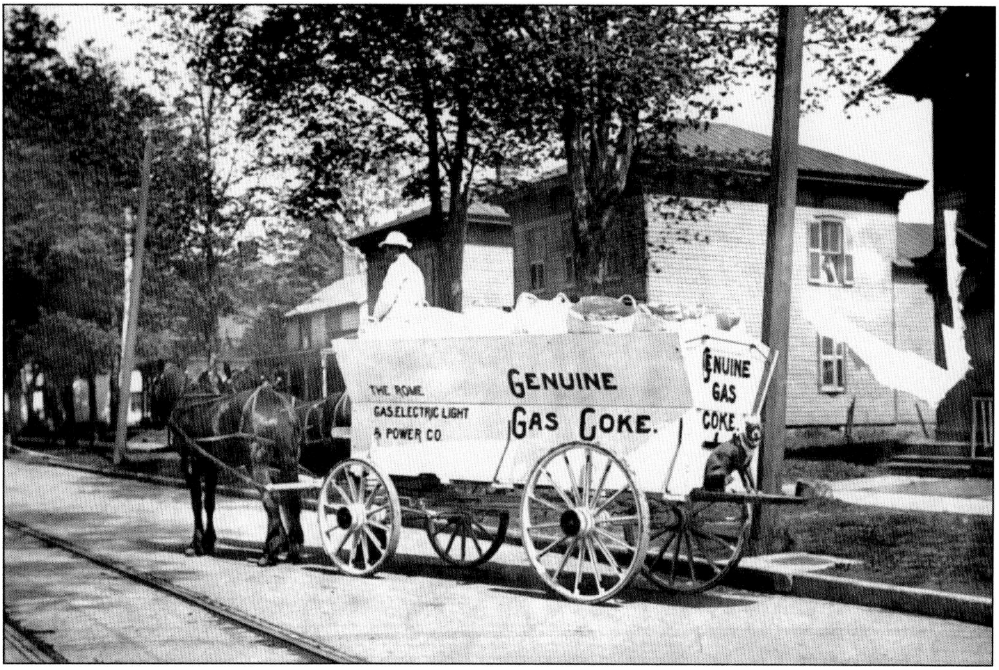

The Rome Gas Light Company, founded in 1852, eventually supplied electricity and gaslight equally and, thus, changed its name to the Rome Gas, Electric Light, and Power Company in 1901. (RHS.)

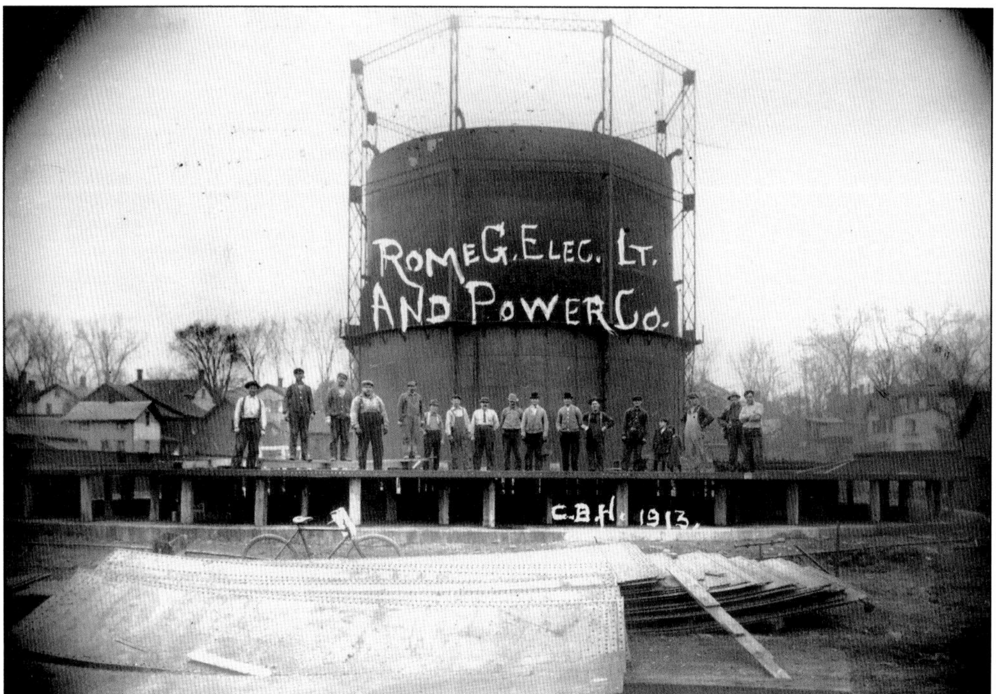

Workers at the Rome Gas, Electric Light, and Power Company pose in 1913. The plant was located on the north side of the Erie Canal, just west of Madison Street. (RHS.)

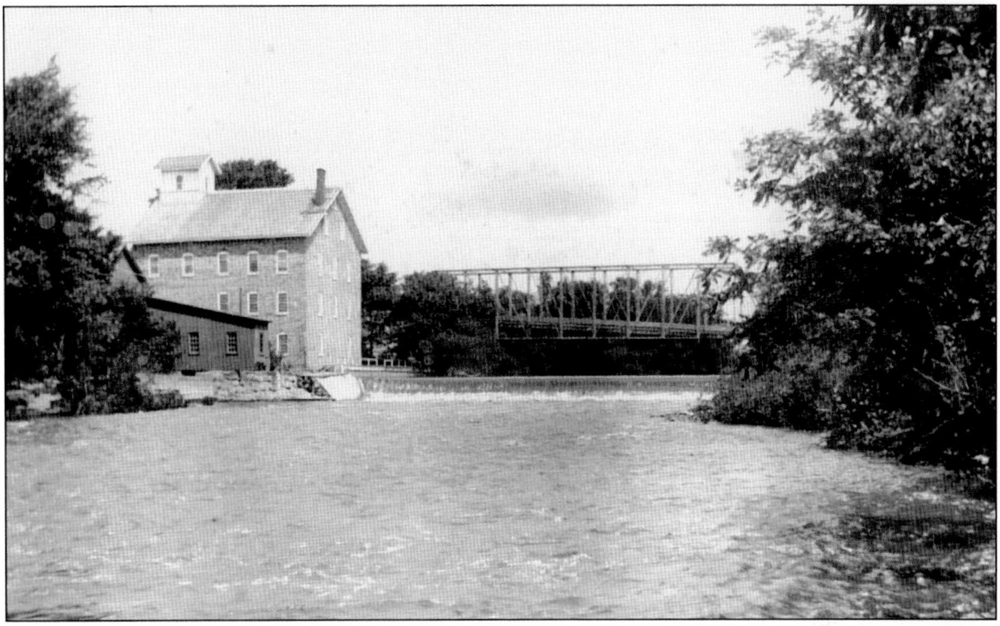

The city instituted a $172,000 bond for the new waterworks in 1872. Shown are the iron bridge over the Mohawk River at Ridge Mills and the Rome City Water Works powerhouse. (RHS.)

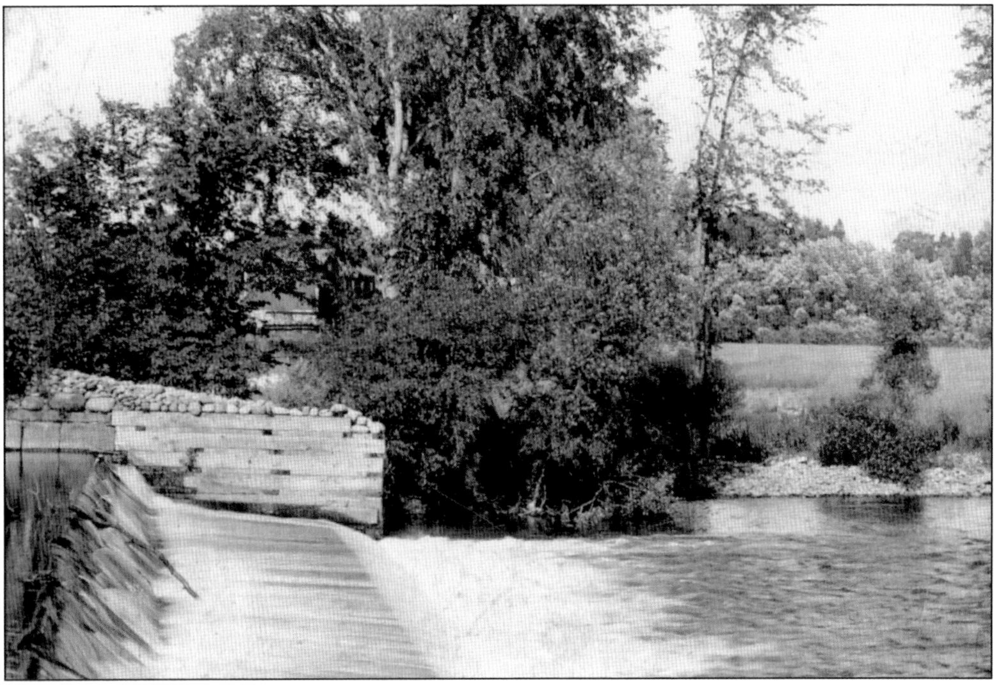

This is a closeup view of the Mohawk River Dam at Ridge Mills. (RHS.)

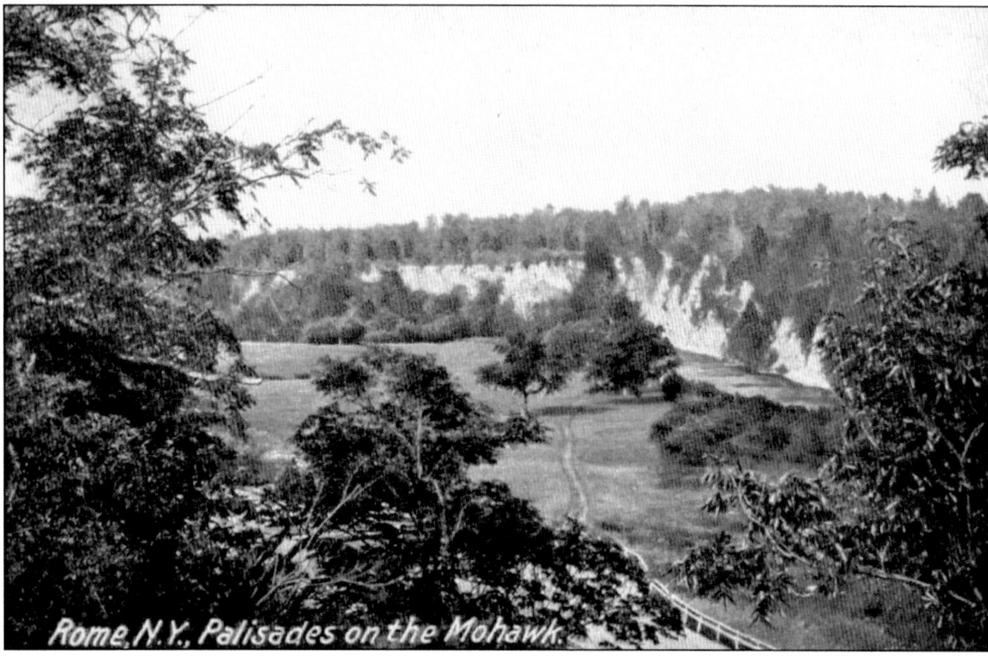

One of the phases of building the Barge Canal involved building a dam and creating a reservoir to regulate the water level. The area of the Palisades on the Mohawk, along with the former town of Delta (approximately 4.3 acres of land), was flooded to make Delta Lake. Before work began on the dam, Delta contained more than 100 buildings and 175 residents. (Portia Vescio.)

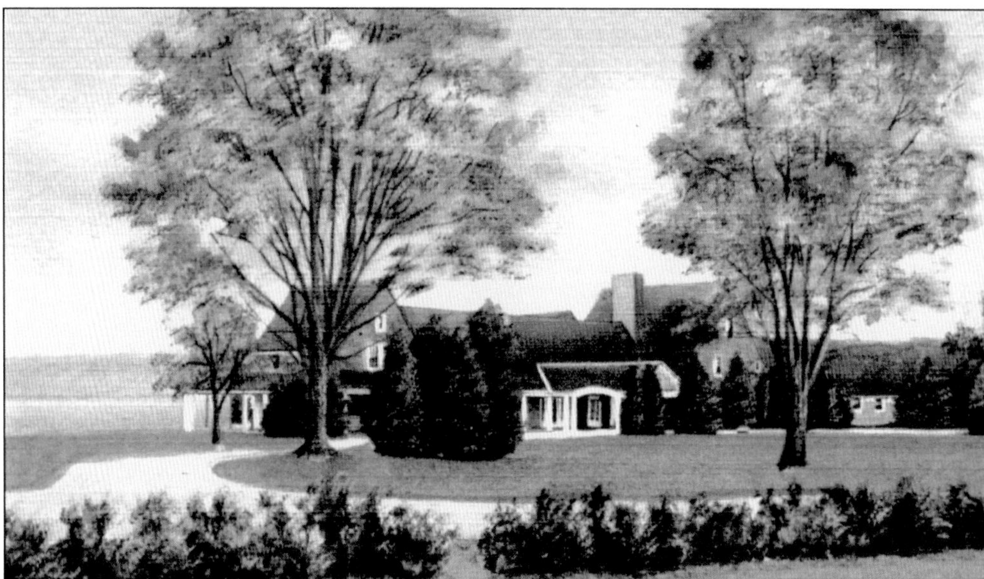

This view shows a representation of the Teugega Country Club, with Delta Lake visible in the background. (Dr. Craeger Boardman.)

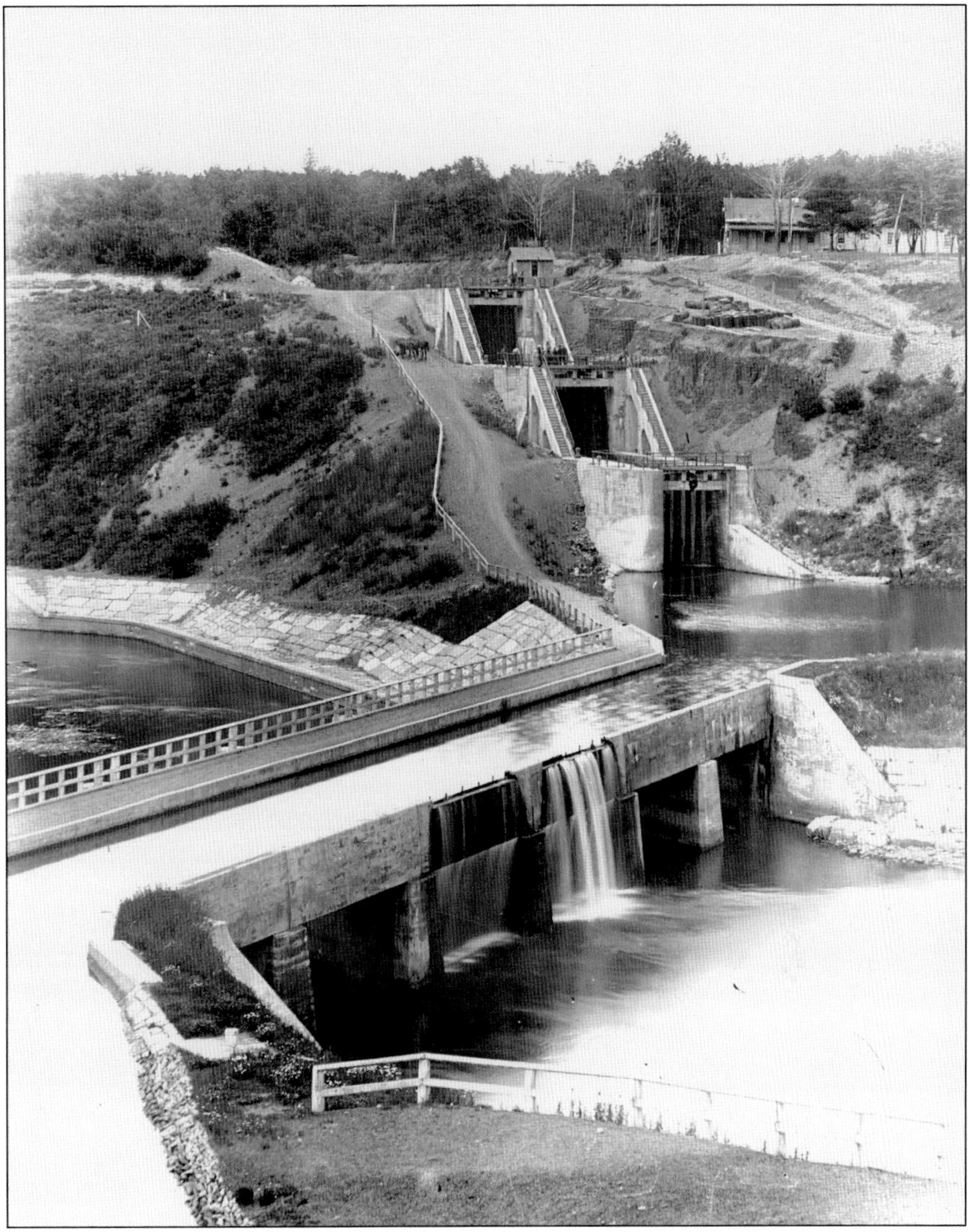

After completion of the Delta Dam, the Black River Canal was carried via aqueduct across the Mohawk River. Some water from the Black River Canal can be seen spilling across into the Mohawk. (RHS.)

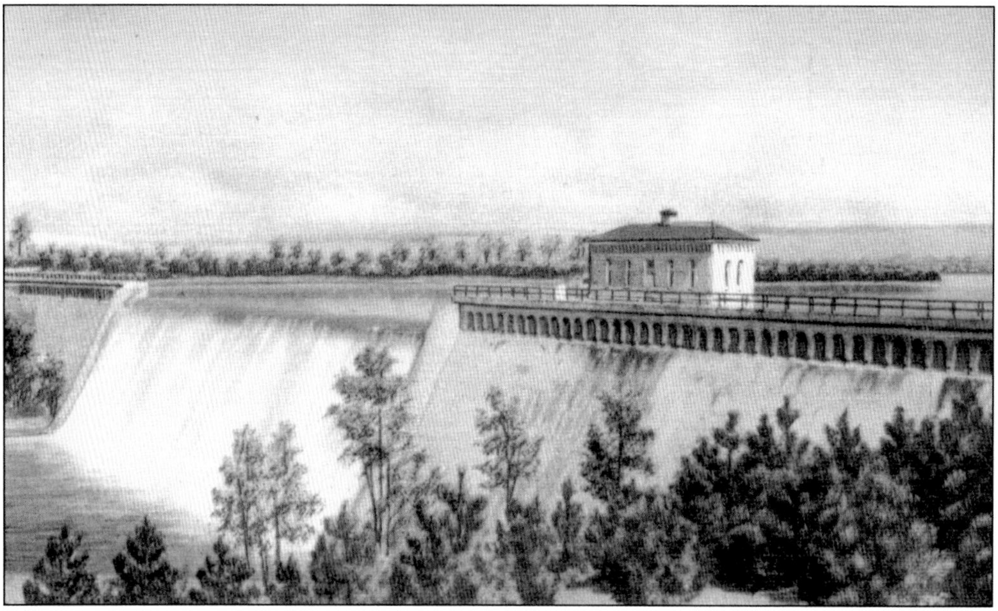

The dam at Delta cost $950,000 and is 1,100 feet long and 100 feet high. One unexpected advantage of the reservoir was that it all but eliminated the floods that used to occur after heavy rains. (Dr. Craeger Boardman.)

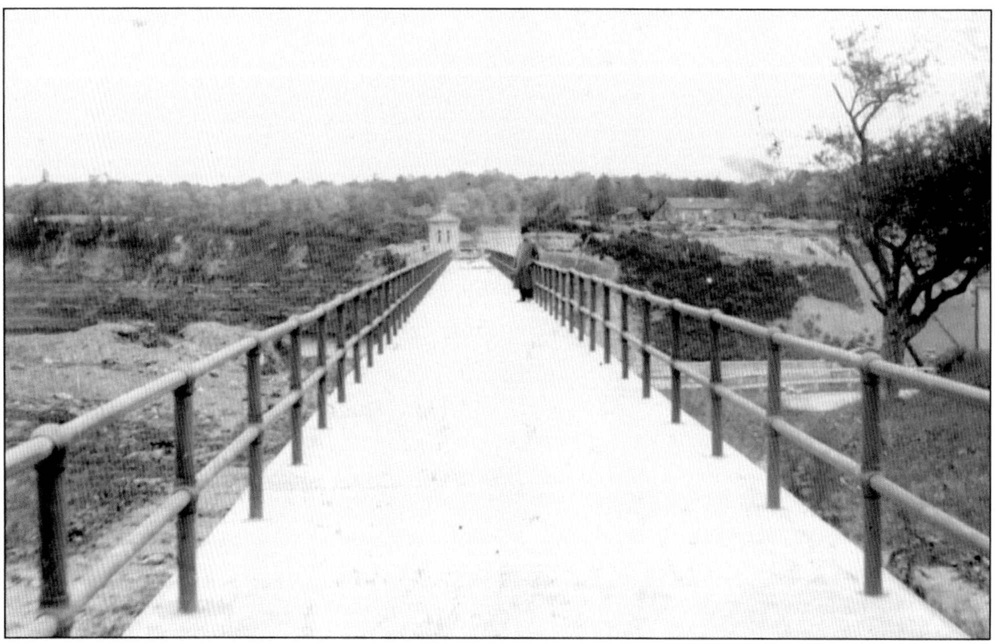

This view looks across the top of Delta Dam. (Richard Wilson.)

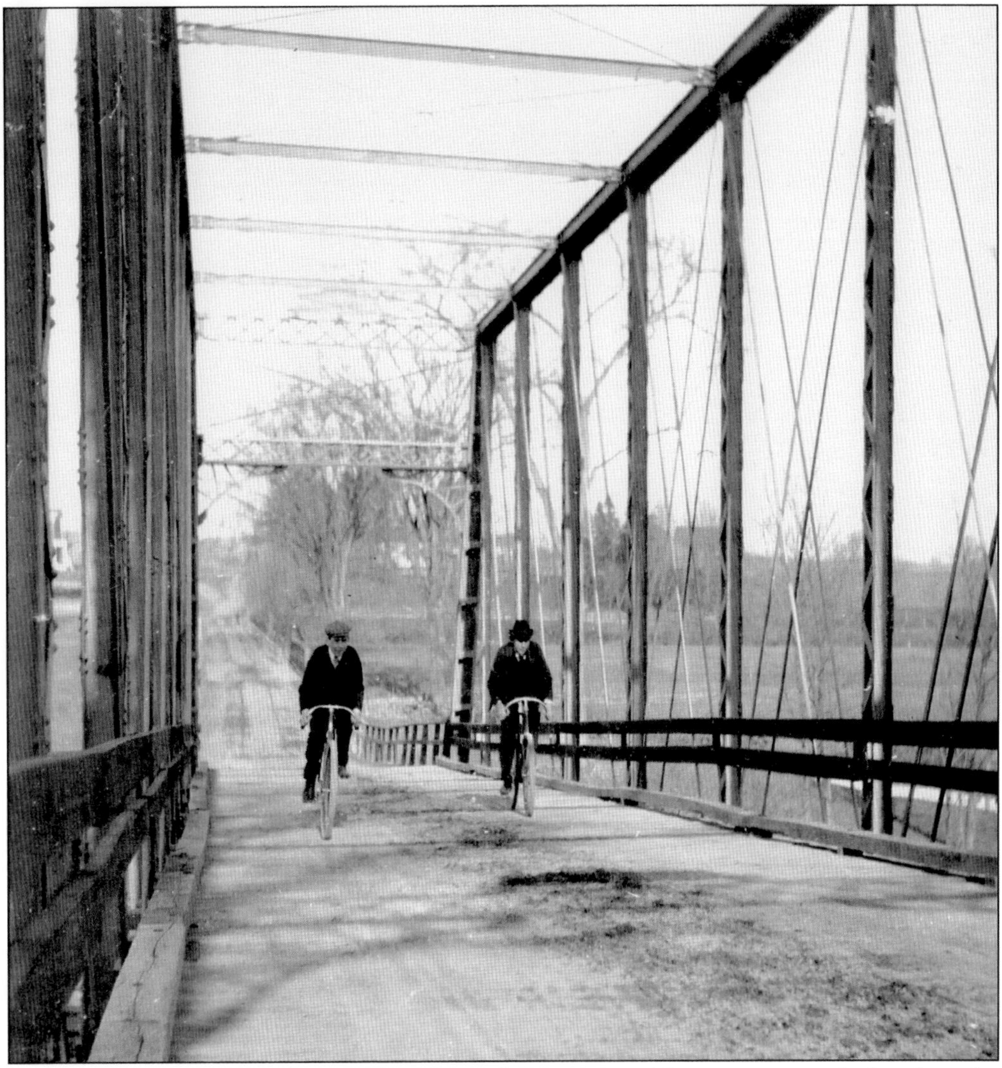

Citizens of Rome grew used to traveling across the waterways. These two men ride their bicycles across a bridge in 1897. (RHS.)

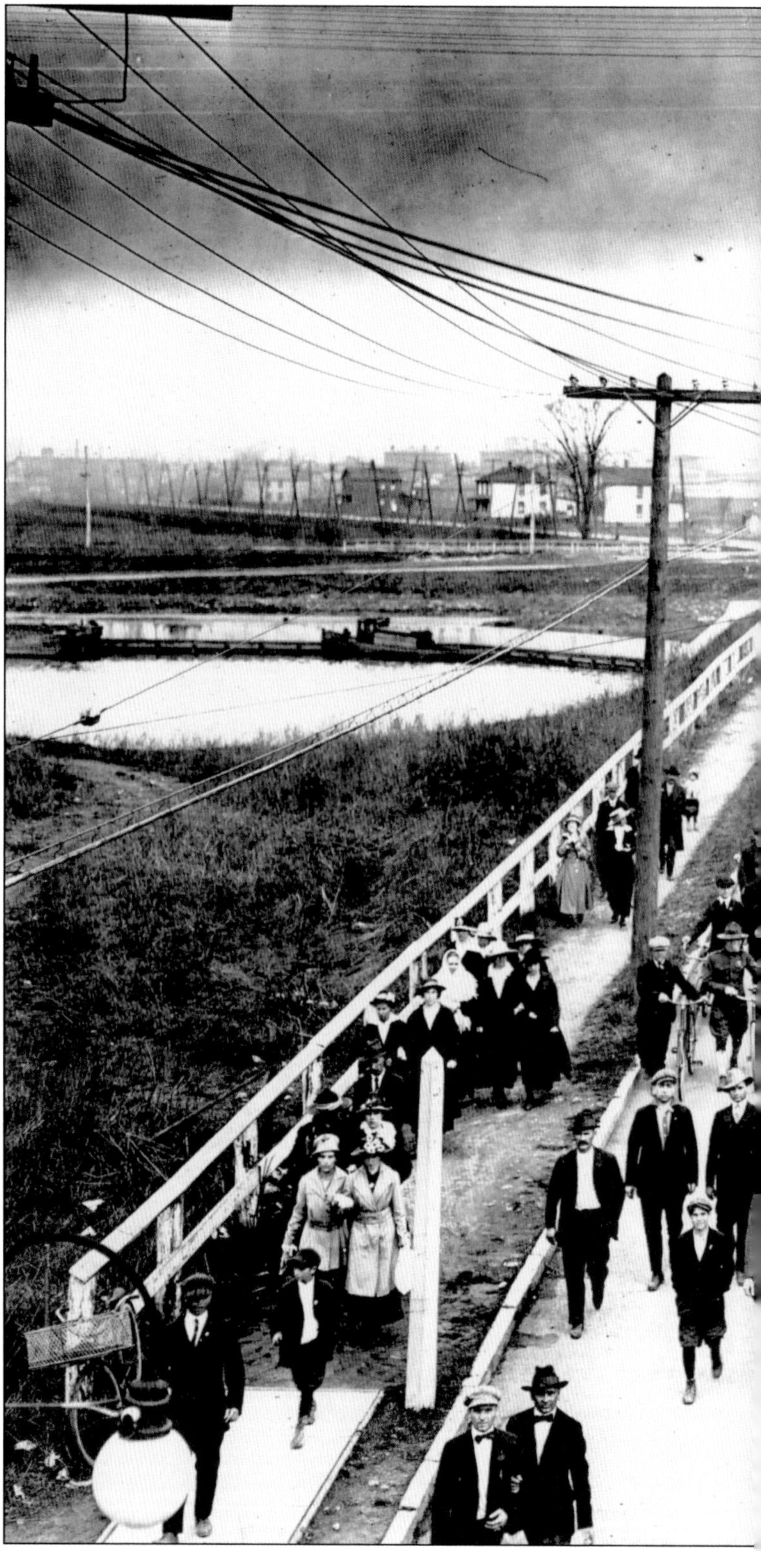

Thirty drafted men march down Mill Street toward the railroad station as they leave Rome for training to fight in World War I. The Mill Street Bridge, which can be seen in the background, carries a sign that says, "1/10 of copper used in United States is manufactured in Rome." The Rome Chamber of Commerce erected the sign in 1914. (RHS.)

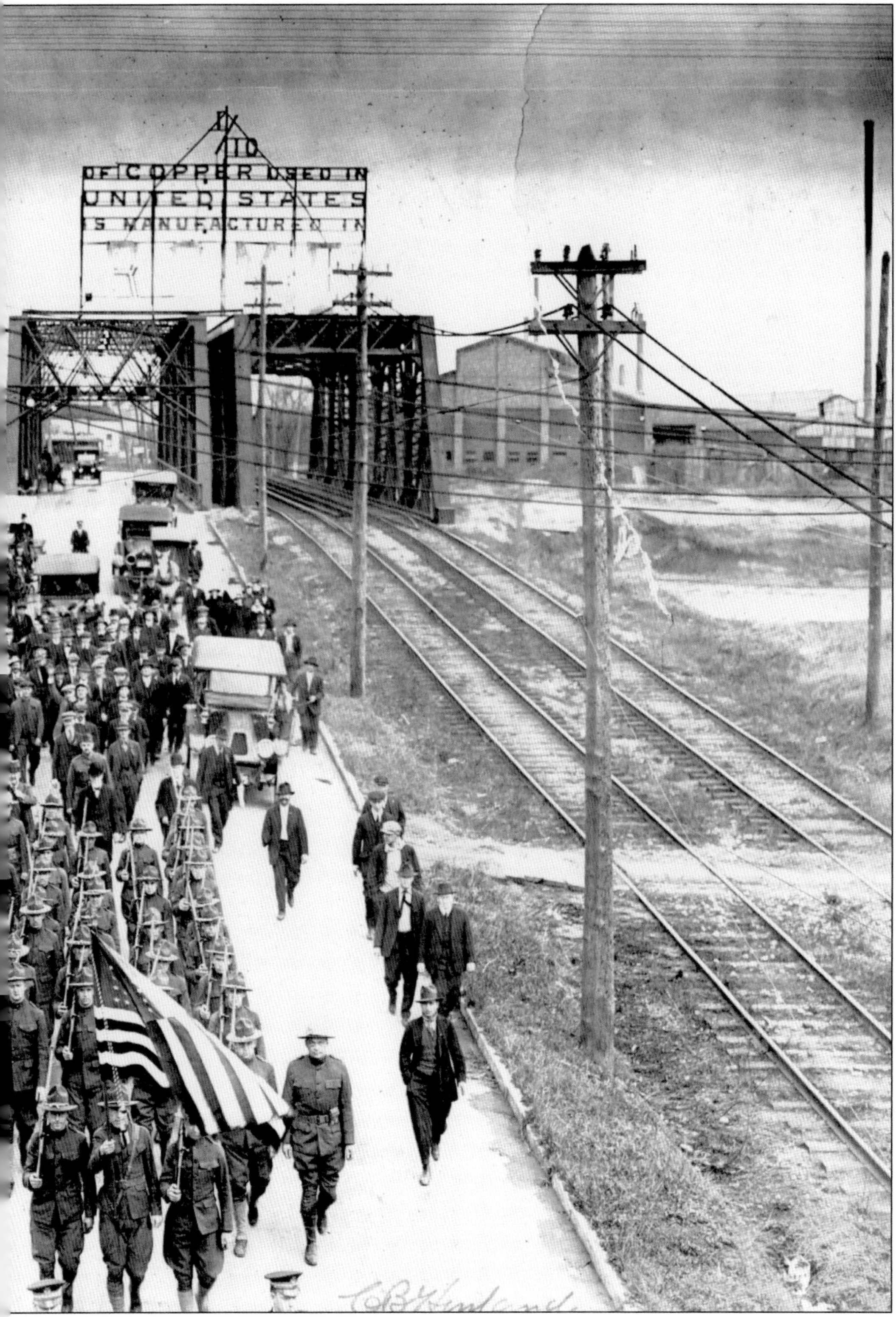
OF COPPER USED IN
UNITED STATES
IS MANUFACTURED IN

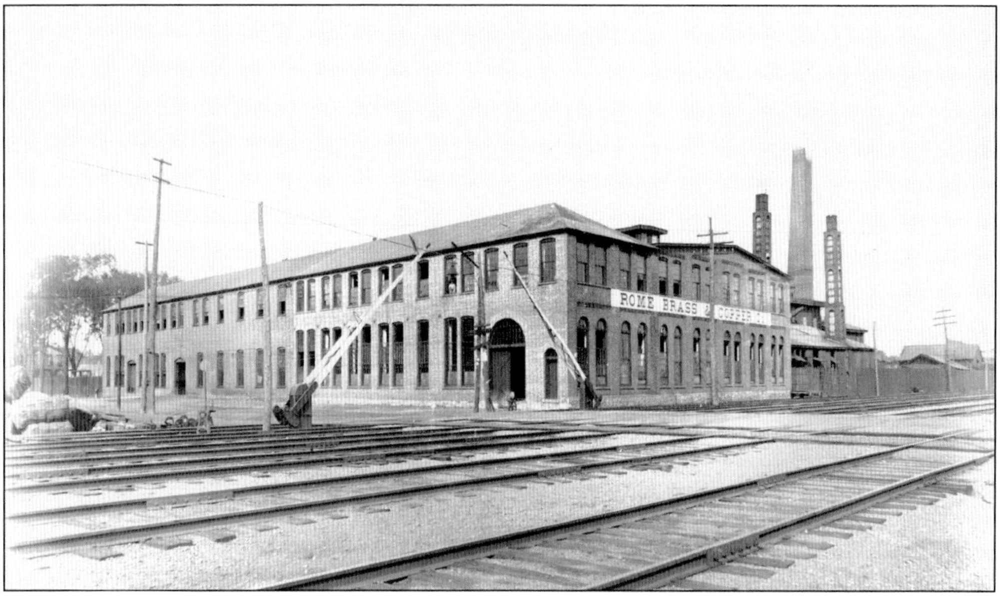

Rome Iron Works began producing copper and brass in response to a diminished demand for iron rails. On October 8, 1891, the company changed its name to Rome Brass and Copper Company to better reflect the output of the company. This factory was located on East Dominick Street at the site now occupied by St. John's Church. (RHS.)

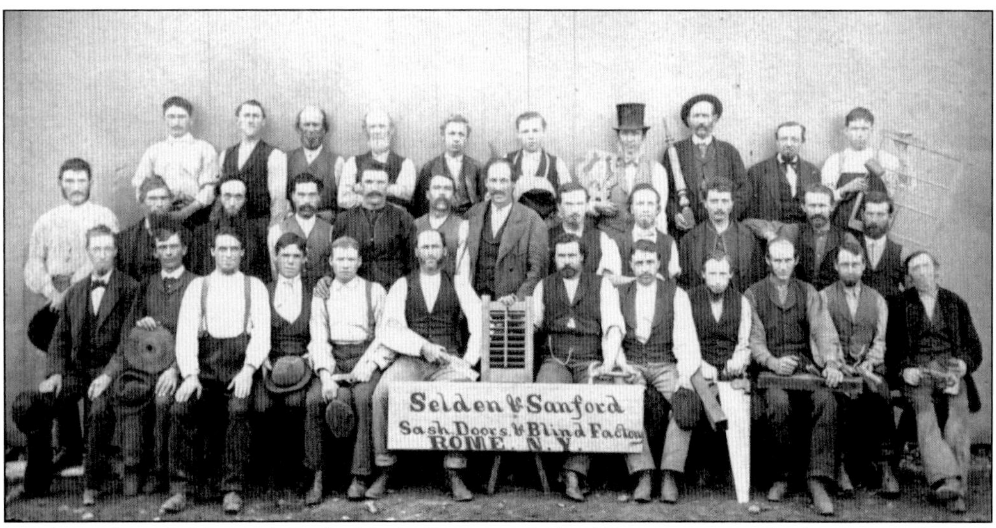

Workmen from Selden and Sanford Sash, Doors, and Blind Factory pose in the late 1880s. (RHS.)

Baum's Castorine Company was relocated to Rome in 1903 from Syracuse, where it was founded in 1883 by the father of L. Frank Baum (the author of *The Wizard of Oz*). This advertisement for Rapid axle grease is from 1900. (RHS.)

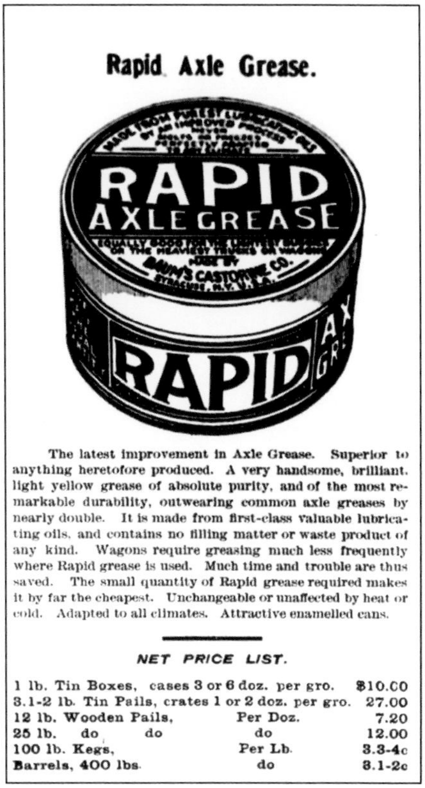

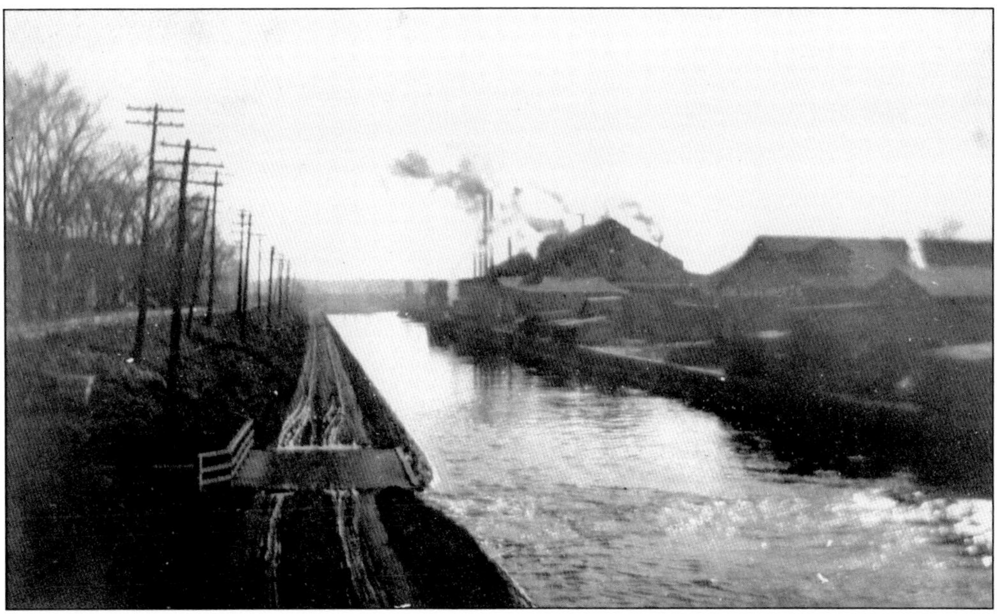

Early industries were dependent upon waterpower. This is the view from alongside the Barge Canal near the manufacturing sector. (RHS.)

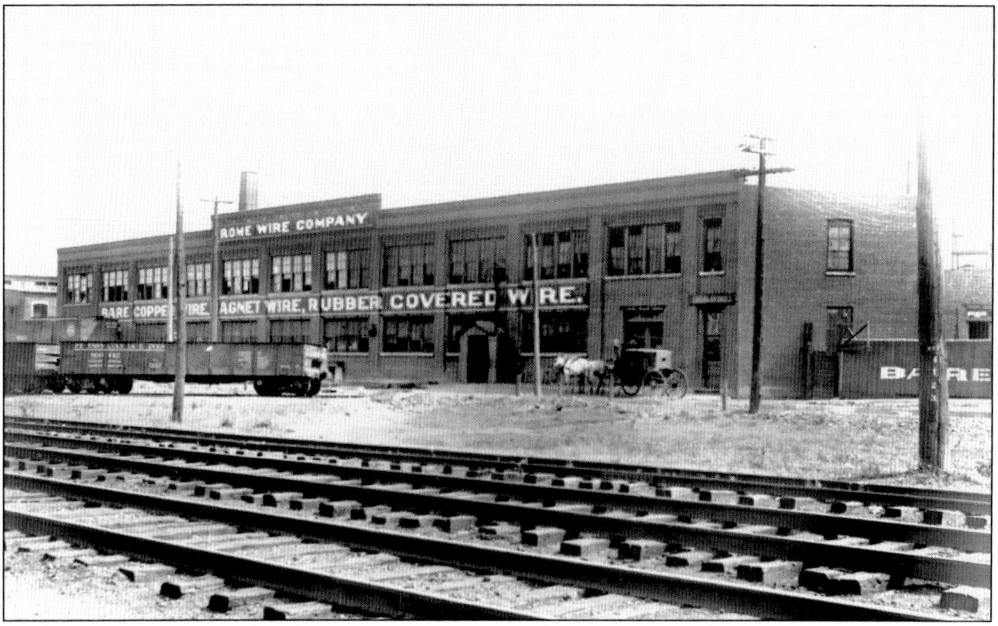

The Wire and Telegraph Company of America was hit hard by a financial depression in 1907. Frustrated with the competition for manufacturing telephones, the company expanded its wire-making facilities. The plant is shown in 1909, shortly after its name was changed to the Rome Wire Company. (RHS.)

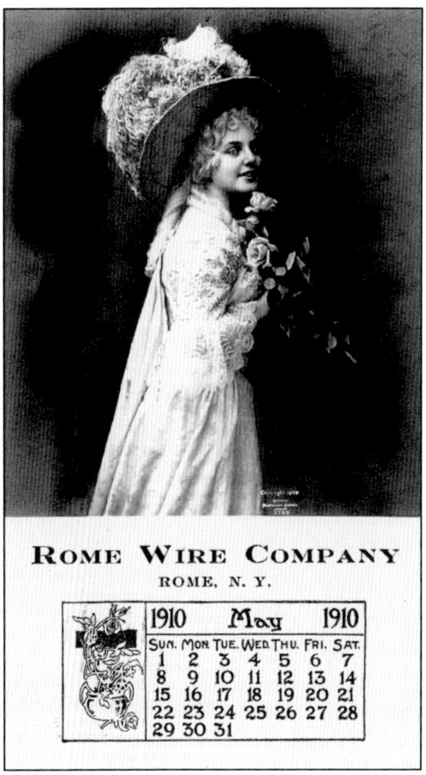

This postcard of a calendar from May 1910 predates the first Rome Wire Company catalog, which was published in June 1910. (Portia Vescio.)

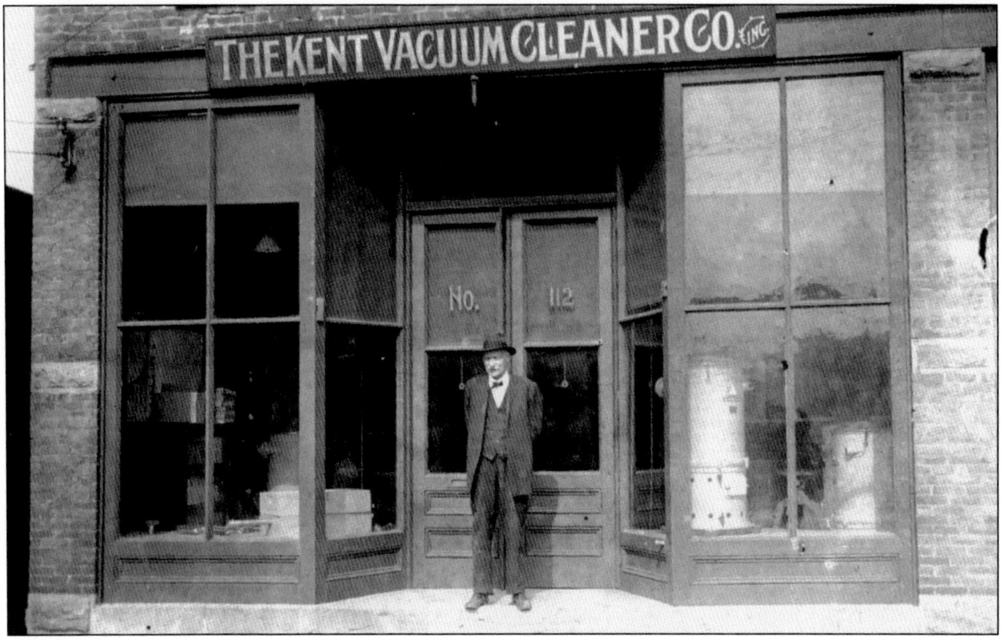

Eugene M. Kent is standing in front of the Kent Vacuum Cleaner Company store at 112 South Washington Street in July 1913, shortly after the company was founded. Kent's company specialized in floor maintenance machinery such as vacuum cleaners and electronic mopping machines. (RHS.)

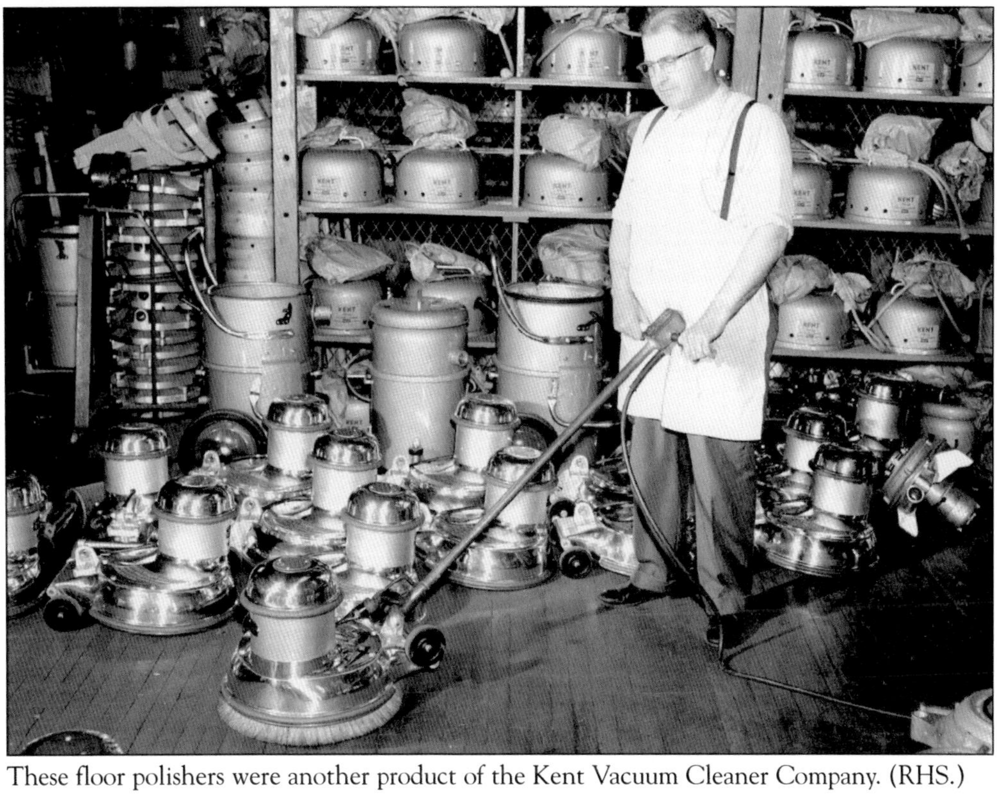

These floor polishers were another product of the Kent Vacuum Cleaner Company. (RHS.)

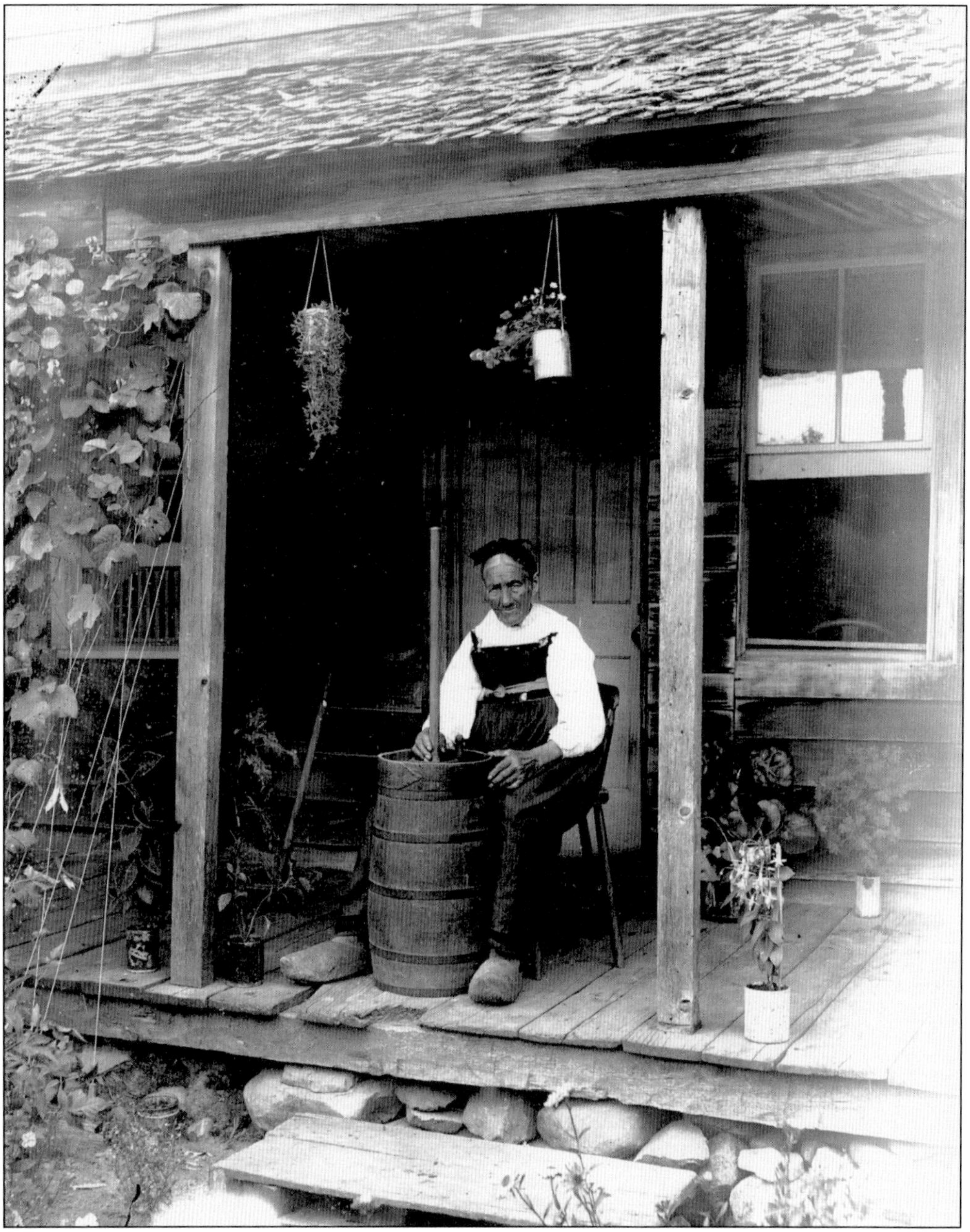

Even with all of the industry in the area, Rome did remain a community with strong ties to agriculture. Soprahia Mertz is seen on her farm with a butter churn. (RHS.)

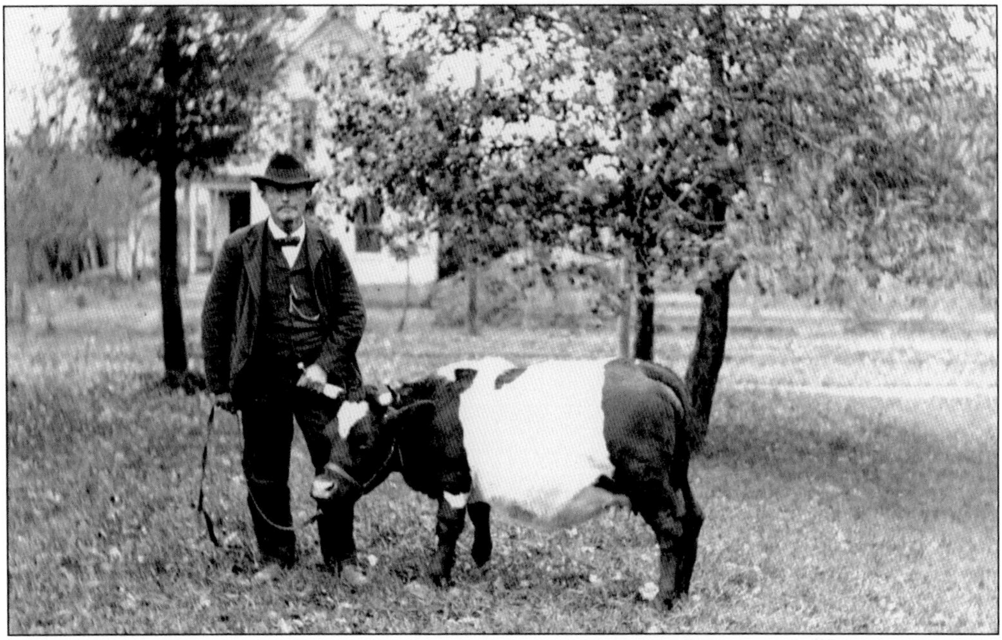

Little Dot was at one time the smallest cow in the world. John H. Jones owned her, and at five years old, she was 32 inches high and weighed 300 pounds. (RHS.)

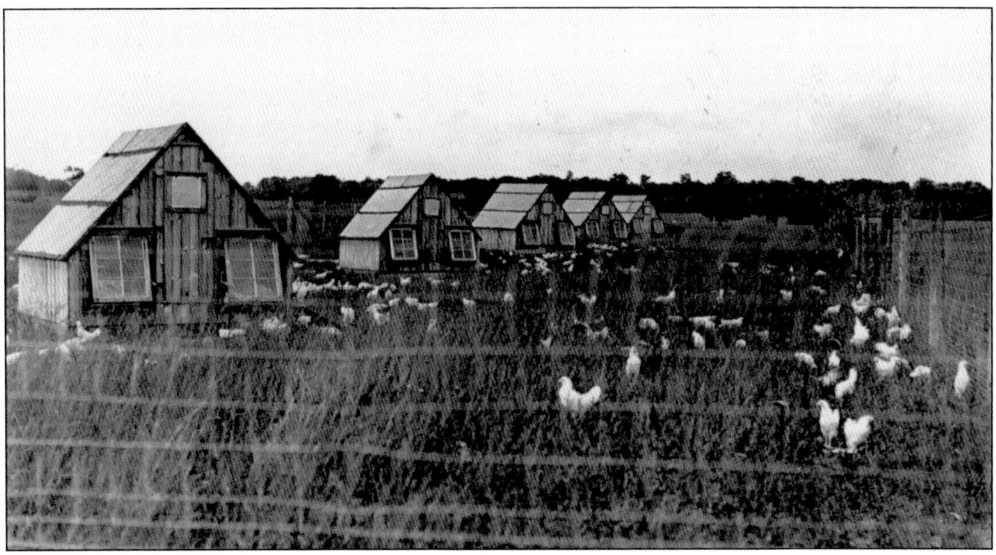

Shown is a small portion of the Huntington Farms chicken farm early in the second decade of the 20th century. The farm was located where Walnut and Oak Streets enter Turin Street today. With a stock of some 5,000 chickens, the farm was considered a large operation at the time. (RHS.)

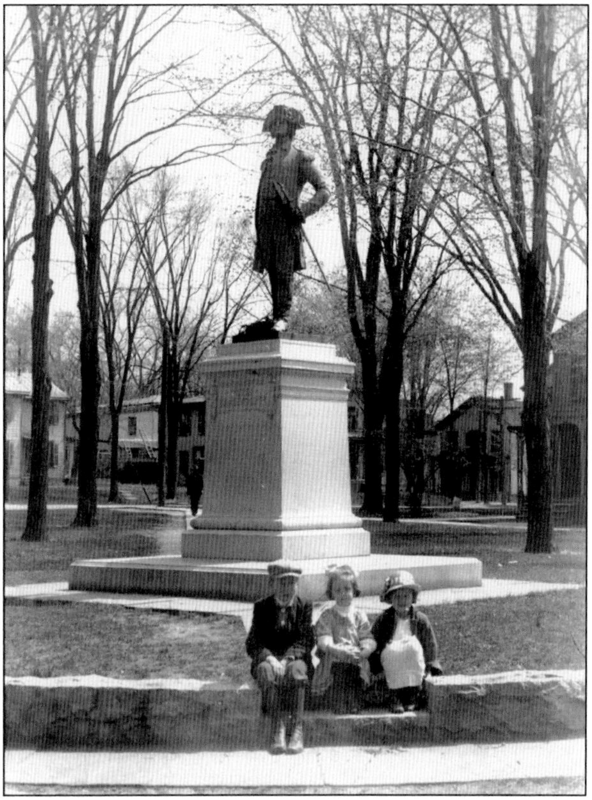

A statue of Gen. Peter Gansevoort was placed in East Park, now Gansevoort Park, in 1907. Located on James Street, the park is surrounded by the courthouse, St. Peter's Church, and the Rome Historical Society. (RHS.)

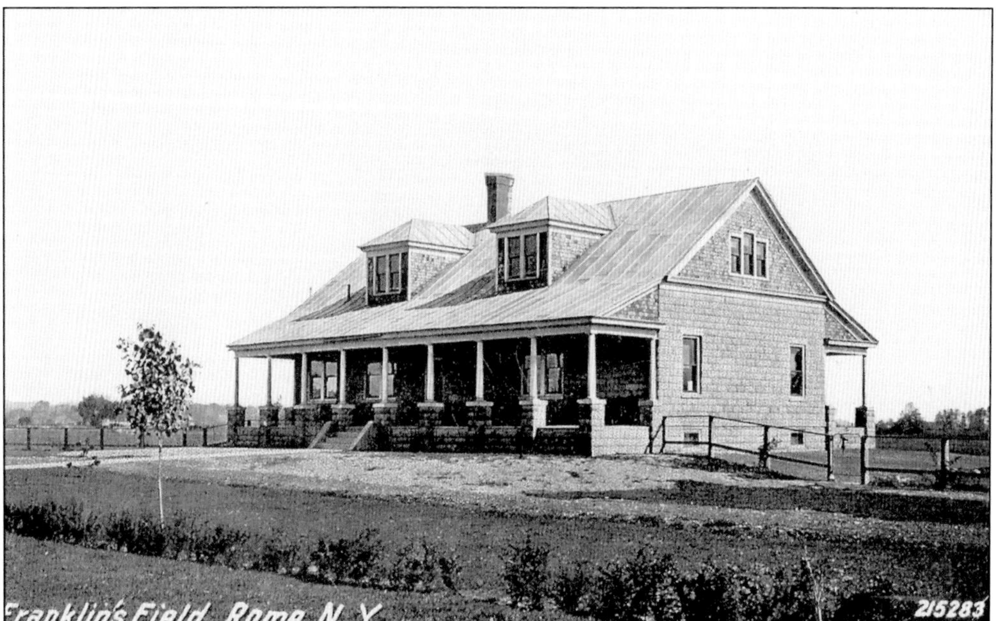

This postcard shows the clubhouse at Franklyn's Field. This park includes play areas, ball fields, and tennis and basketball courts. It is located on North James Street. (Richard Wilson.)

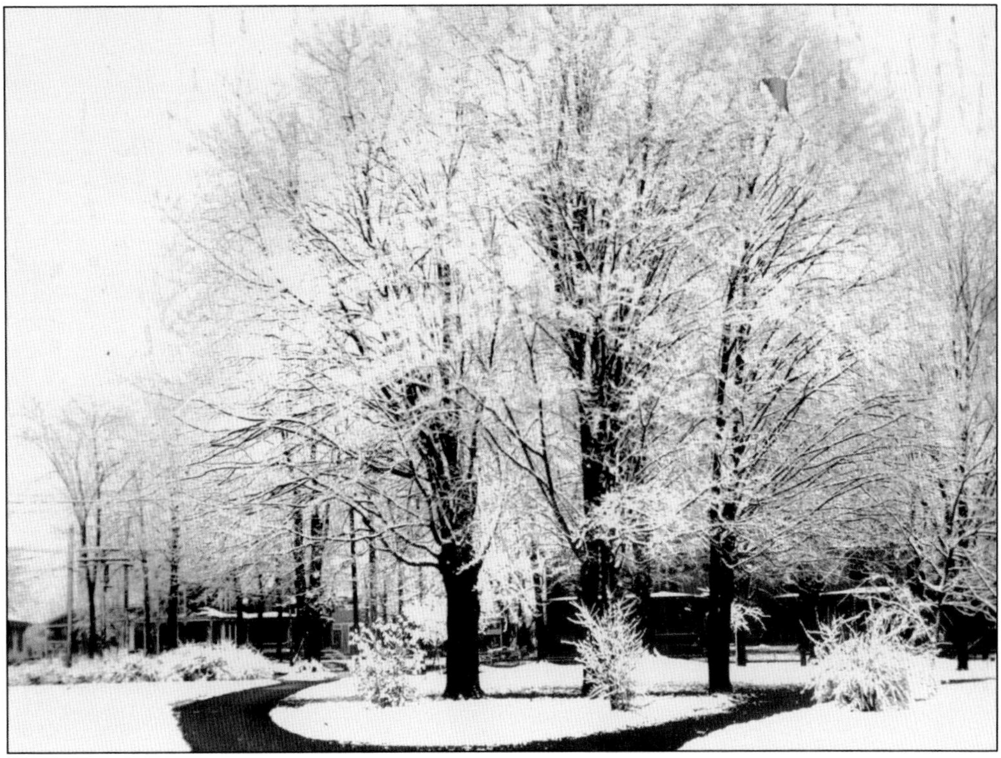

Rome's weather can be unpredictable. This photograph was taken after a late-season snowstorm on May 11, 1907. (RHS.)

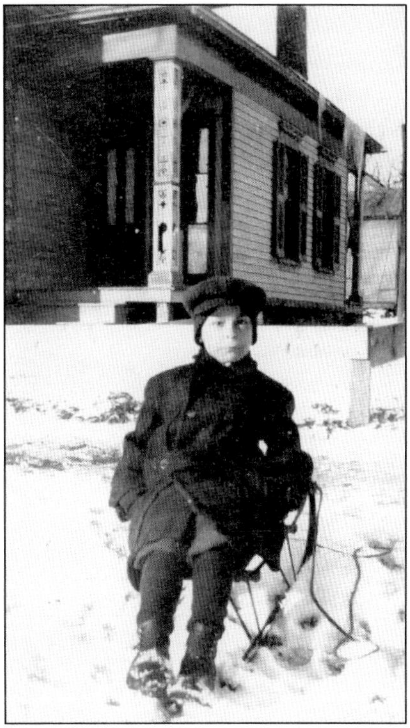

Children like Ted Grimm probably enjoyed the unpredictable weather. Grimm sits on his sled in front of a neighbor's Calvert Street yard in the winter of 1915. (Melody Kiepert Milewski.)

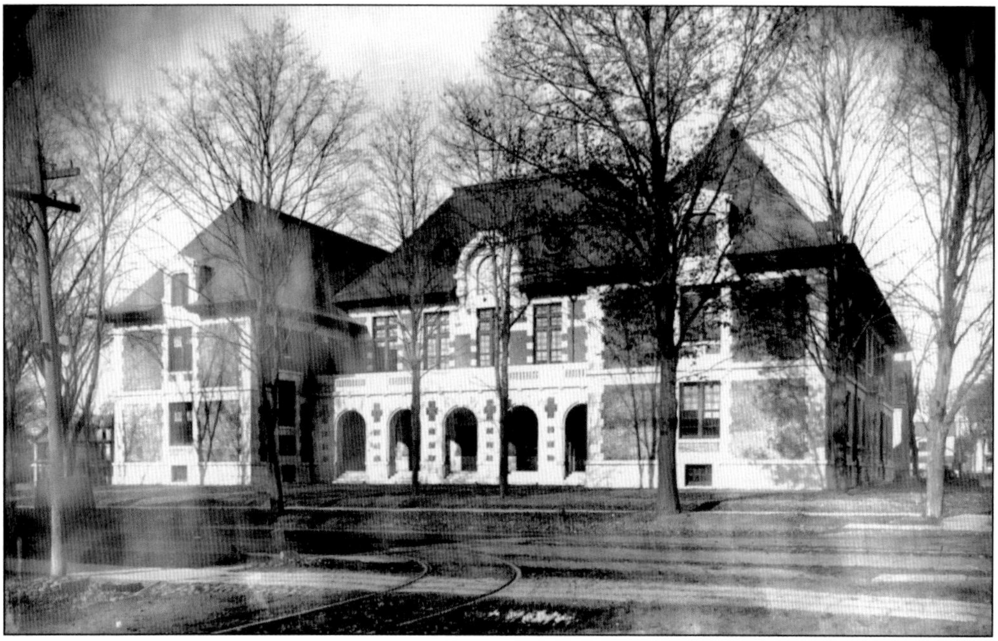

With a growing student population, the Rome Free Academy opened a new building on James Street in 1899. This Chateau-style building cost $80,000 to build. At first, the upper floor was used only for the high school, with the lower floor hosting the Court Street School. The building was torn down in 1960 to make room for the Justice Building. (RHS.)

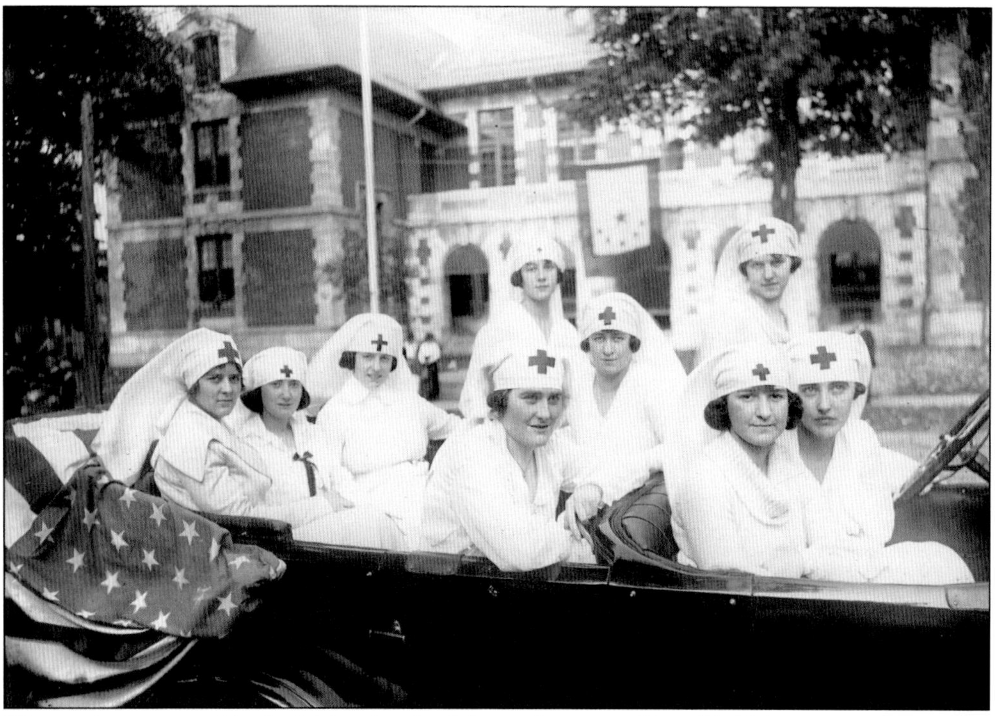

Women in a car outside the high school celebrate Armistice Day. (RHS.)

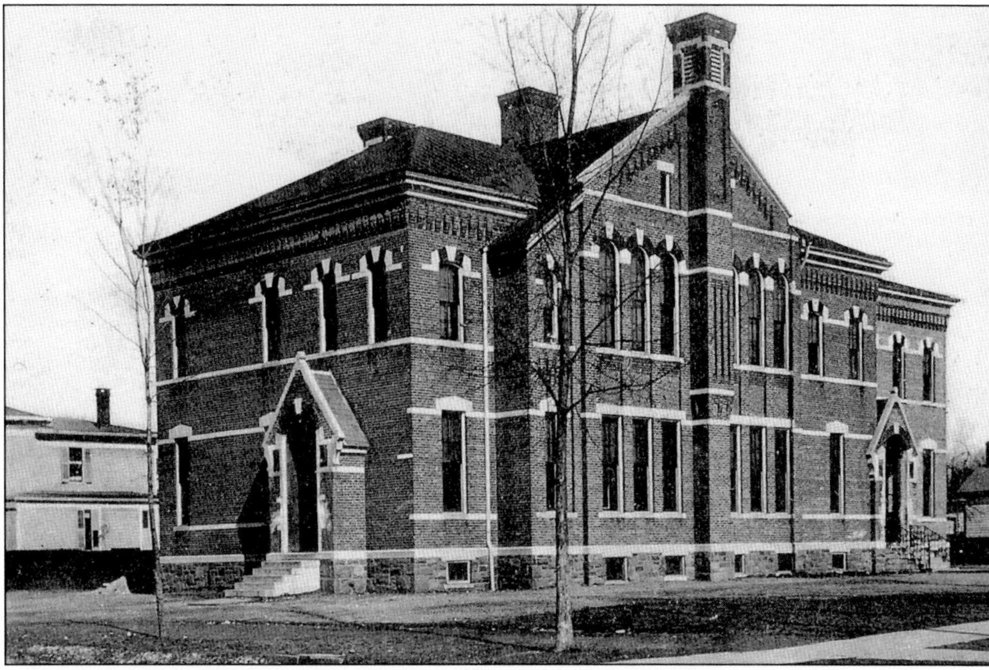

The Jay Street School, on the corner of Thomas and Jay Streets, opened in 1878. The original building, before additions, cost $8,000 and held primary and intermediate level classes. (Richard Wilson.)

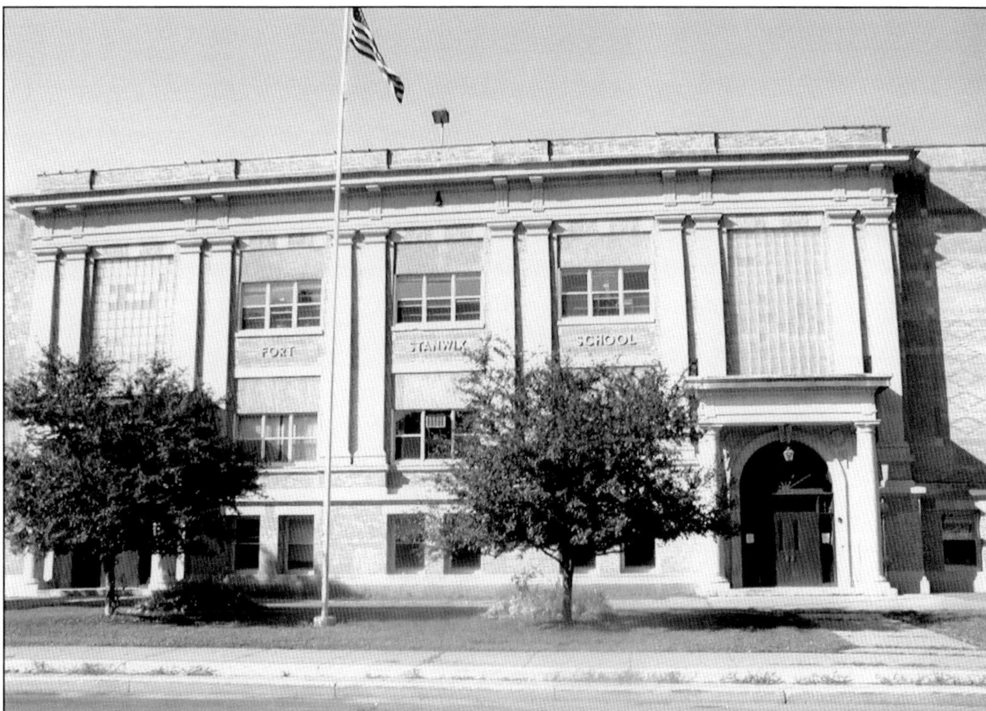

Fort Stanwix Elementary School, on West Linden Street, was built in 1921 and renovated in 1937. (Portia Vescio.)

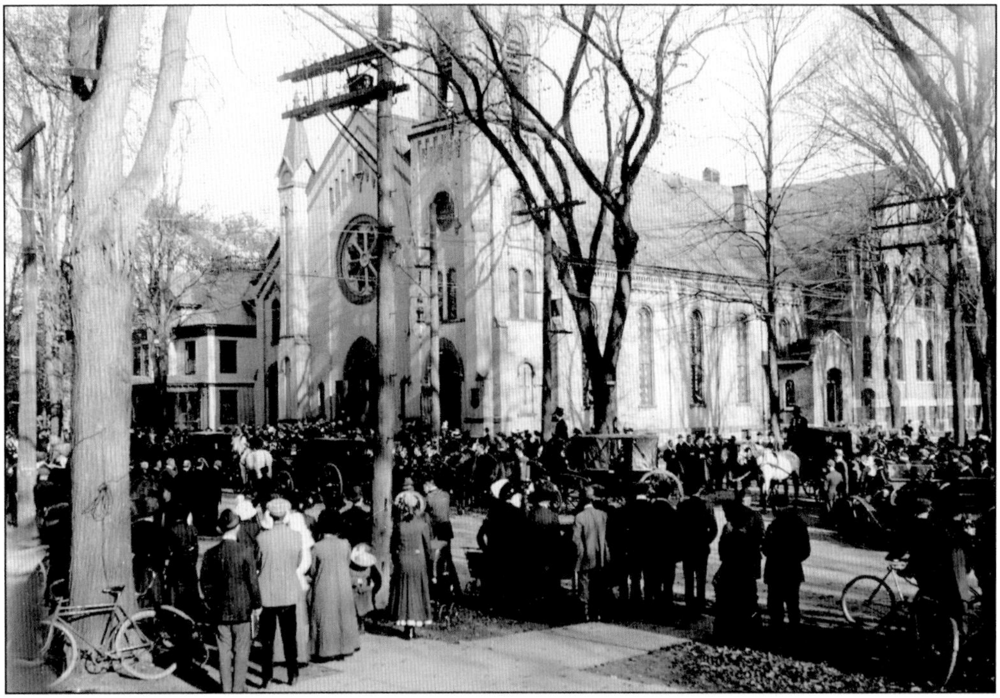

The First Methodist Church is located on the corner of West Embargo and North George Streets. The First Methodist Society in Rome dates back to 1799. (RHS.)

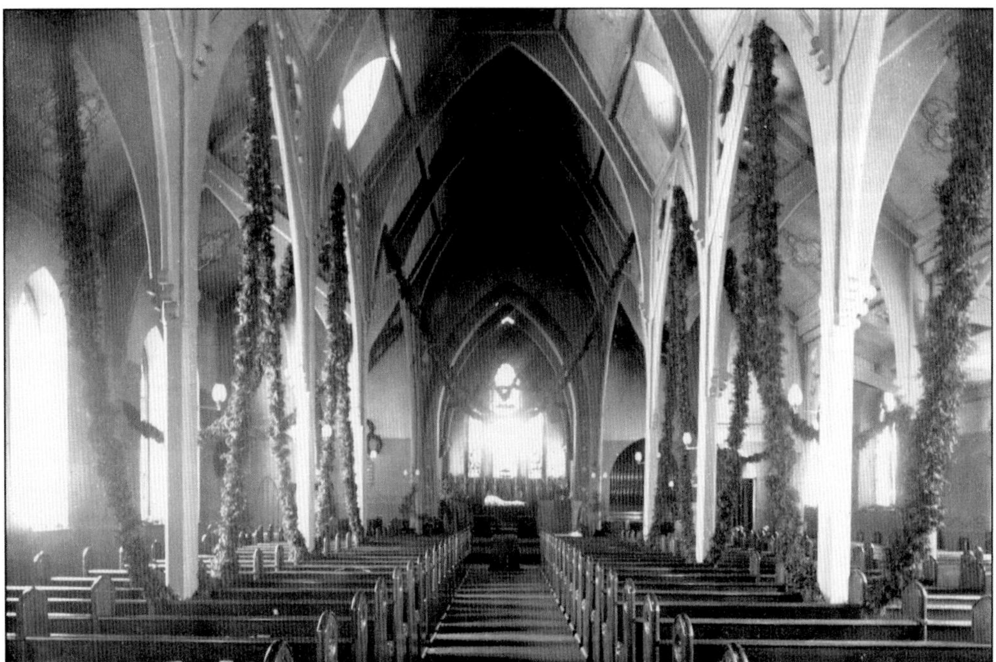

The Zion Episcopal Church was incorporated in Rome in 1825. Architect Richard Upjohn conceived the Gothic design of the building, in which the first service was held on August 17, 1851. (RHS.)

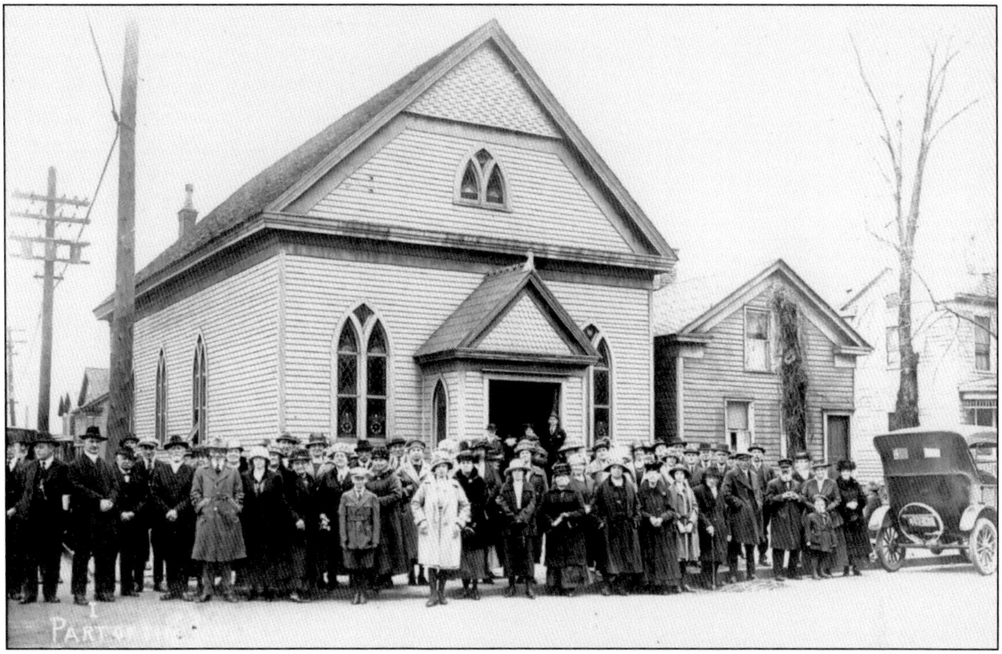

Part of the congregation of the Trinity Evangelical Church gathers outside for the 75th anniversary of the building of the church. (Melody Kiepert Milewski.)

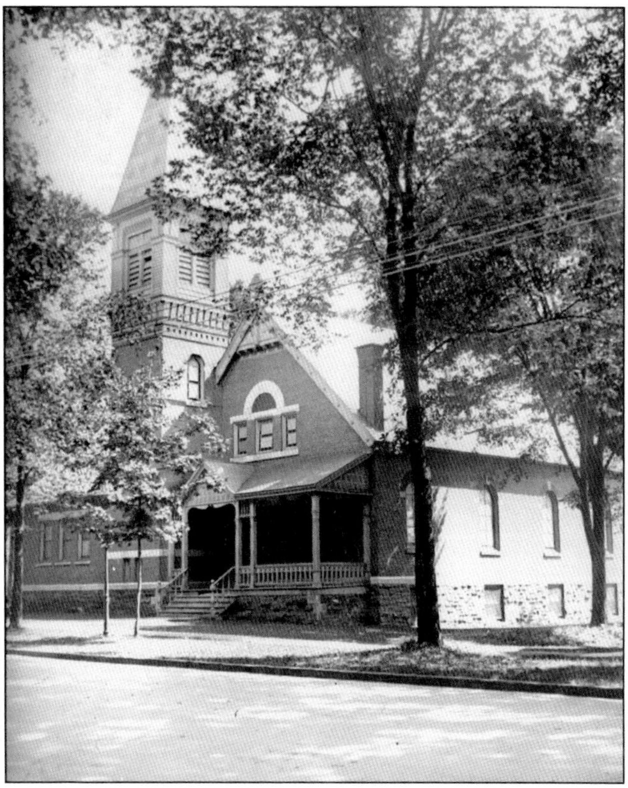

This building on North Washington Street was once a Welsh Presbyterian church. Later, the building was used for the Masonic temple. (RHS.)

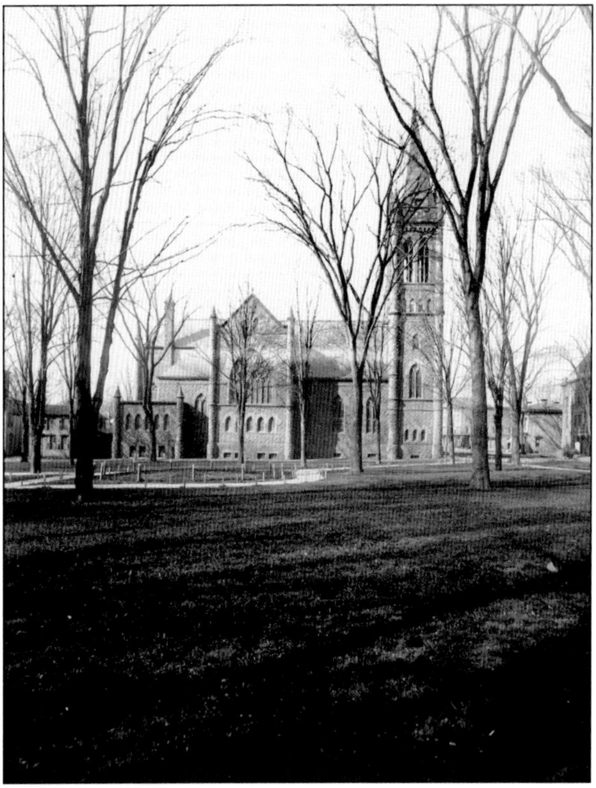

St. Peter's Church, on North James Street, was begun in 1893 and cost approximately $150,000. The building was consecrated in 1897. (RHS.)

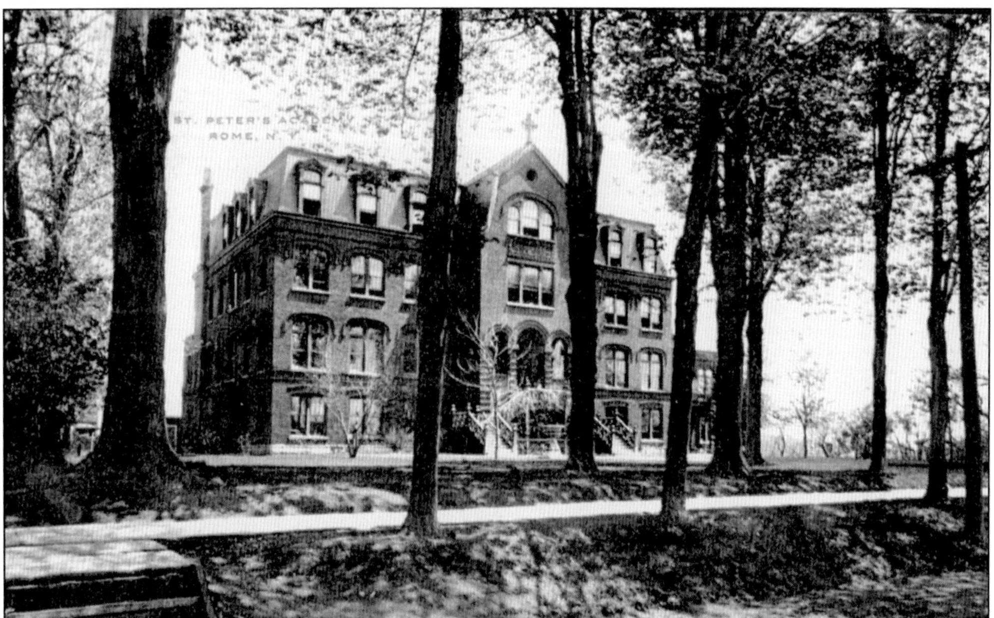

Shortly after the end of the Civil War, the Sisters of the Holy Names established the St. Peter's Academy for young ladies. The Sisters of the Holy Names later opened the Academy of Holy Names, on St. Peter's Avenue at the head of River Street. (Dr. Craeger Boardman.)

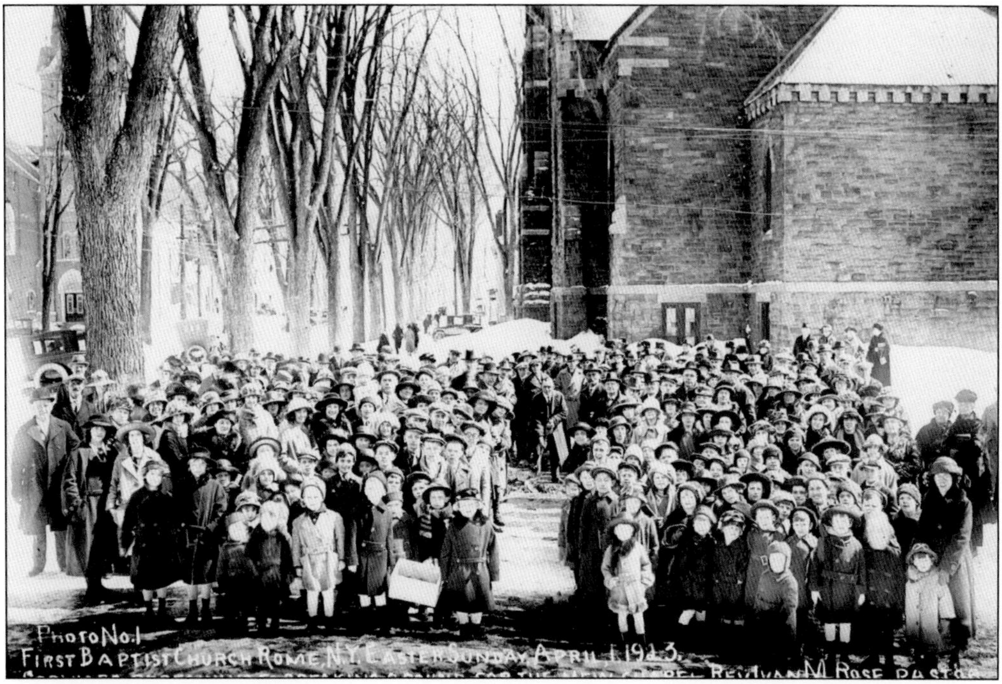

The First Baptist Church congregation stands outside on Easter Sunday, April 1, 1923, to celebrate the groundbreaking for a new chapel. (RHS.)

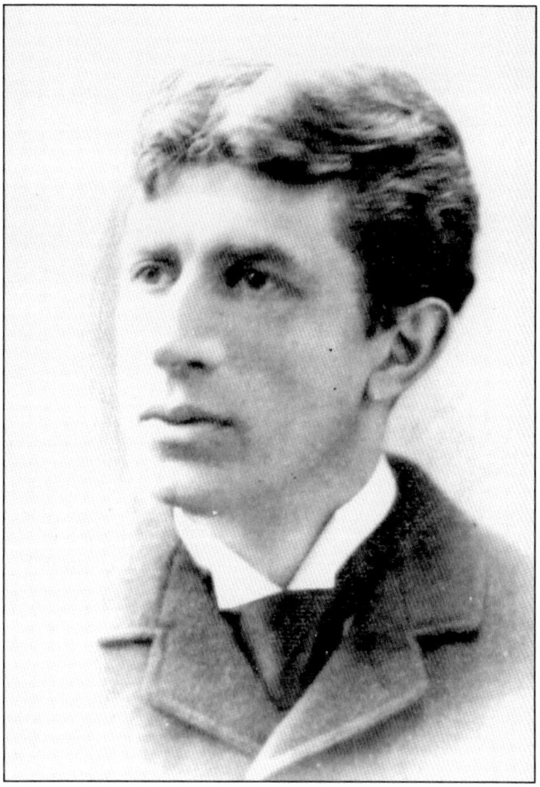

Francis Bellamy (1855–1931) was the son of a pastor of the First Baptist Church in the 1860s. Bellamy was also a minister and worked for *Youth's Companion* when the owners were promoting a national public celebration of Columbus Day. Bellamy wrote a salute to the flag, which later became known as the Pledge of Allegiance. Bellamy's original 23 words went as follows, "I pledge allegiance to my flag, and to the republic for which it stands; one nation indivisible with liberty and justice for all." (RHS.)

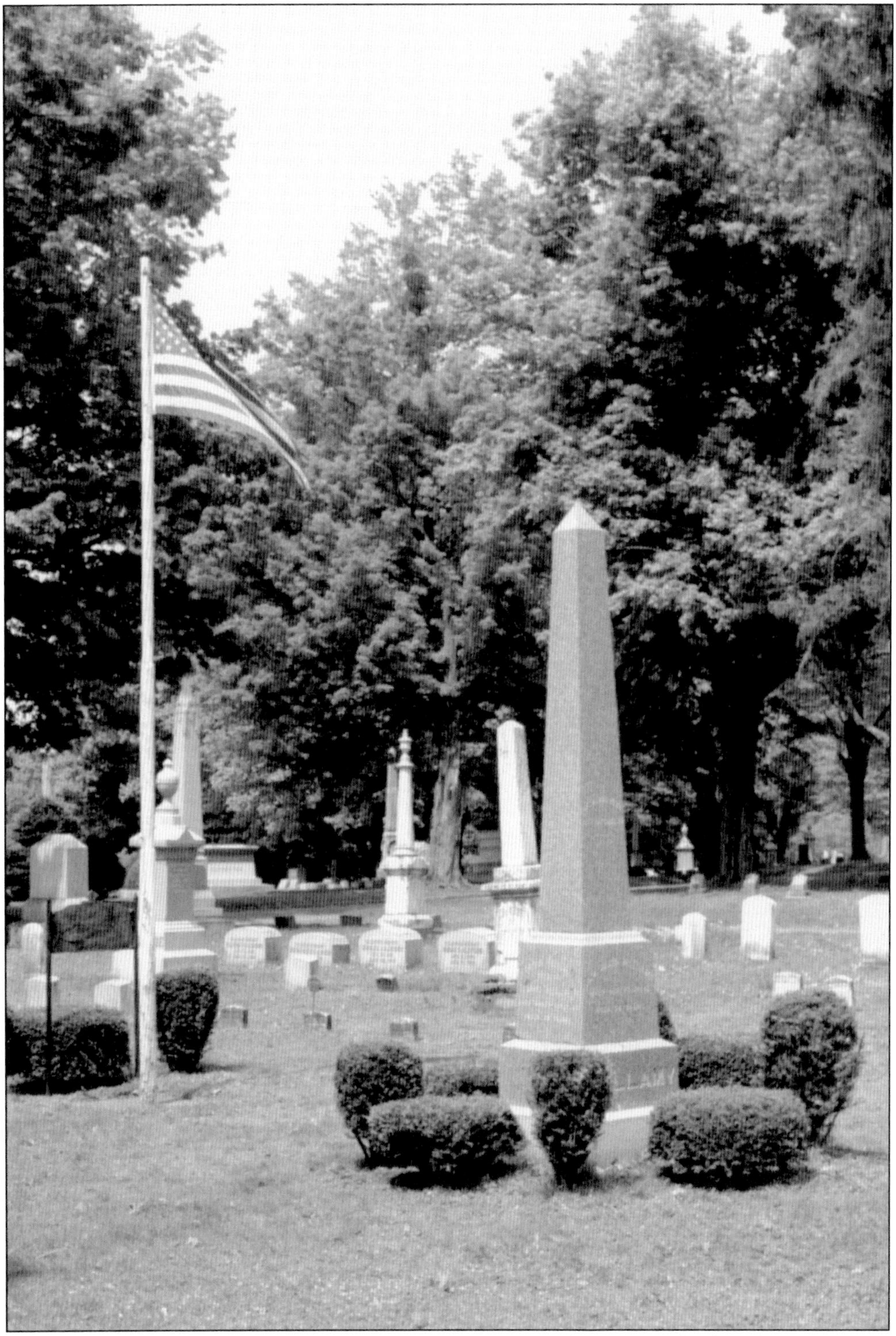

Located in the Rome Cemetery is a monument to Francis Bellamy. Inscribed on the monument is Bellamy's text for the Pledge of Allegiance. (RHS.)

Three

THE COPPER AGE

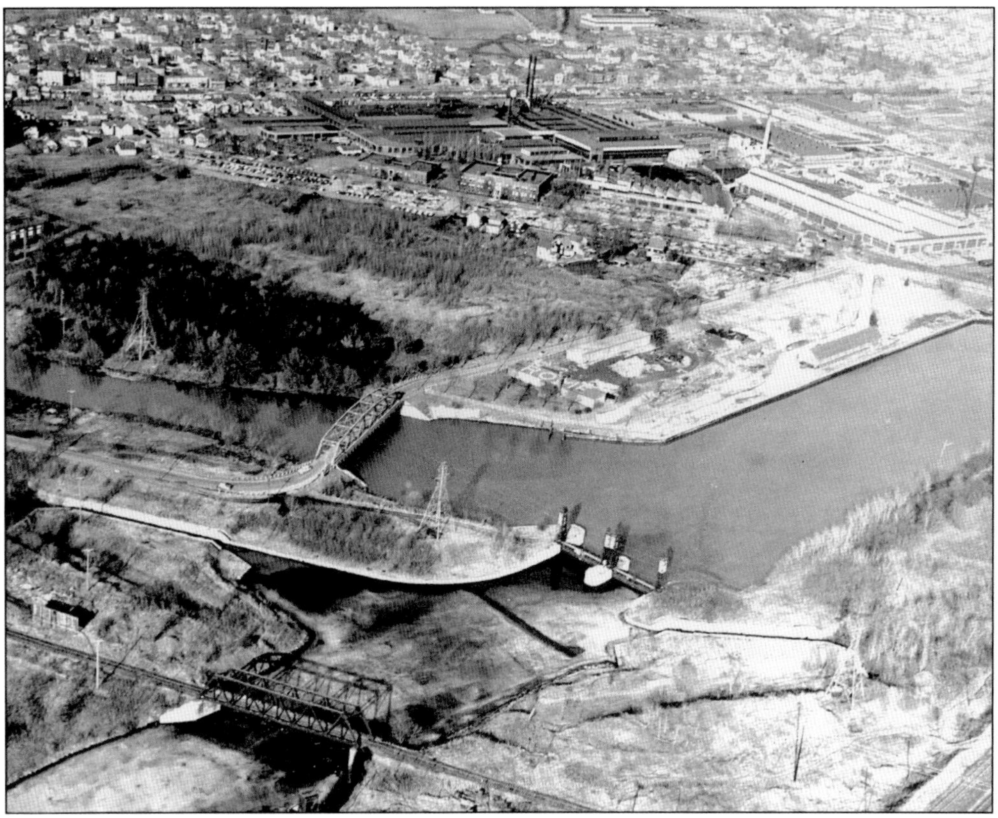

This aerial view of the Barge Canal shows the industrial section of Rome in the 1930s. The period from the 1930s to the 1960s was the golden age of Rome. Many industries flourished during these years, and the population continued to grow, reaching a peak of more than 50,000 people. Rome's association with Revere Copper and Brass earned the city the nickname of Copper City. It was also during this period that Griffiss Air Force Base opened in Rome. (RHS.)

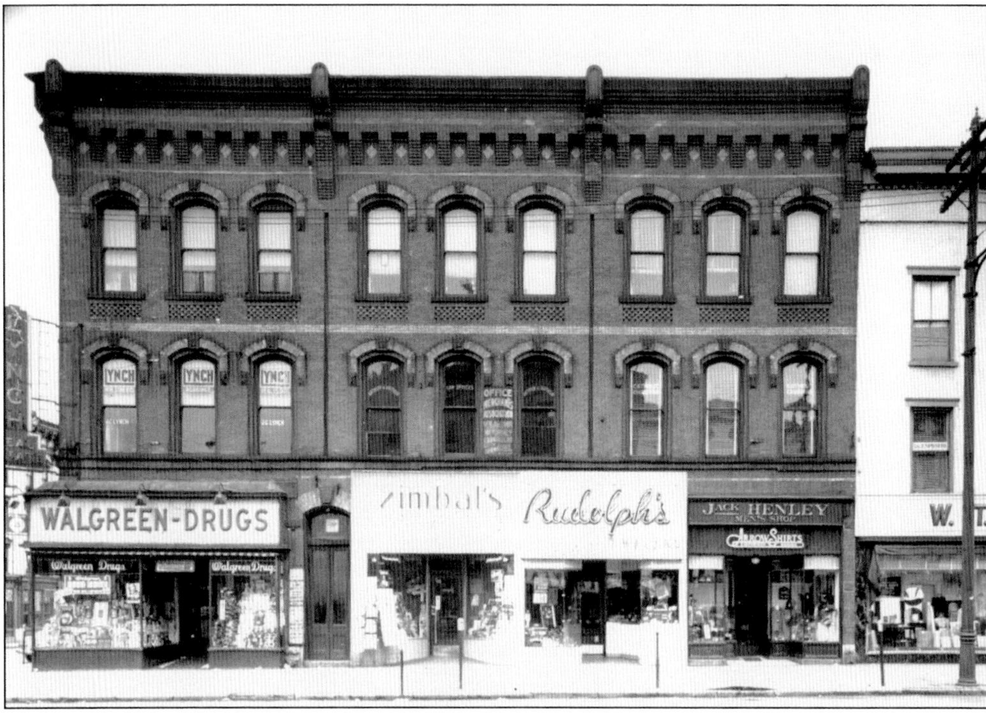

These four photographs show what residents of Rome would have seen while looking at the south side of Dominick Street in the 1950s. (RHS.)

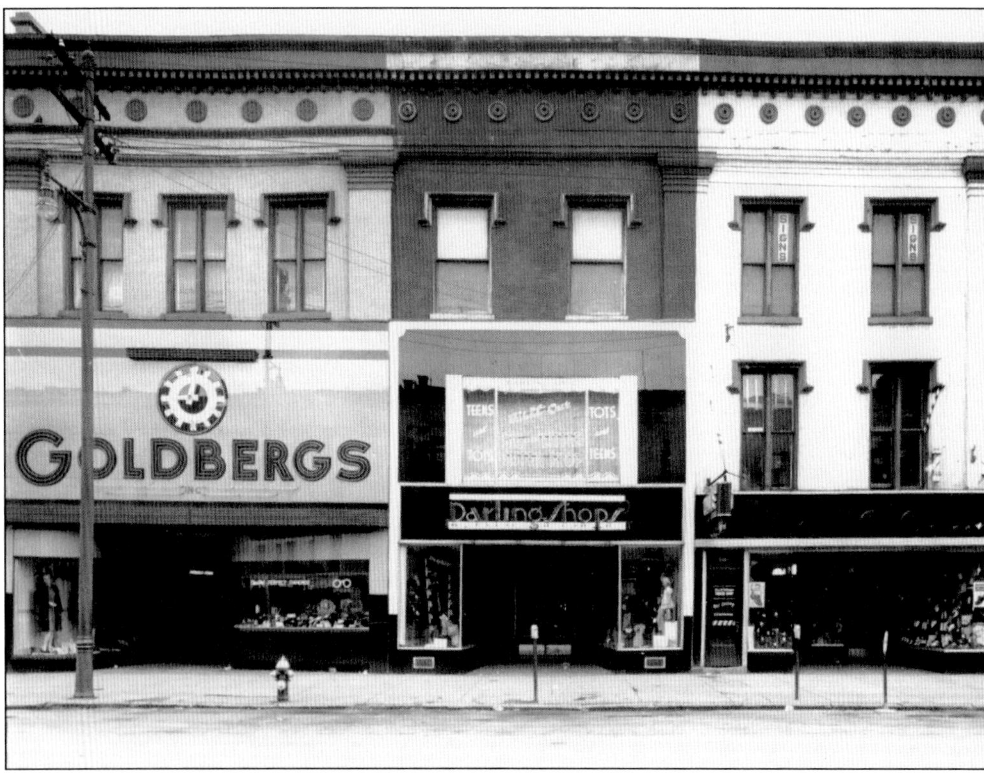

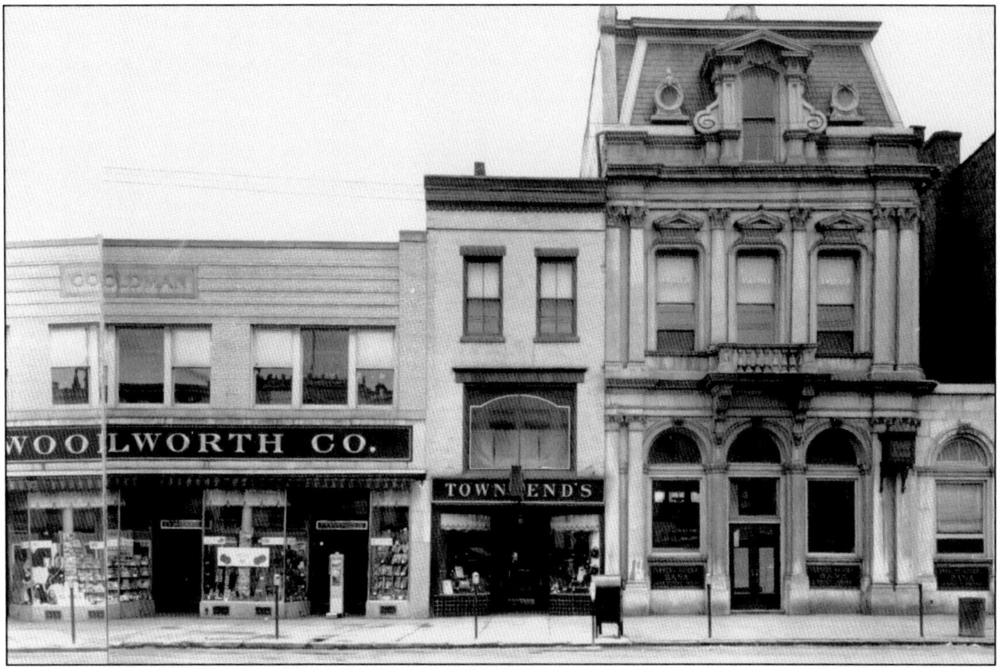

Though the tenants in these buildings changed over the years, the buildings themselves remained relatively unchanged from the time at which they were originally built. (RHS.)

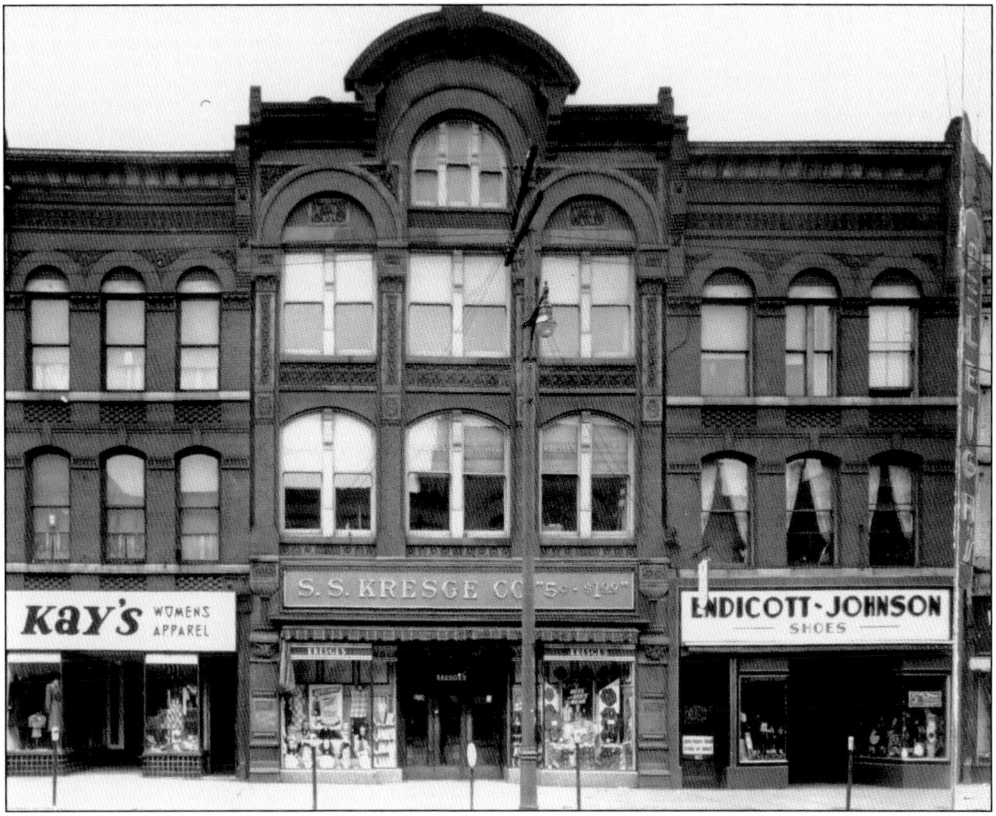

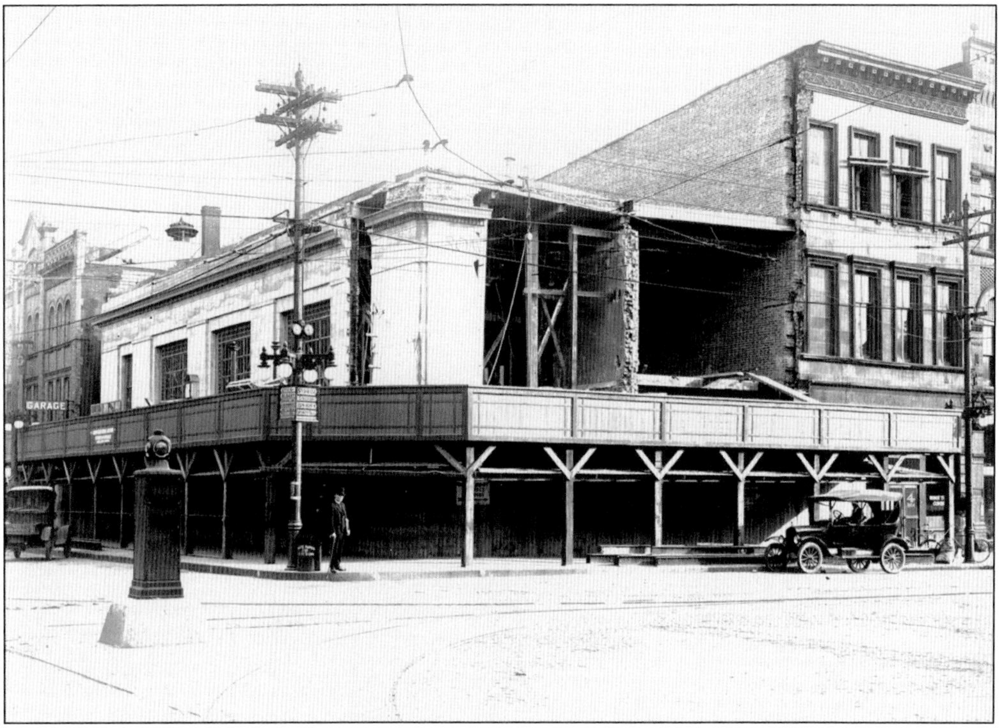

This series of photographs shows the evolution of the southeast corner of Dominick and James Streets where the Rome Trust Company resides. In these first two photographs, the building is under construction and the corner is still developing. (RHS.)

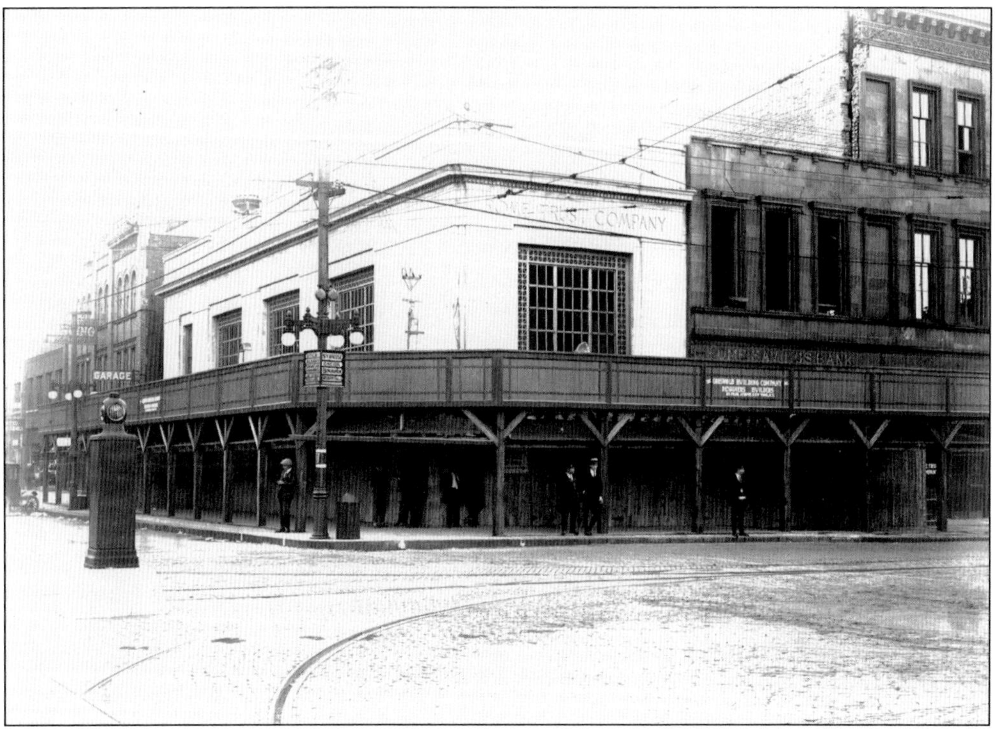

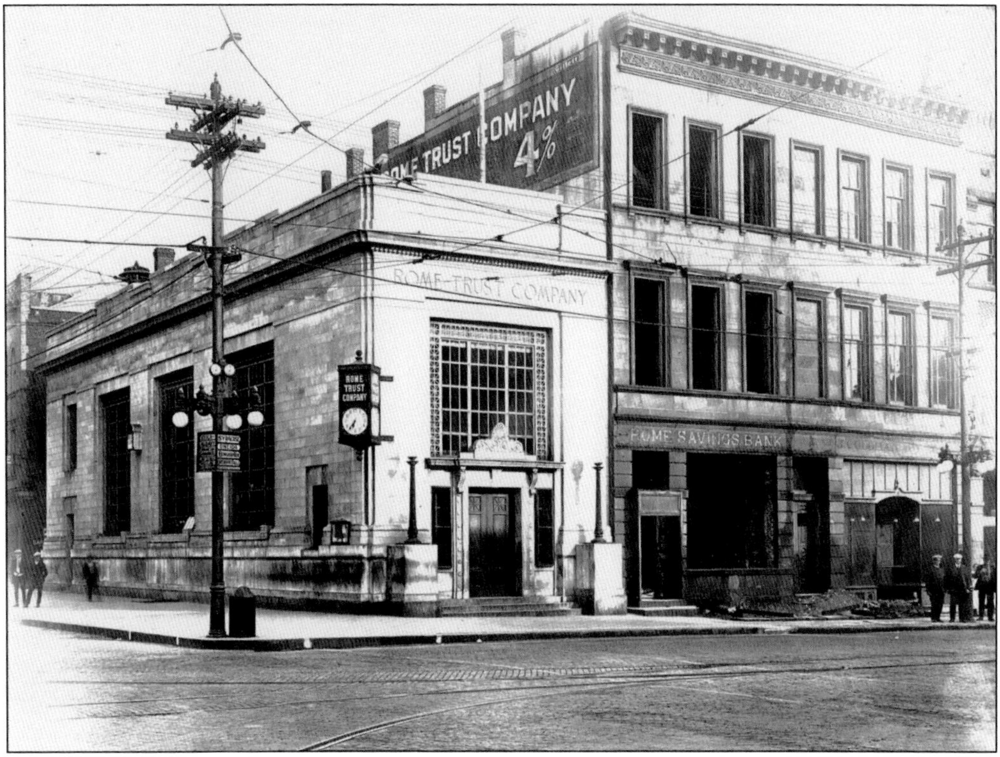

In these two photographs, the building is finished and the Rome Trust Company is open for business. The street sign, visible in the 1923 photograph above, is absent from the photograph below, taken in the 1950s. The sign did not list streets but rather pointed the direction to major cities such as Utica, Albany, Syracuse, Oneida, and Binghamton. (RHS.)

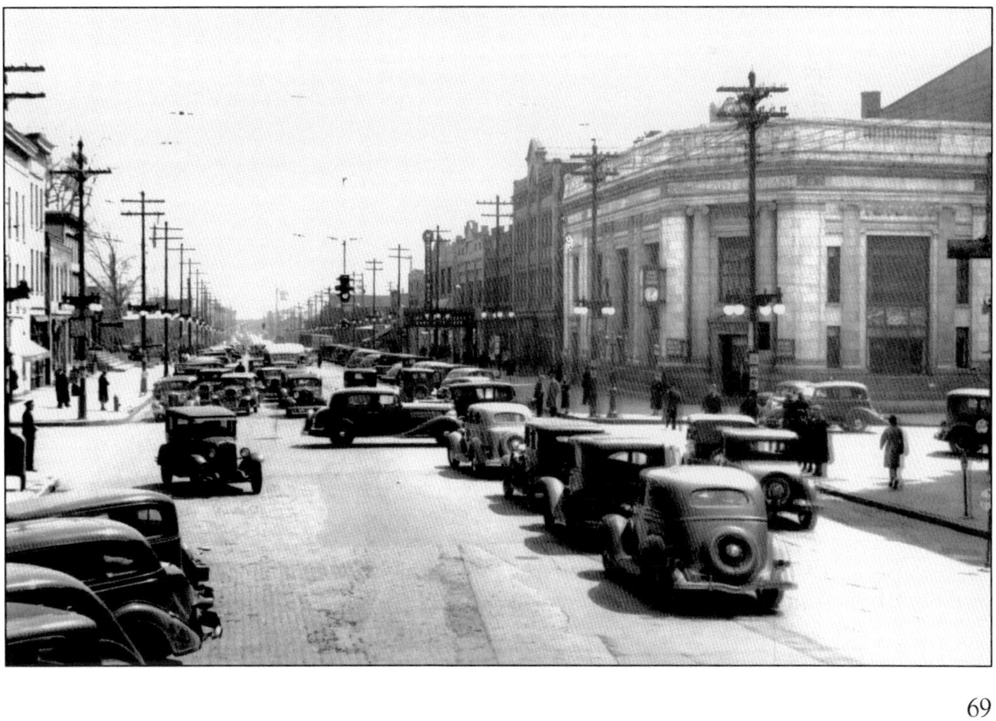

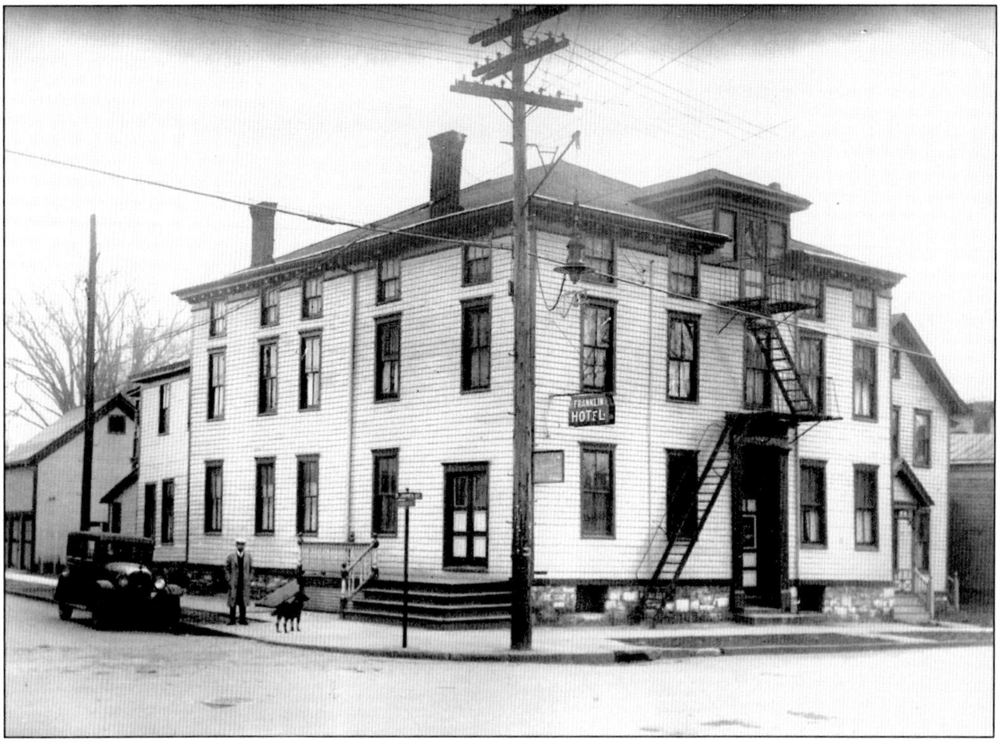

The Franklin Hotel, located on the corner of James and Lawrence Streets, was another early hotel in Rome. Today, the Franklin Hotel is a popular restaurant. (Phil Vescio.)

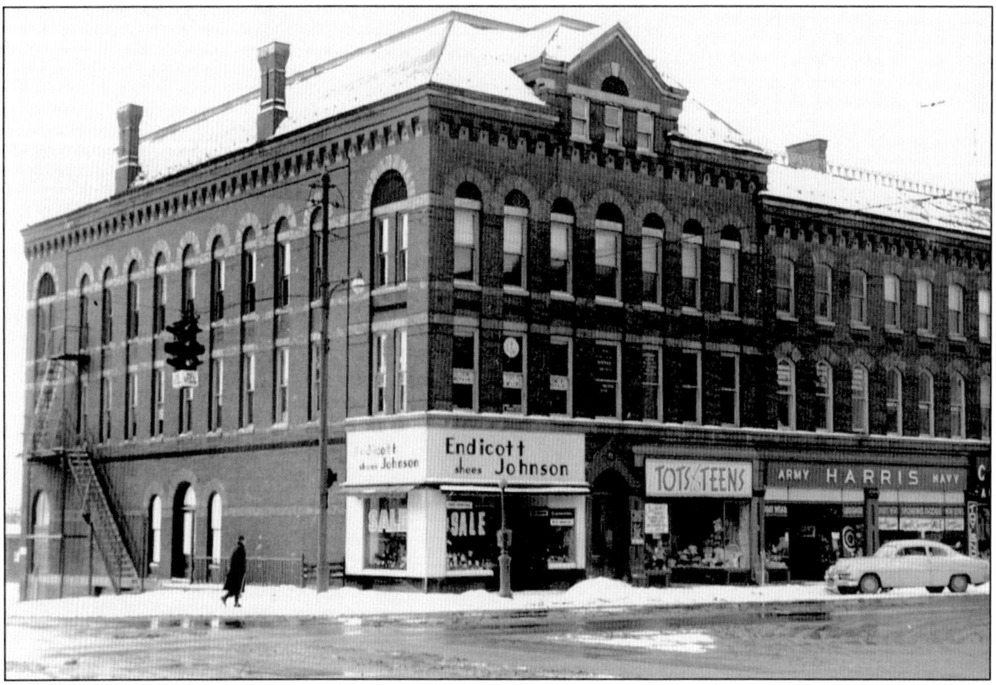

This is the corner of Dominick and Washington Streets known as the Glesmann-Hower Block. This is the same corner where the Rome Business Institute once resided. (RHS.)

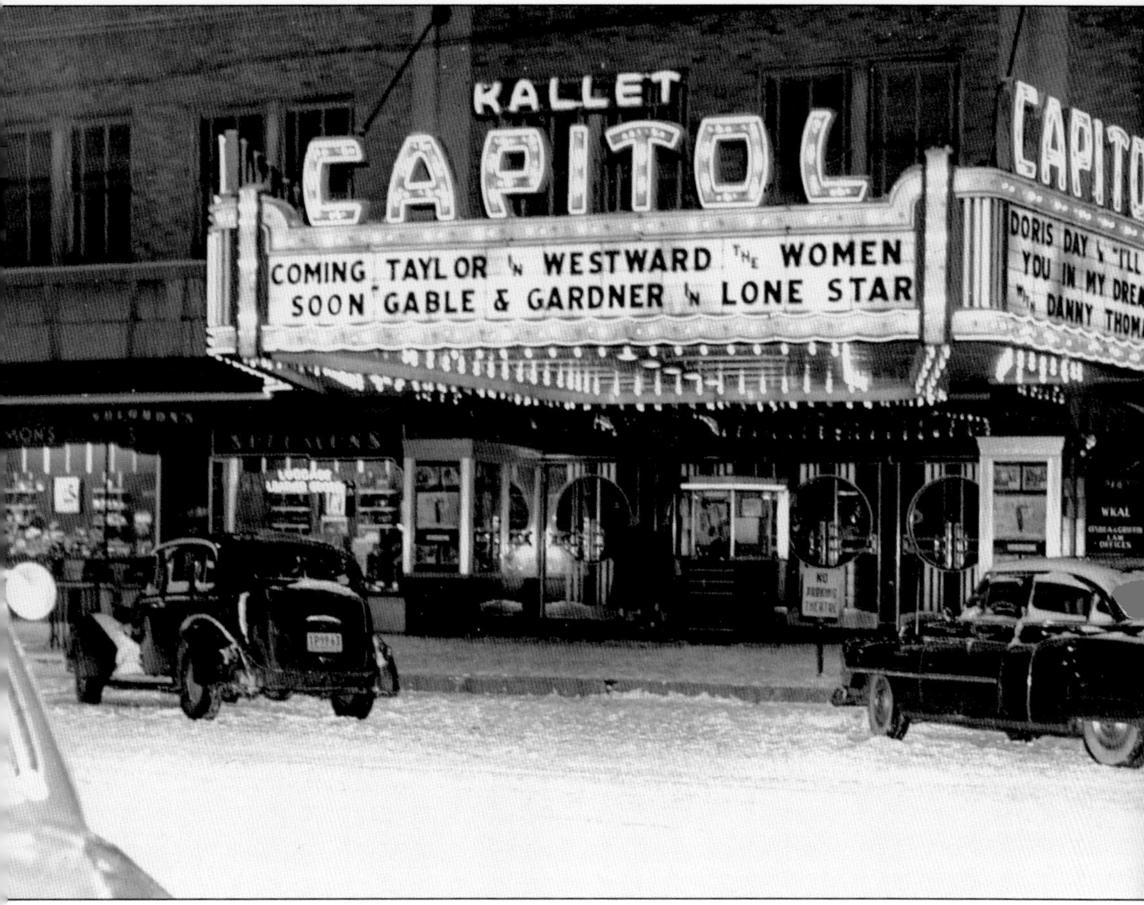

For many years, the Kallet Capitol Theater provided residents with a nice night out at the cinema. The theater opened on December 10, 1928 and showed first-run movies until the 1970s. (RHS.)

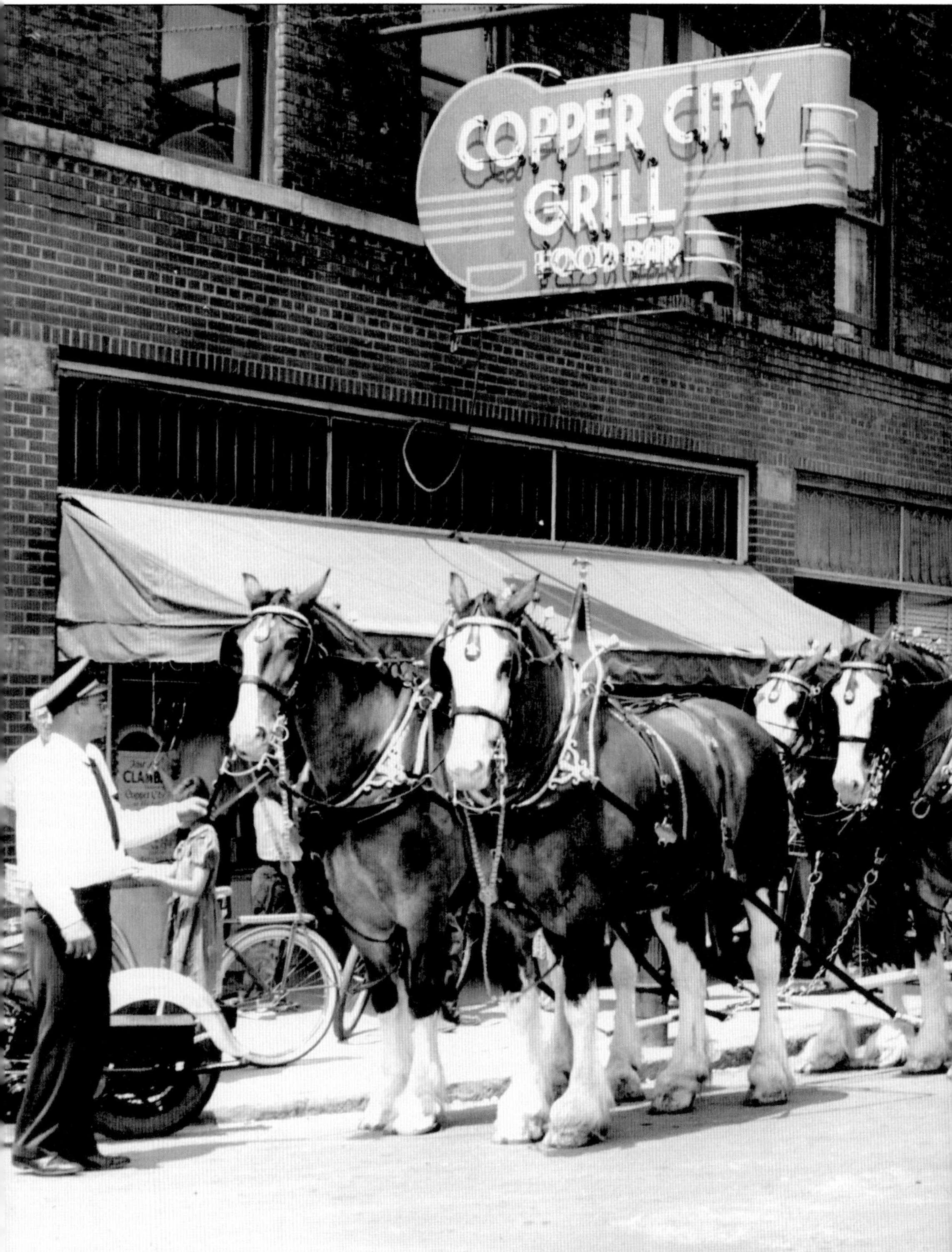

The Clydesdale horses from Anheuser-Busch pause in front of the Copper City Hotel and the

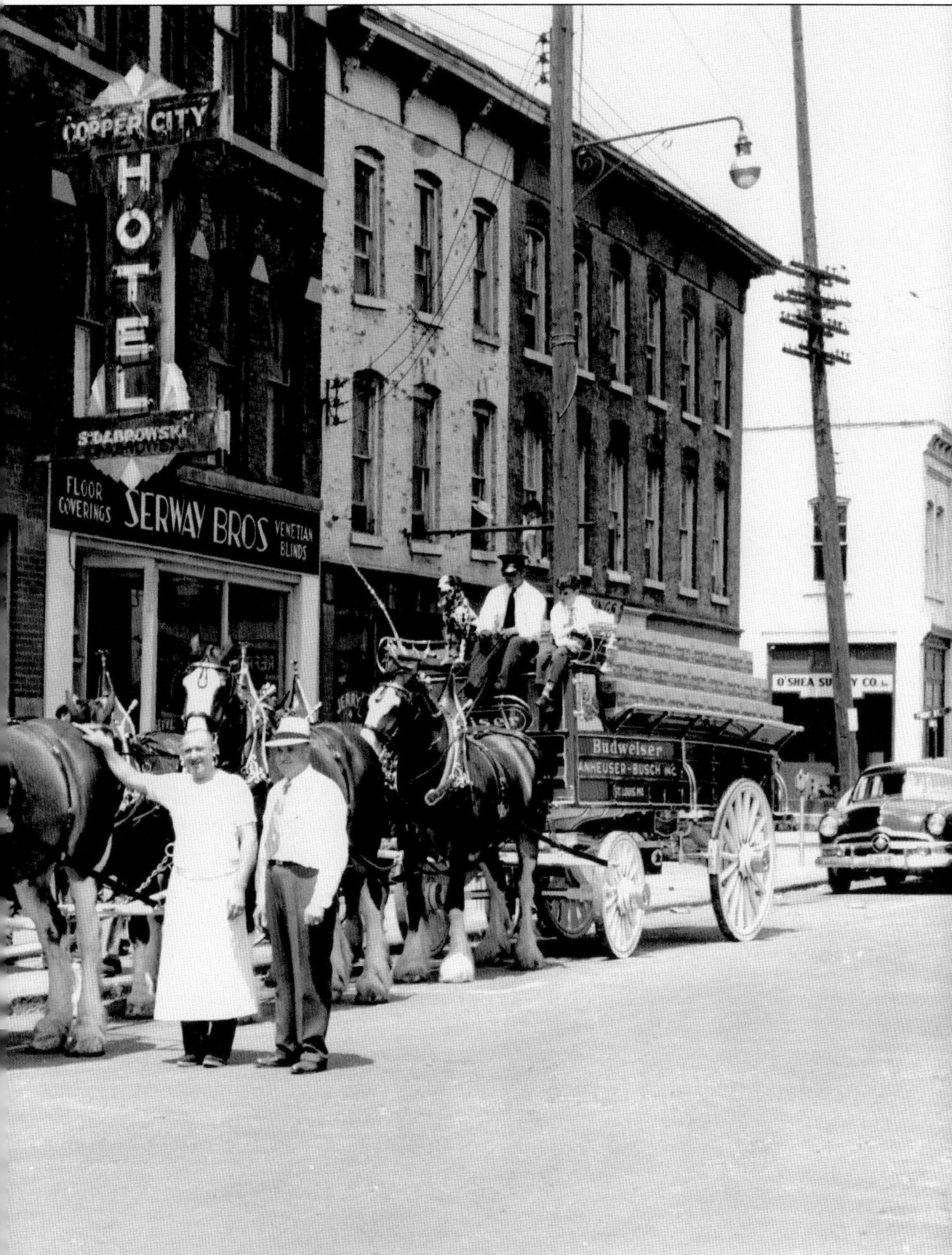

Copper City Grill on their march along James Street. (RHS.)

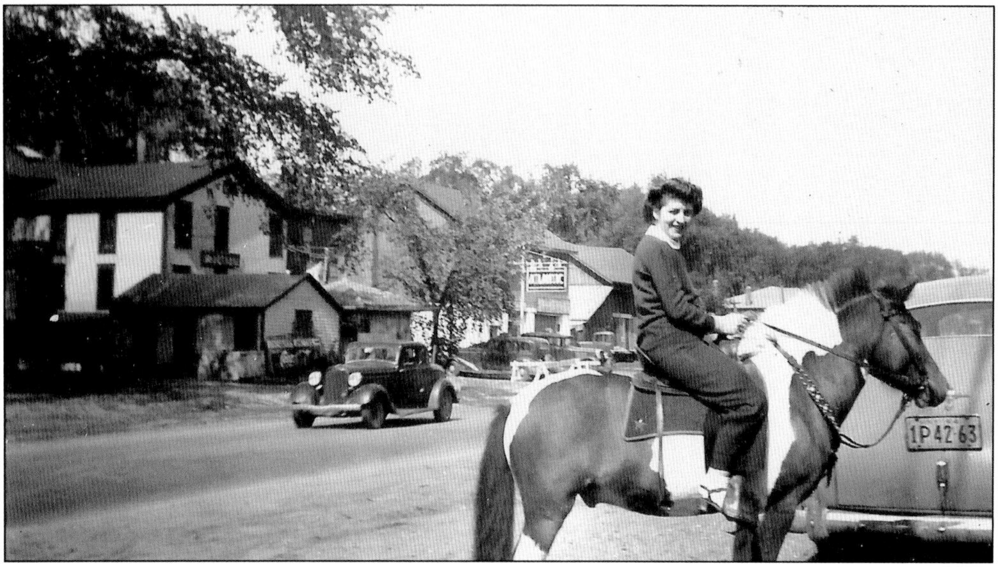

Black River Boulevard was built over the old Black River Canal. The road was not opened to traffic until 1954. Frances Scerra rides a horse on Black River Boulevard before it was paved. (Patty Hudak.)

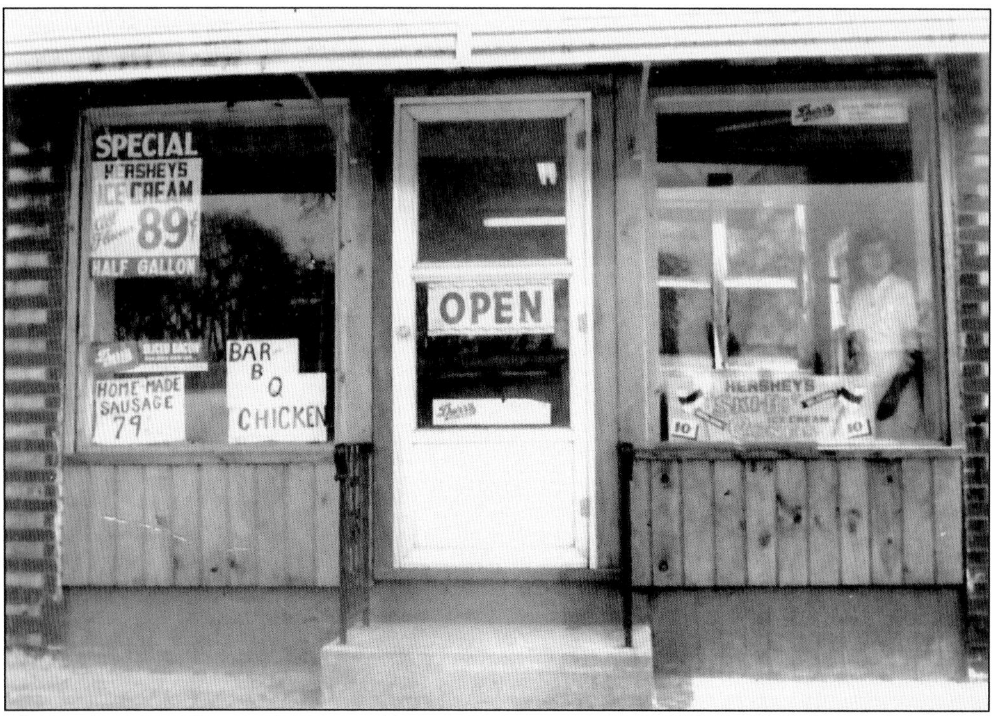

The Boulevard Poultry Market, owned by Rose Baptiste, was located on the Black River Boulevard. This photograph was taken a week after the market opened on May 6, 1956. (Patty Hudak.)

After the creation of the reservoir at Delta, the worst flood Rome experienced occurred in October 1945 following an unusually wet September and three days of continuous rain. This is a view of the corner of Dominick and River Streets after the rains stopped. (Patty Hudak.)

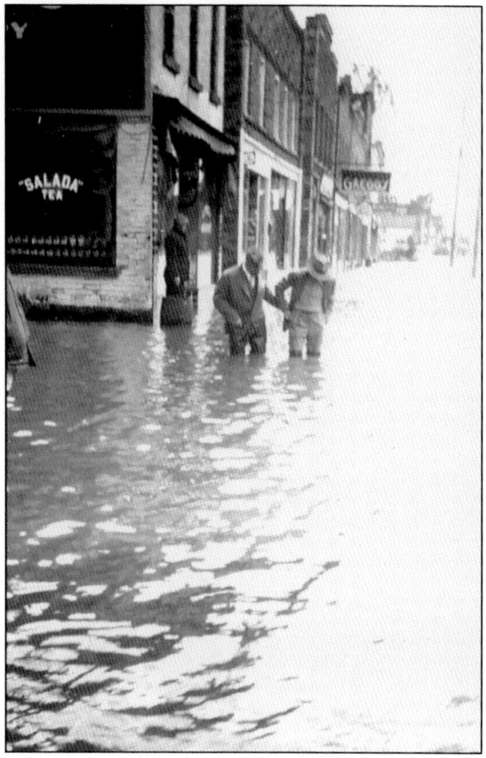

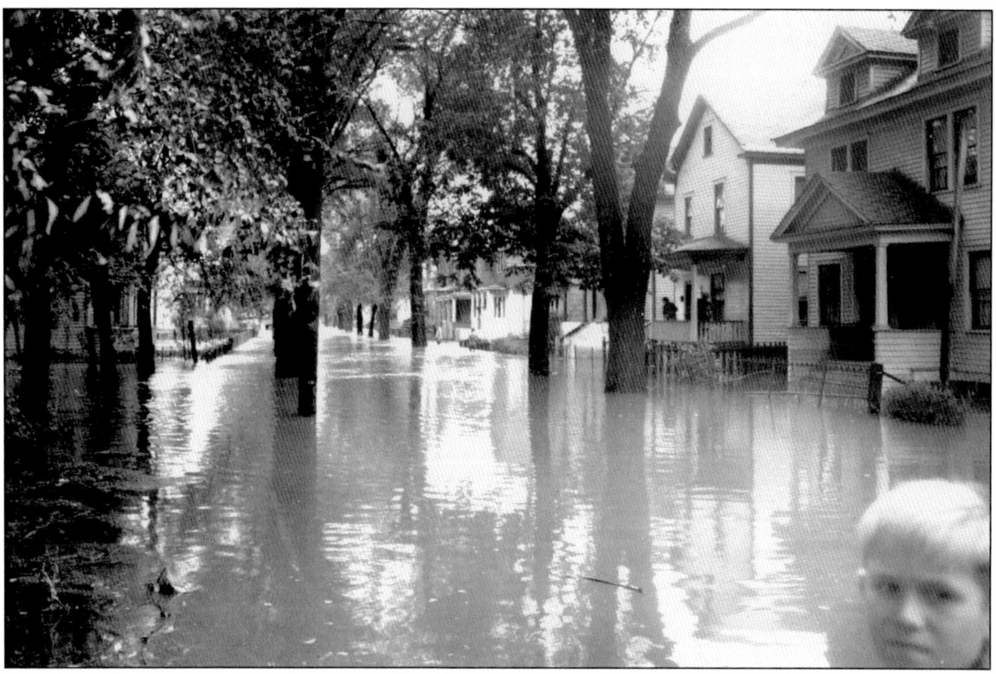

Residential areas were flooded, as well as businesses. (RHS.)

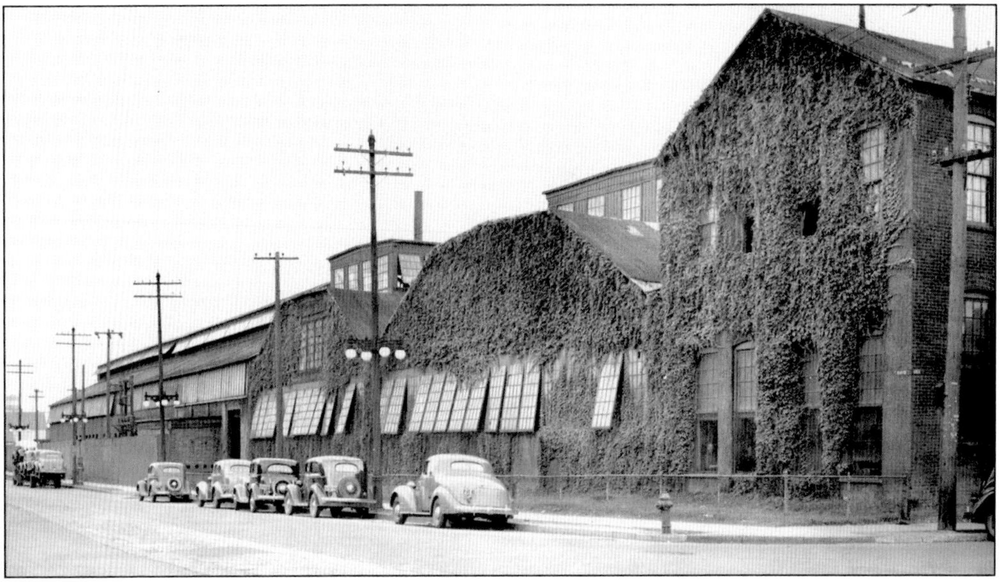

Rome Brass and Copper Company and five other companies merged in 1928 to form Revere Copper and Brass. The company changed its name to Revere because it had its roots in the copper company founded by Paul Revere in Canton, Massachusetts, in 1801. Barton Haselton, who was head of Rome Brass and Copper, became chairman of the board of the new corporation. The Revere building is pictured in 1935. (RHS.)

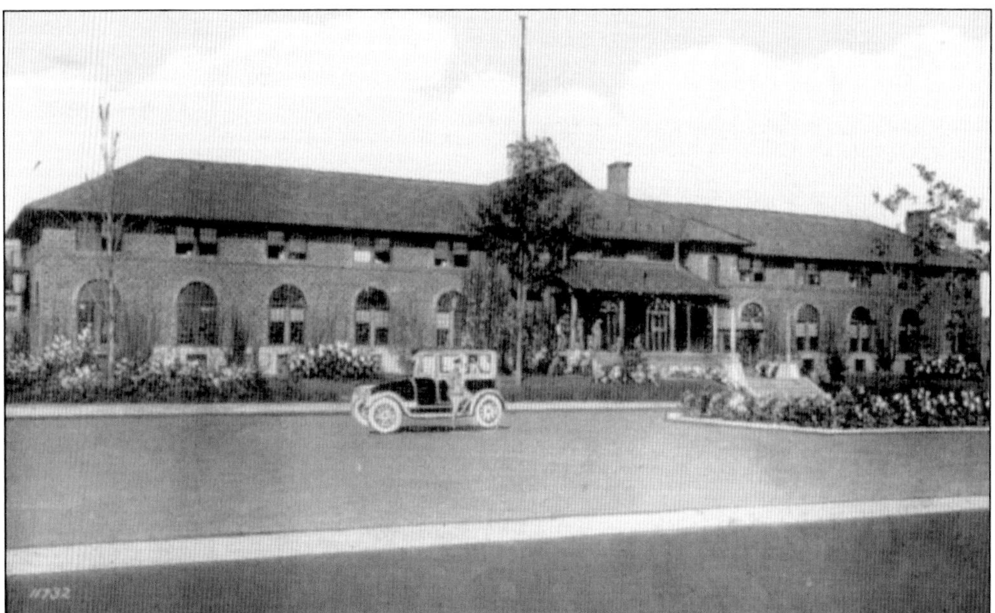

The headquarters of the new Revere Copper and Brass were in Rome, with the executive offices located in the old Riverdale Club House. (Portia Vescio.)

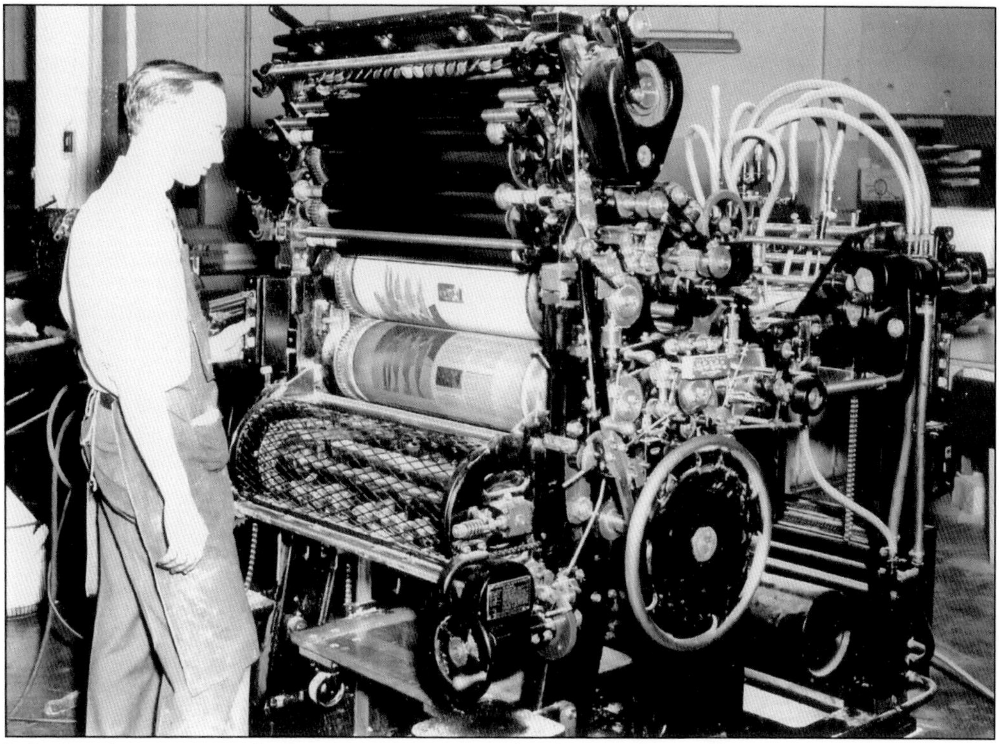

Lyle Beach operates a large printing press at the Revere Print Shop at 100 Bouck Street. (Steven Beach.)

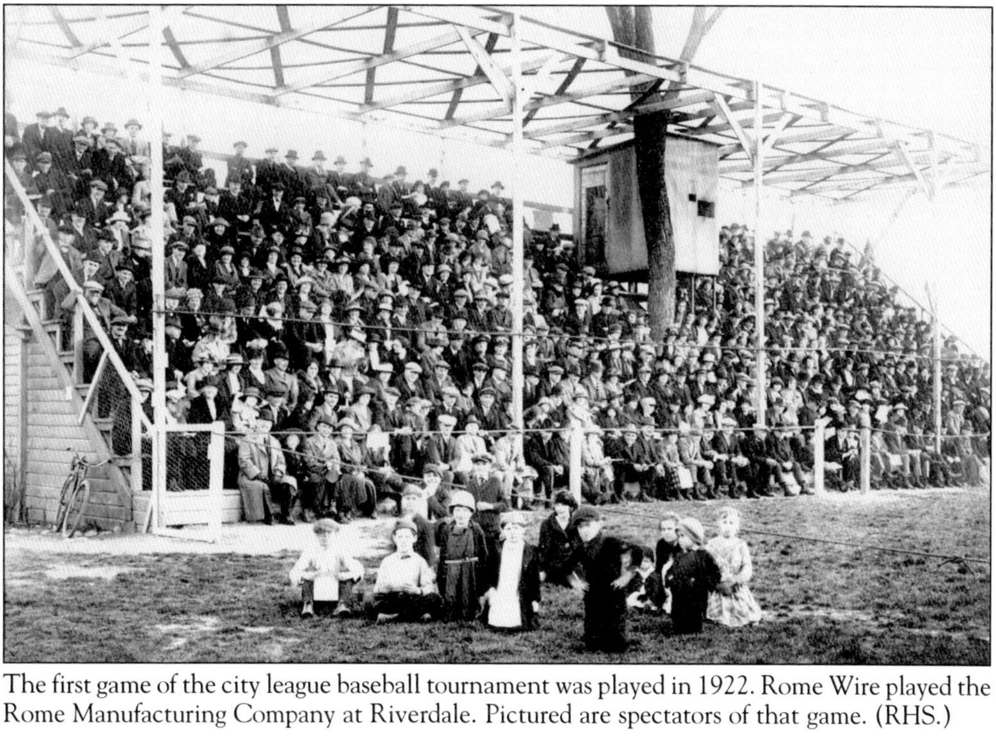

The first game of the city league baseball tournament was played in 1922. Rome Wire played the Rome Manufacturing Company at Riverdale. Pictured are spectators of that game. (RHS.)

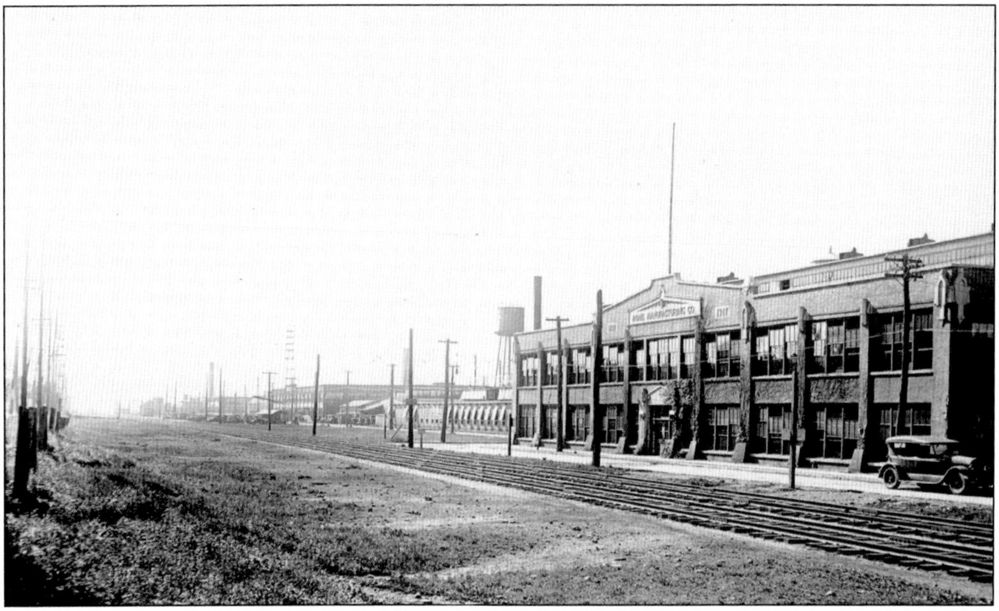

The Rome Manufacturing Company began in 1893 with the production of various household items. Rome Brass and Copper Company bought the Rome Manufacturing Company the year before the Revere merger. Rome Manufacturing became its own division within Revere in 1929 and, in 1936, started producing cookware known as Revere Ware. (RHS.)

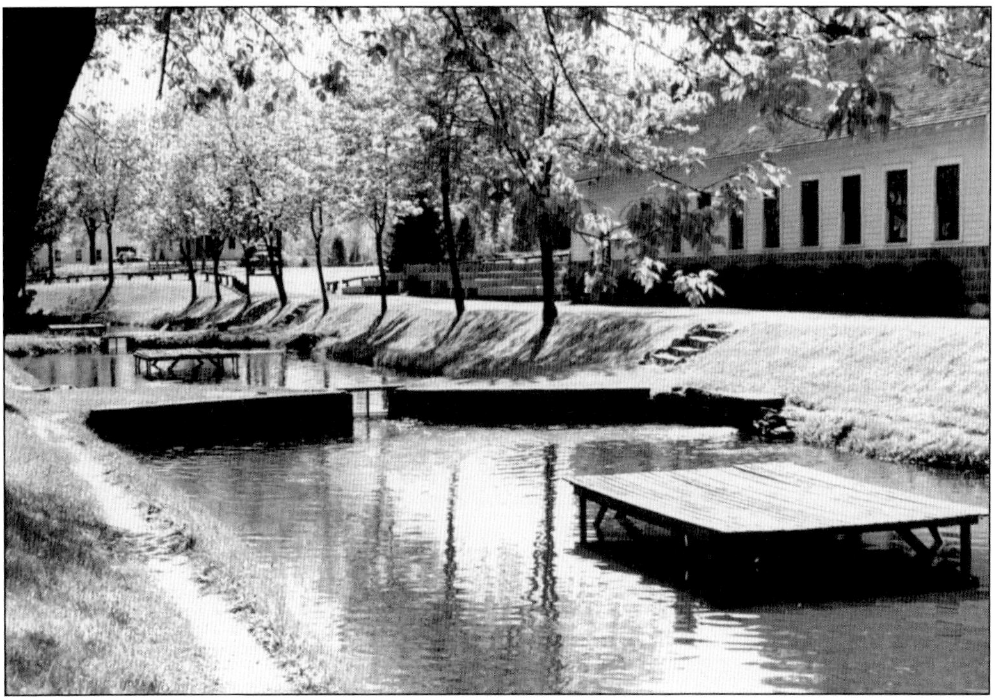

Rome Brass and Copper, Rome Manufacturing, Rome Metallic Bedstead, and Rome Wire purchased the trout hatchery of the Rome Fish and Game Protective Association for the enjoyment of the community. Ownership of the hatchery was transferred to the state of New York in 1932. The New York State Fish Hatchery is seen in 1946. (RHS/Margo Studio.)

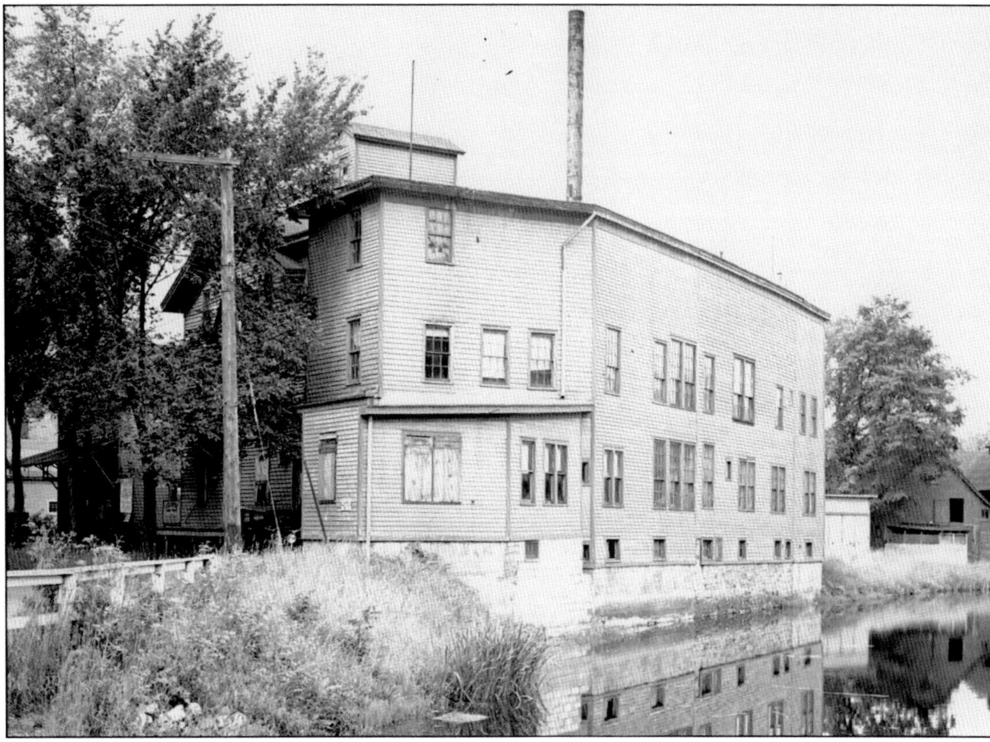

Textile factories were common in Rome. Organized in 1895, the Rome Textile Company occupied a former flour mill located on Wood Creek at Thron's Pond. (RHS.)

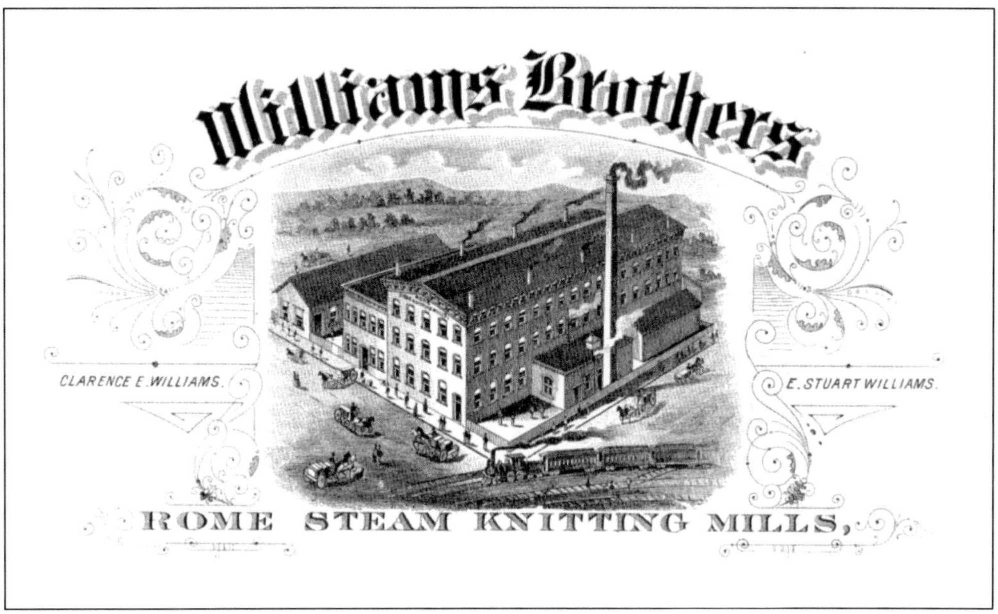

The Williams Knitting Mill, which manufactured lightweight underwear, moved from Utica to Rome in 1878. The company adopted the name Williams Brothers Manufacturing Company in 1902 and became a division of Johnstown Knitting in 1940. The plant closed in 1963. (Dr. Craeger Boardman.)

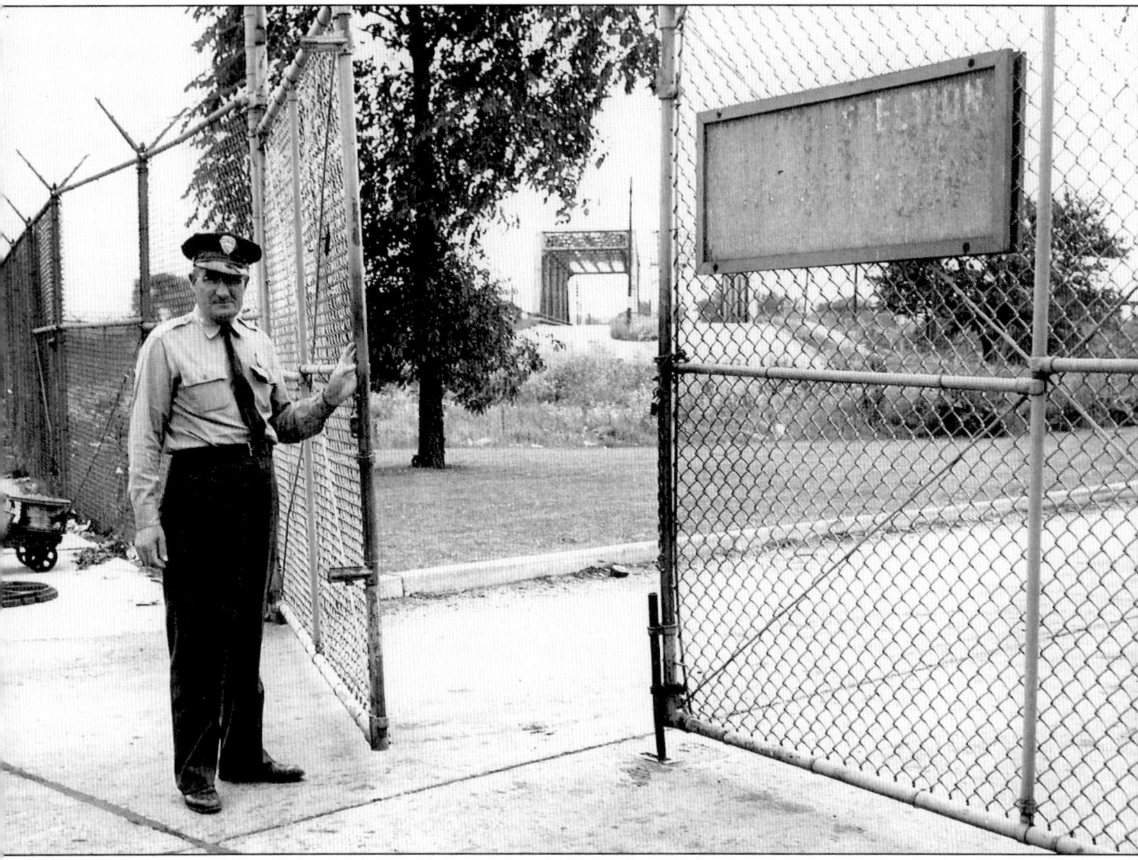

Paul Nittka worked as a guard for General Cable Company in 1942. The Mill Street Bridge can be seen in the background. During World War II, General Cable was a major supplier of communications cable to the armed forces. As a result, the Rome plant received the Army-Navy E award for outstanding wartime production. (Melody Kiepert Milewski.)

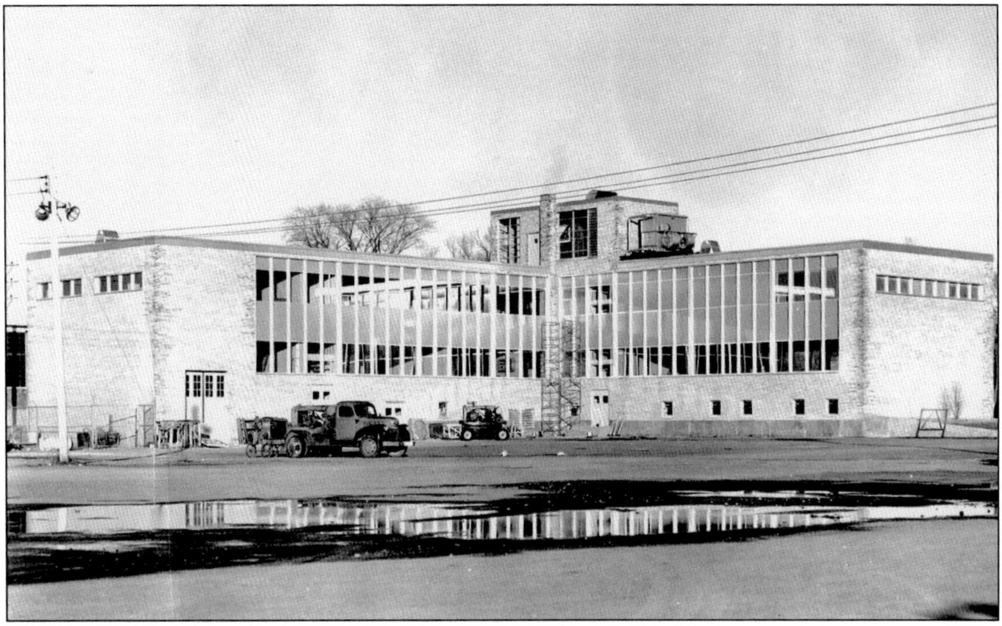

Rome Cable Corporation was first organized in 1936. As the company grew rapidly, it built an additional plant in Torrance, California. When the electronics industry needed aluminum wire and cable, Rome Cable added these products to its inventory. (RHS.)

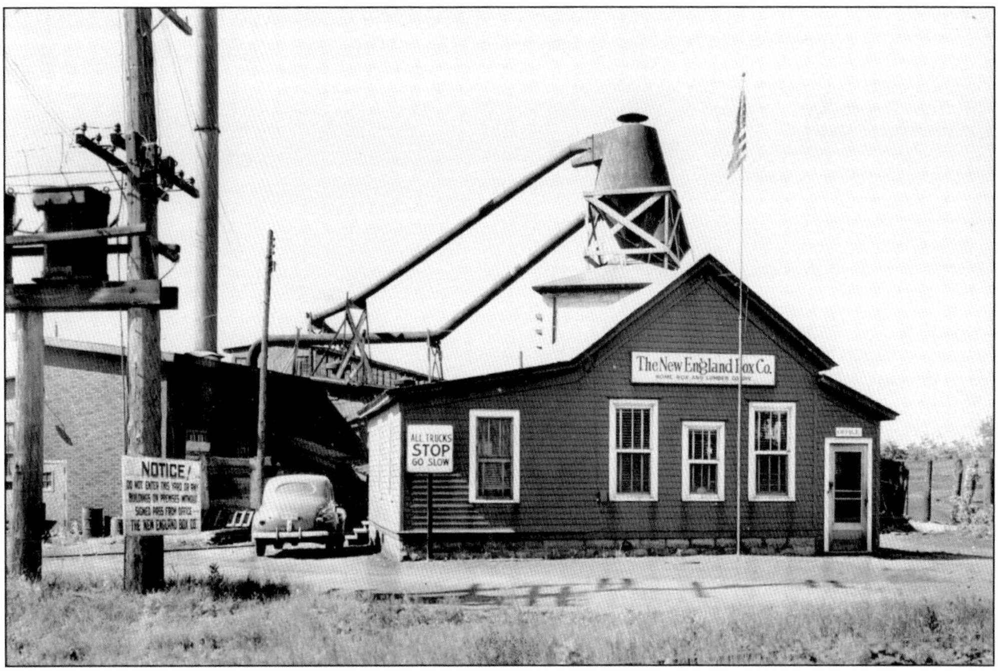

The New England Box Company, located on Railroad Street, is pictured in 1945. (RHS.)

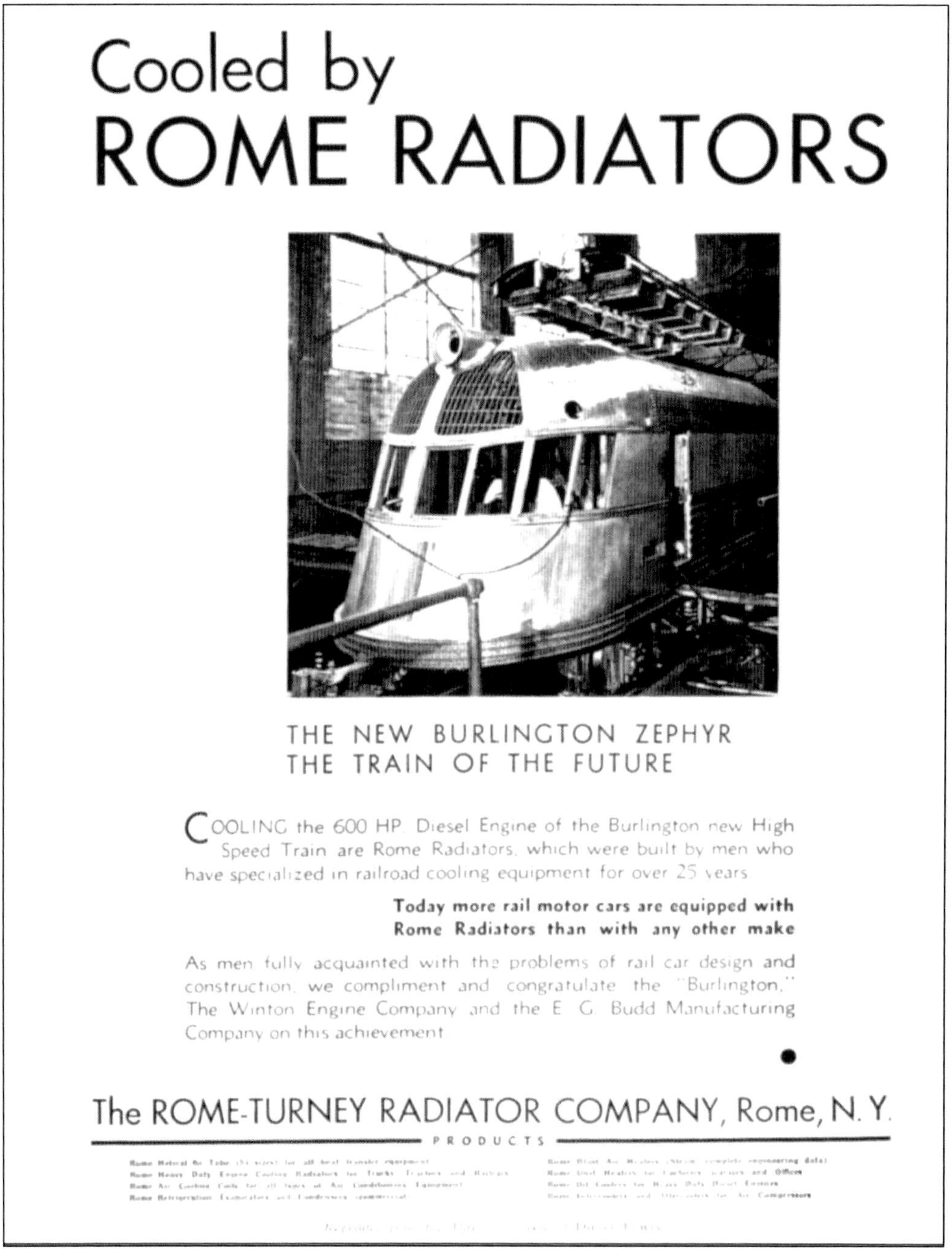

The Long-Turney Radiator Company was established in 1905 to manufacture radiators for the new automotive industry. The name changed to Rome-Turney Radiator Company in 1908. The first person hired by the company was William Lynch, who was the bookkeeper. Lynch eventually purchased the company in 1921. He ran the company until his death in 1965, when his son, William Lynch Jr., took over. (RHS.)

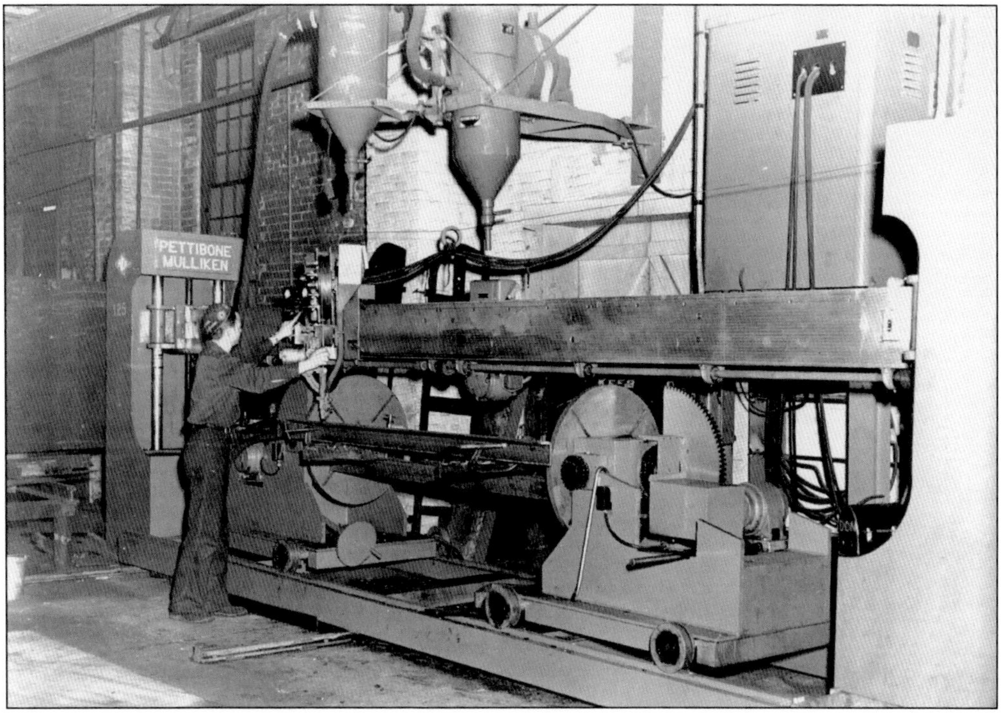

Pettibone-Mulliken Corporation specialized in the manufacture of mobile cranes for industrial and construction work. The company moved into the old headquarters of the New York Locomotive Works in east Rome. (RHS.)

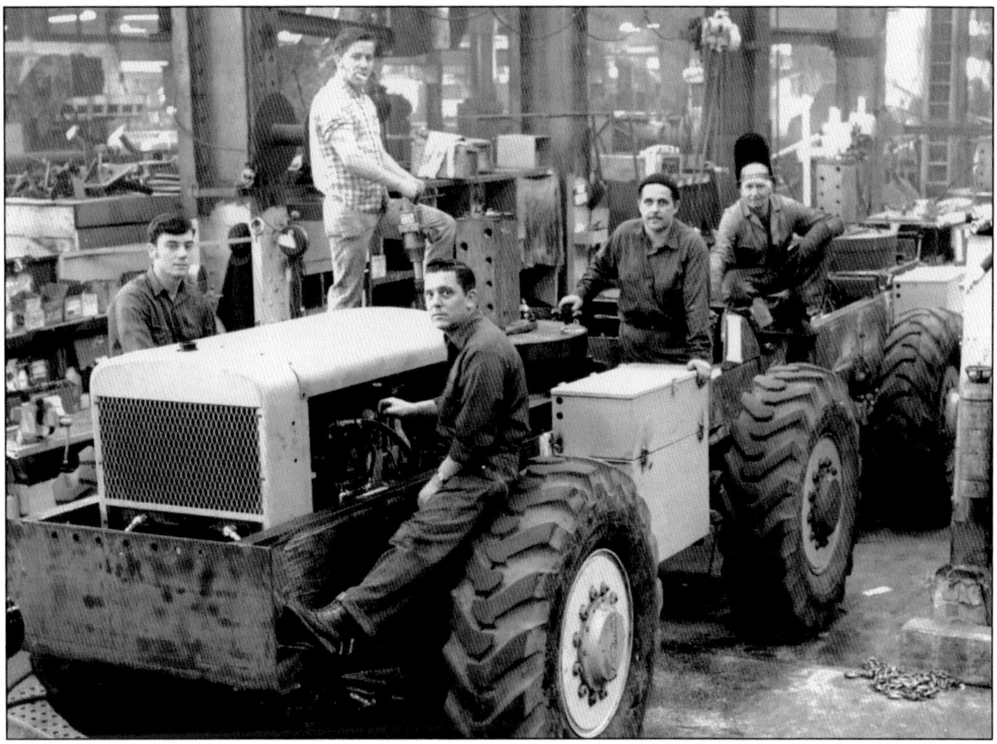

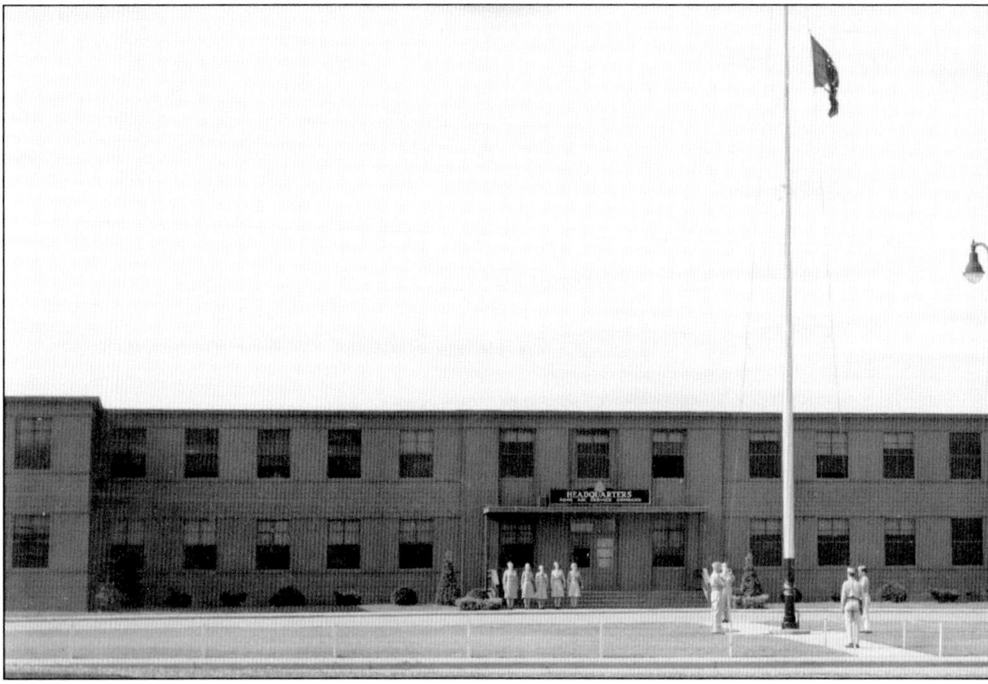

The Rome Air Depot was officially established on February 1, 1942. The inauguration ceremonies were held at the headquarters on November 7, 1942. (RHS.)

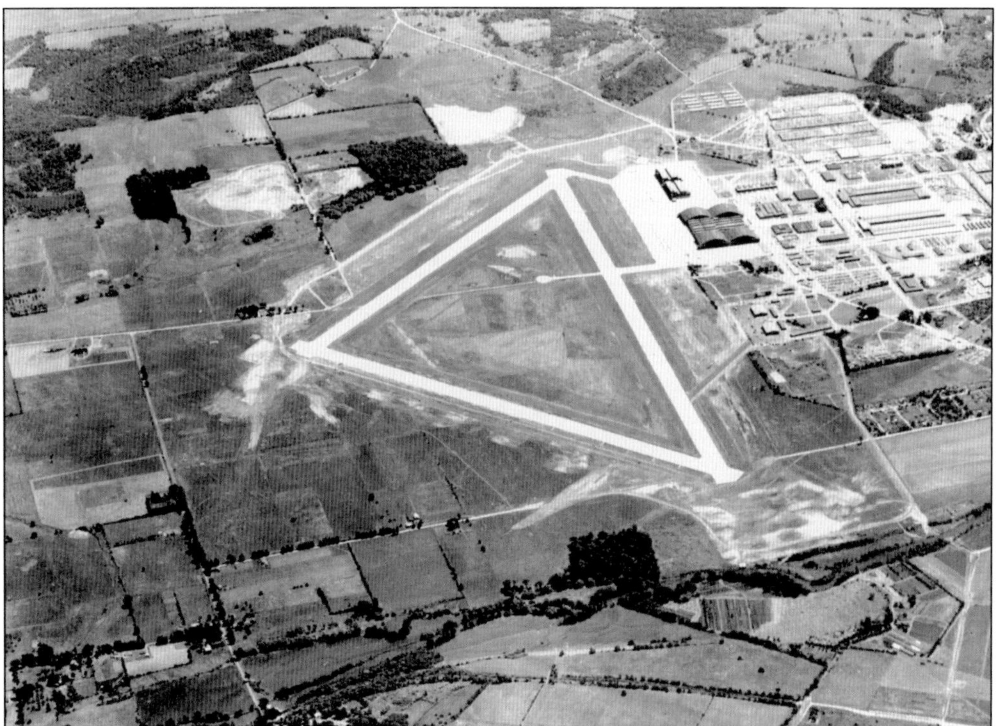

The first runway was completed in October 1942, despite two weeks of rain, snow, and cold weather. (RHS.)

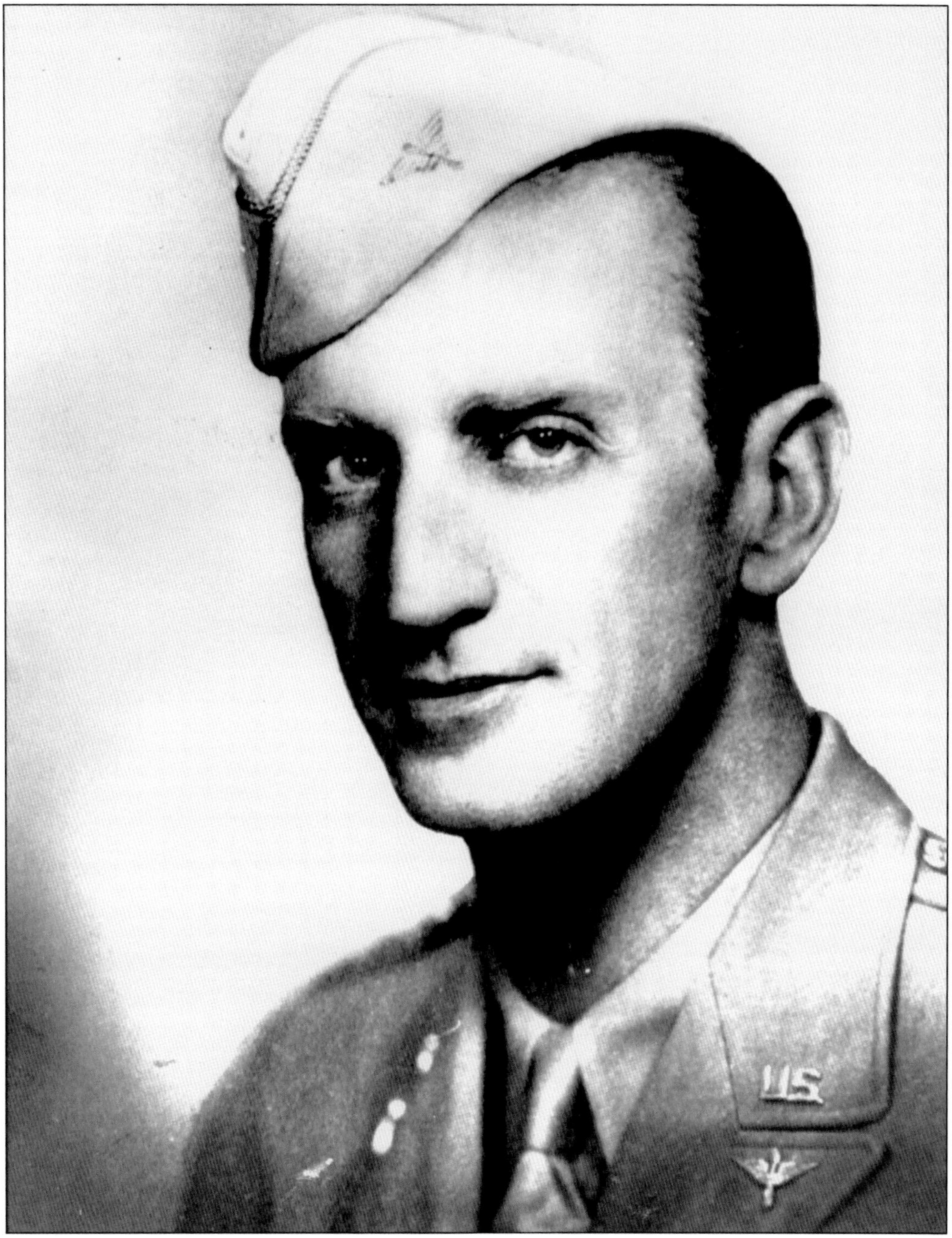

Griffiss Air Force Base was named after 1st Lt. Col. Townsend E. Griffiss of Buffalo, who was the first U.S. soldier killed in the line of duty in Europe during World War II. Rome Army Air Field was renamed on September 20, 1948, in his honor. (RHS.)

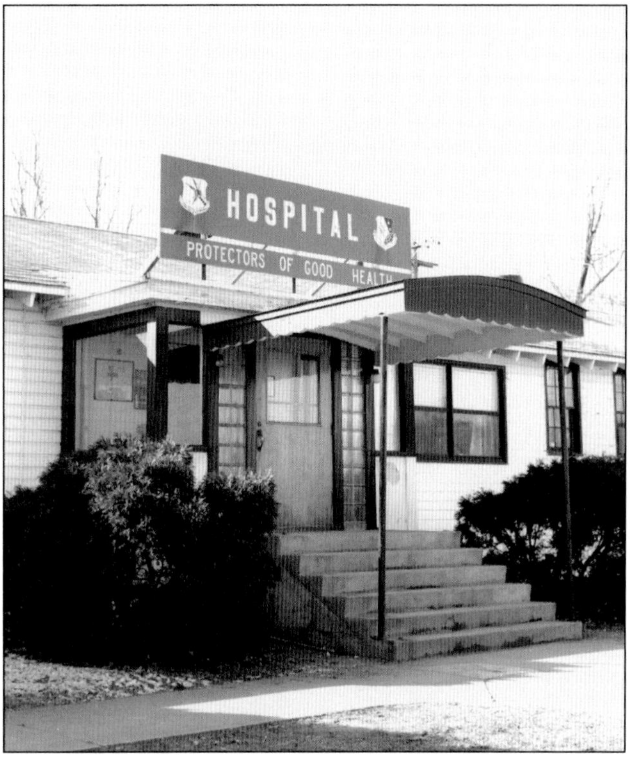

This view of the main entrance of the hospital was taken in the early 1960s after the 416th Bombardment Wing came to GAFB. (RHS.)

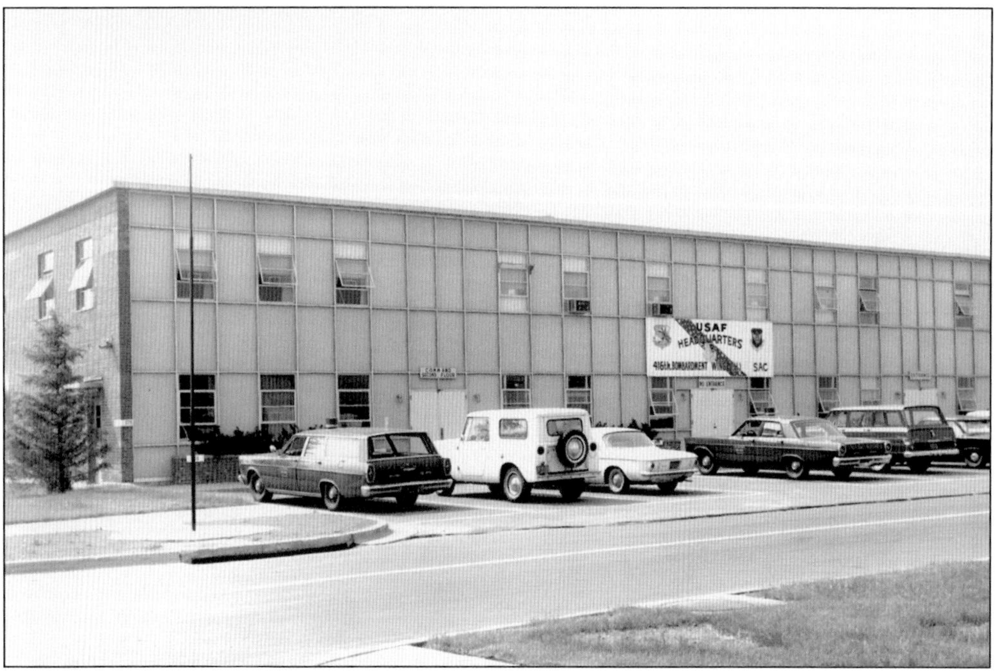

Building 778 on the Griffiss Air Force Base served as headquarters for the 416th Bombardment Wing. The 416th was originally activated in February 1943, inactivated in October 1945, and reactivated in 1963 as part of an Air Force program to reestablish outstanding World War II units. (RHS.)

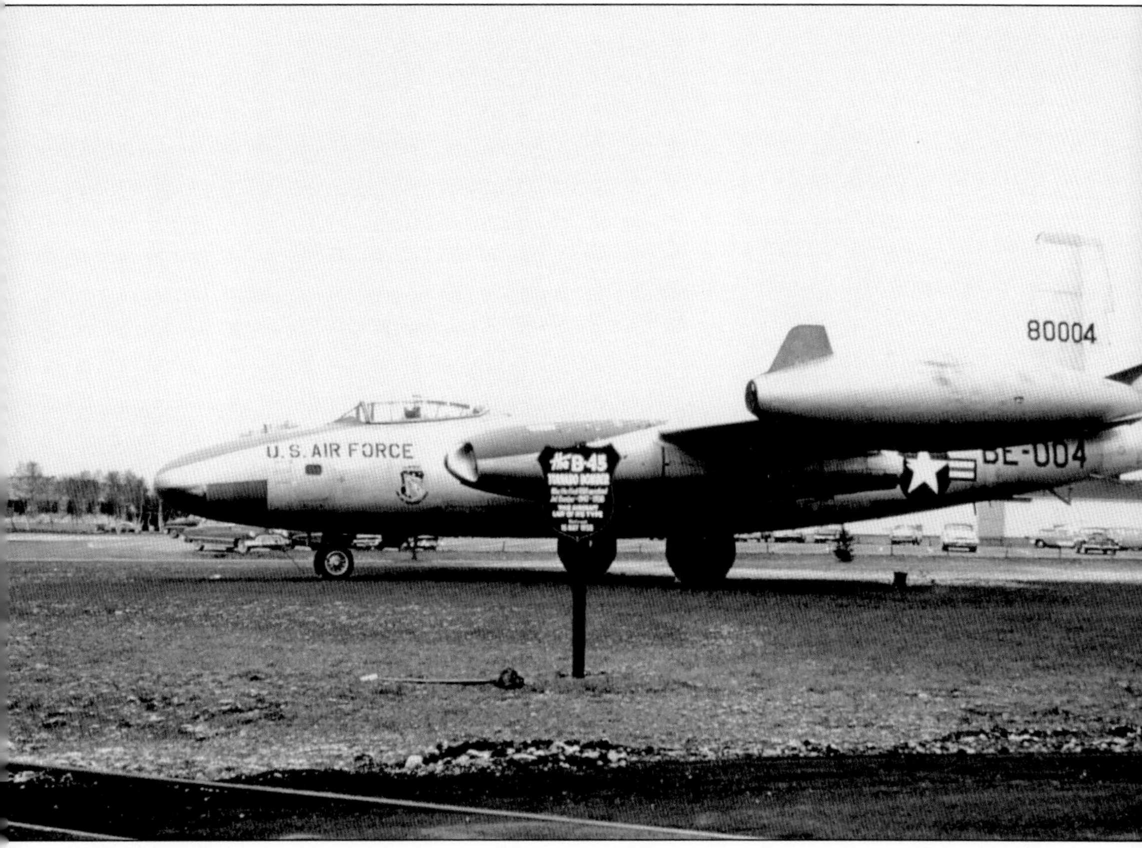

A B-45 bomber was put on display in the center of base. The sign in front of the bomber reads, "The B-45 Tornado Bomber was the first USAF operated Jet Bomber – 1947-1958. This Aircraft last of its type. Retired 16 May 1958." (RHS.)

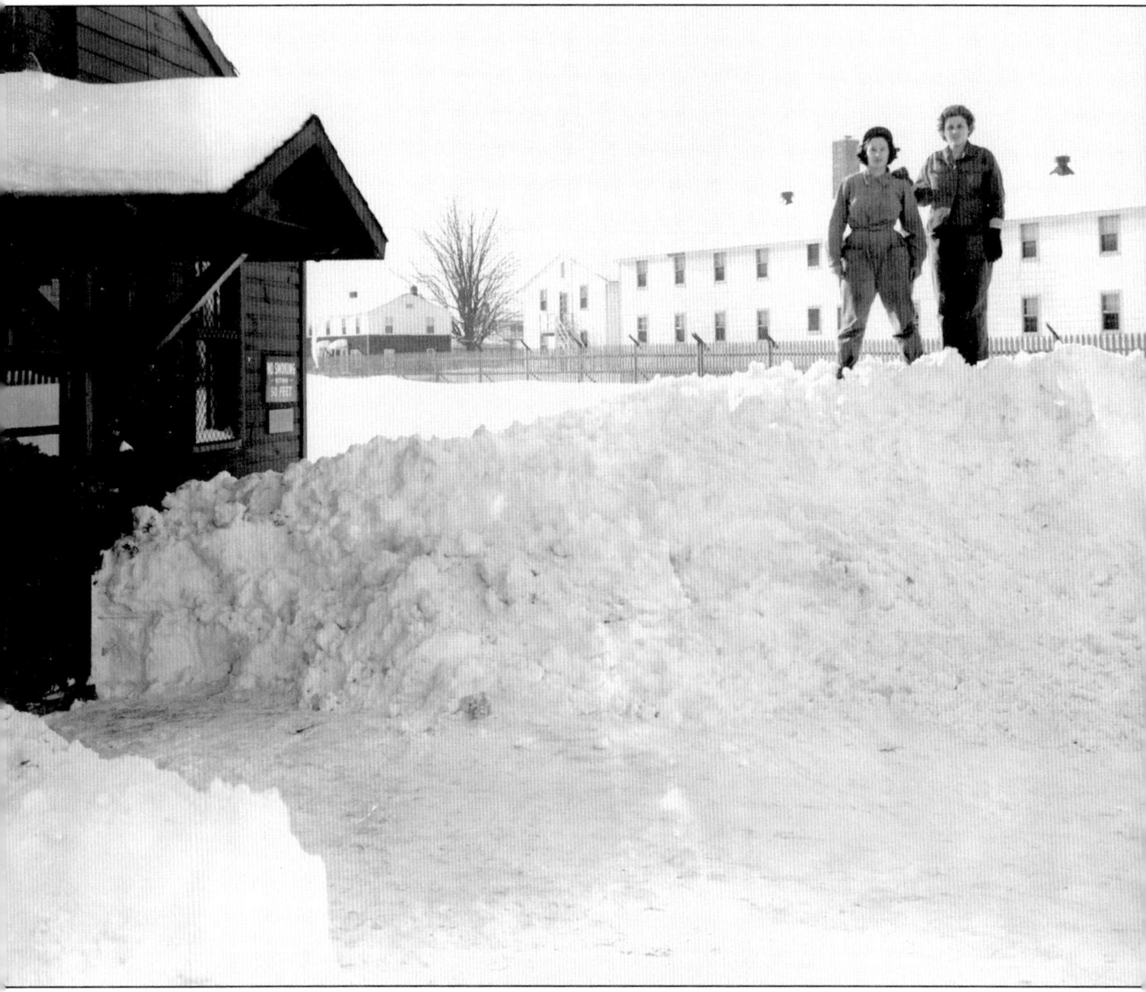

The first woman assigned to Griffiss Air Force Base arrived on August 26, 1943. In April 1944, the Rome Air Service Command presented a television show featuring Women's Army Corps (WAC) recruiting on a Schenectady public station. (RHS.)

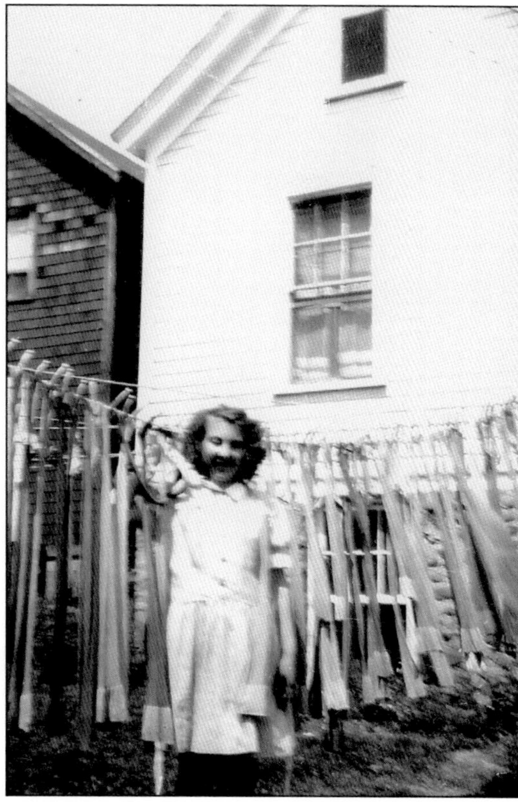

Civilian women also pitched in to help the war effort. Nylon was used by the army for parachutes, so alternative materials for stockings had to be found. Elsa Nittka proudly displays her "victory stockings" in 1943 at her Dominick Street house. (Melody Kiepert Milewski.)

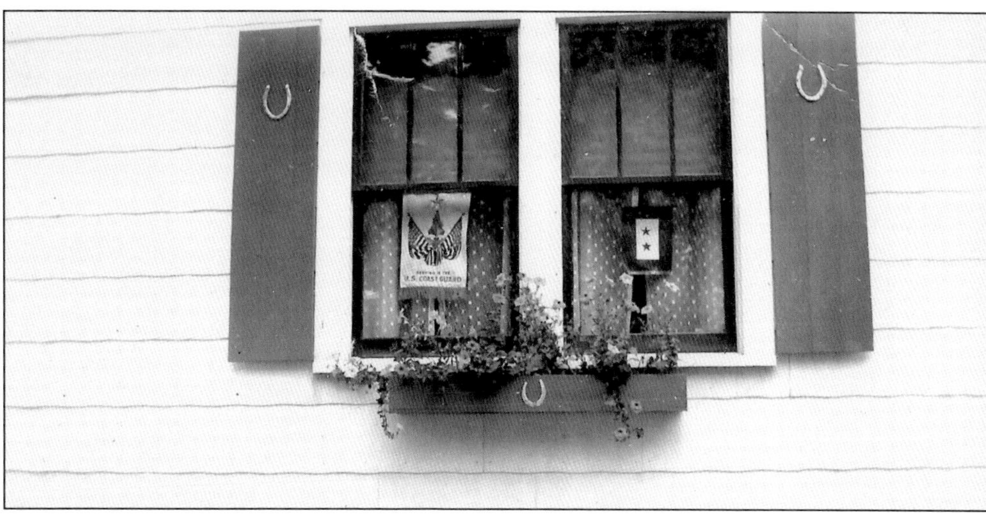

The Taubert family displays a star banner in the window. Blue stars on a white background show that two men from the household were fighting in World War II. (Sophie Taubert.)

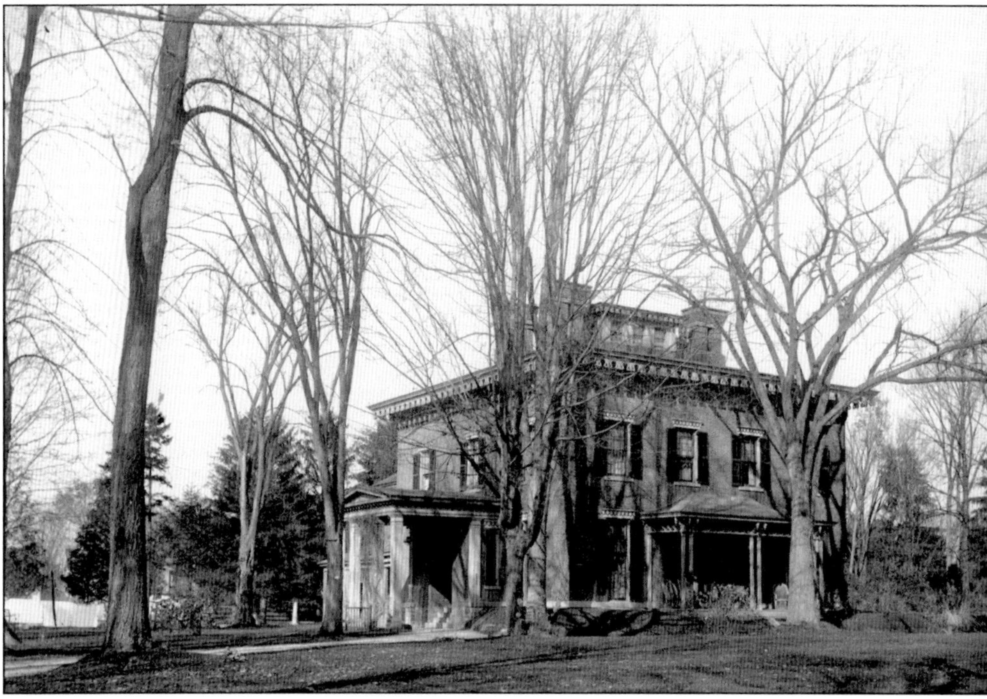

The old Thron house, at 506 West Embargo Street, became the Murphy Memorial Hospital in 1920. This became a maternity hospital in 1929, when the city of Rome took over the management. The building was later torn down, and the Kennedy Ice Arena now occupies the site. (RHS.)

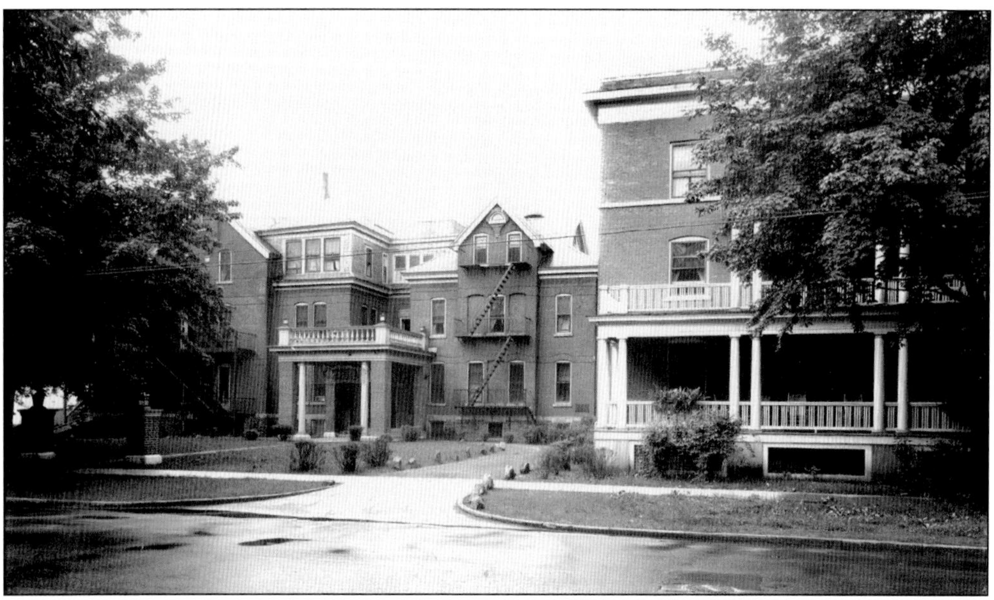

The Rome Hospital was located on East Garden Street. It is pictured in 1928; the building on the right is likely a residence. (RHS.)

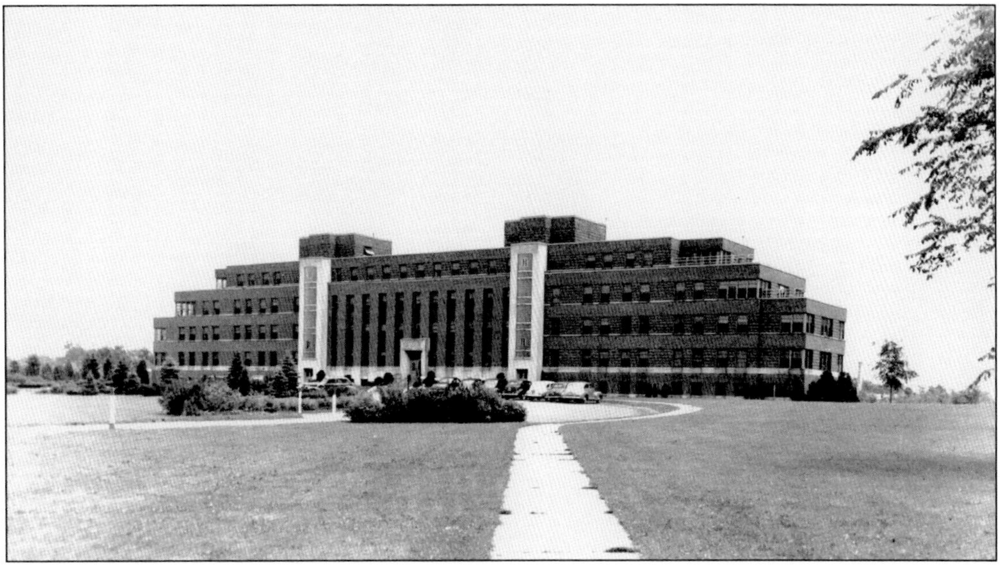

By 1935, both the Rome Hospital and the Murphy Memorial Hospital were run-down and overcrowded. The city combined the two hospitals into one building on James Street. The new Rome-Murphy Memorial Hospital opened on April 10, 1940. (RHS.)

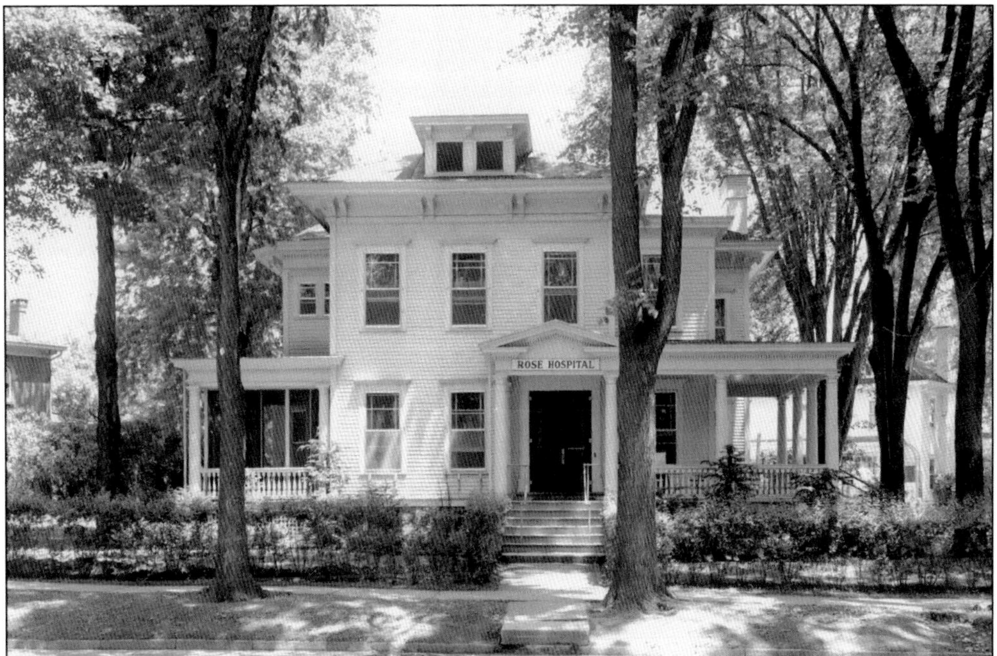

The Rose Hospital is pictured in July 1948. This building stood where the Valentine Apartments currently stand on Turin Street. (RHS.)

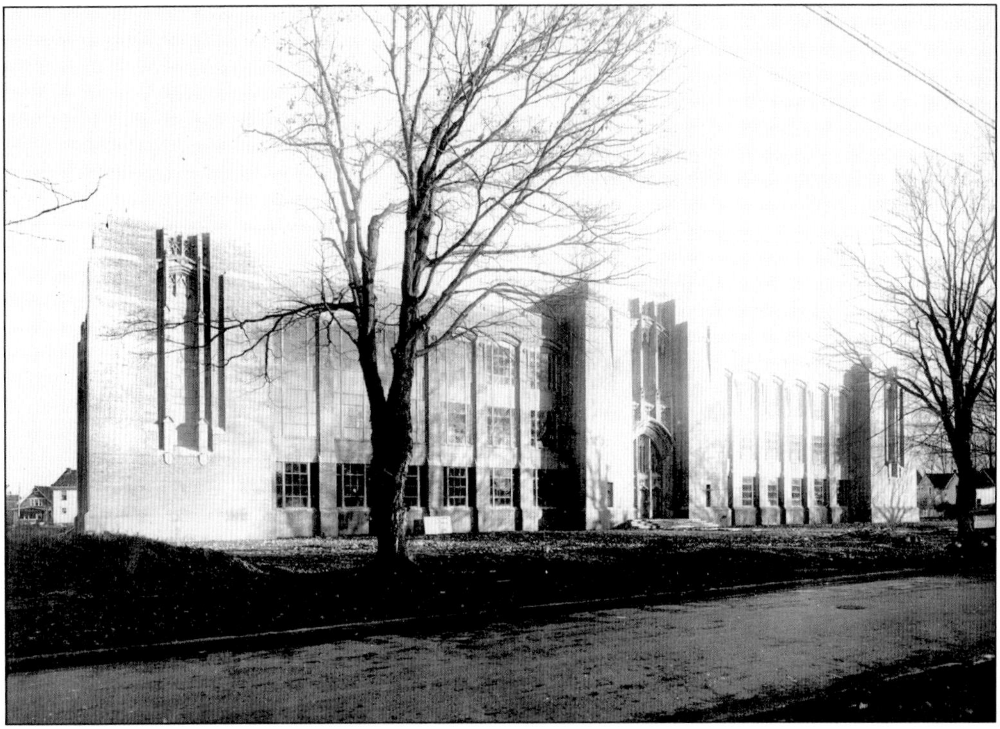

The third building for Rome Free Academy opened its doors in April 1926. This building on Turin Street cost $400,000 to build. The school was for grades 10 through 12. A fire ripped through the interior of the building in 1938, causing the need for a complete interior reconstruction. (RHS.)

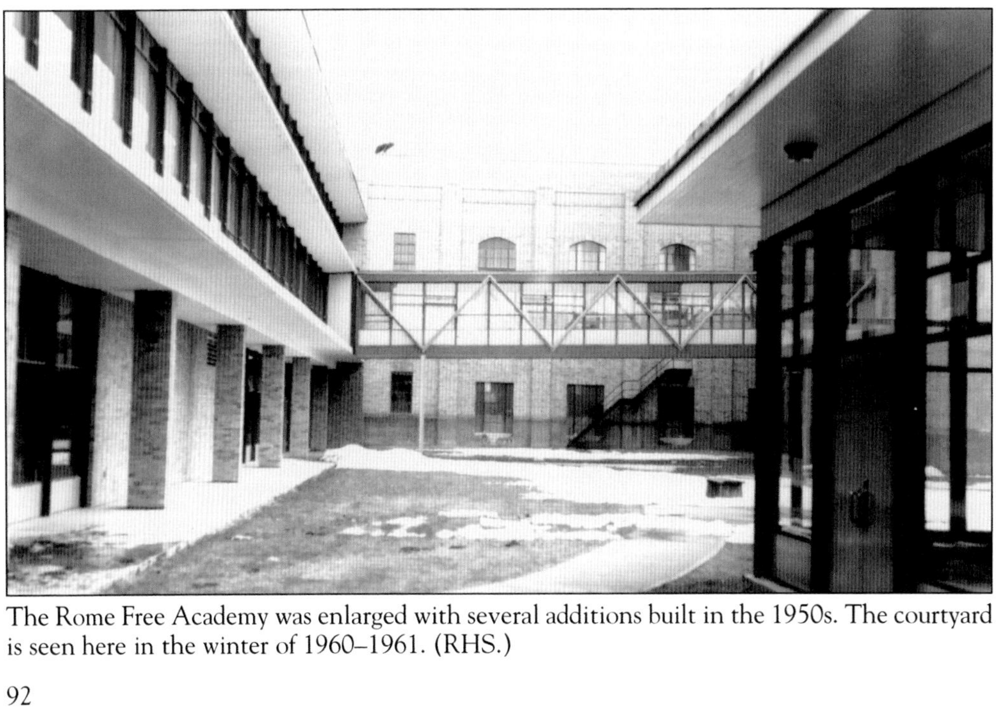

The Rome Free Academy was enlarged with several additions built in the 1950s. The courtyard is seen here in the winter of 1960–1961. (RHS.)

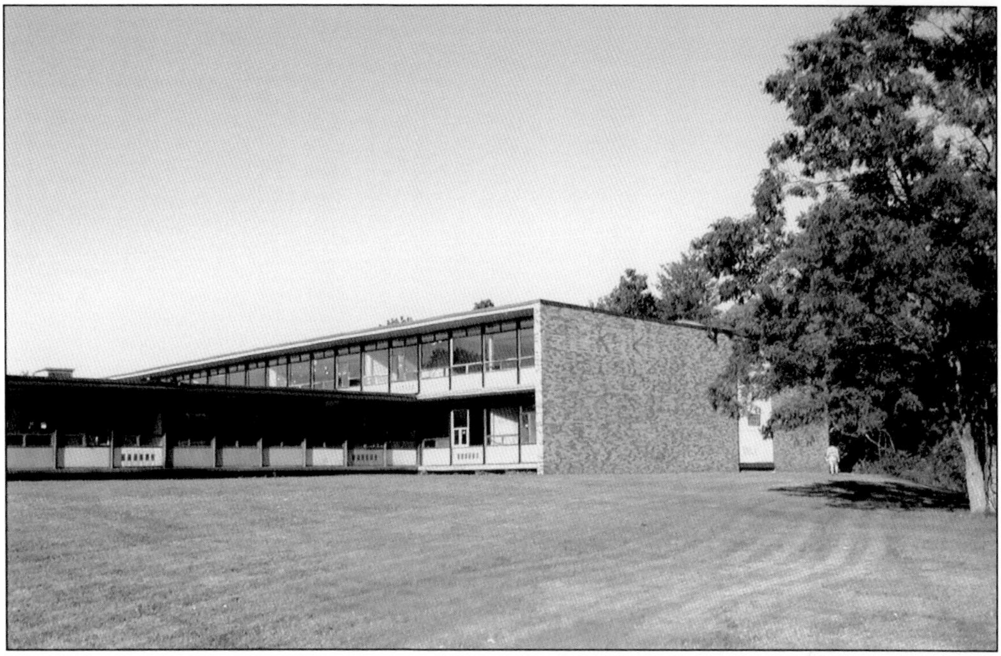

Staley Junior High School opened on East Bloomfield Street in 1958. The school was named after George R. Staley, who was superintendent of schools from 1912 to 1945. The brickwork of the school reflects the era in which it was built. Below is a closeup of "I Like Ike," the Dwight D. Eisenhower presidential campaign slogan, which was set in the brickwork. (Joseph Vescio, Portia Vescio.)

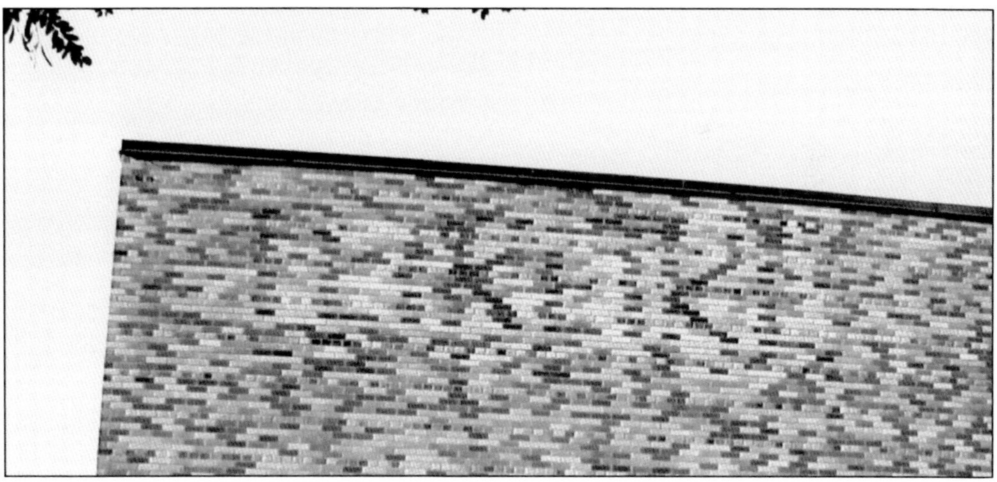

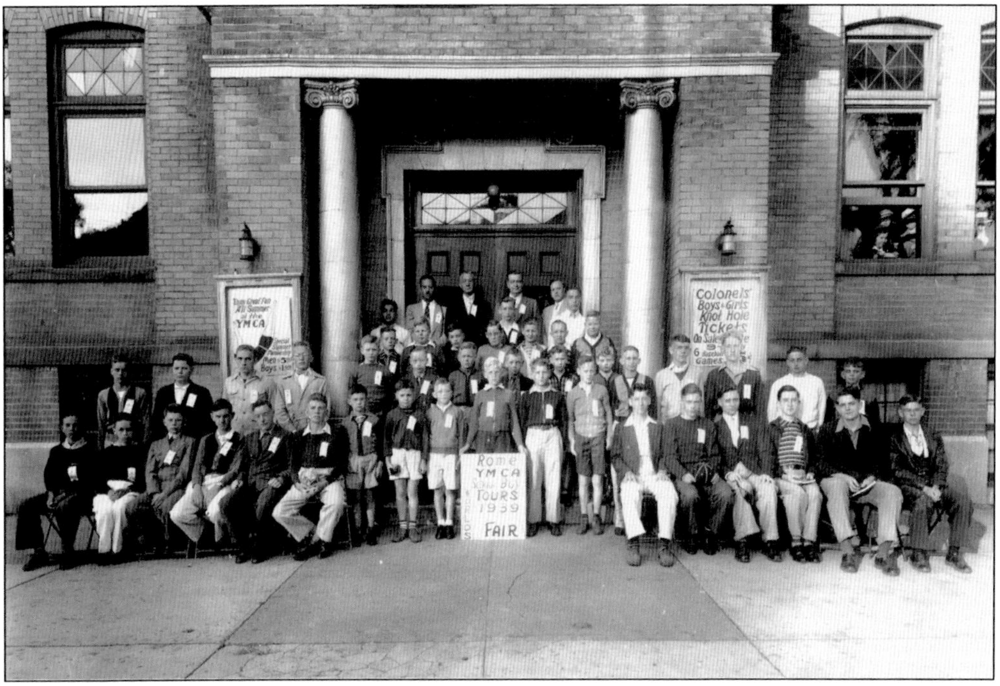

The YMCA began in Rome in June 1872. This photograph of the Rome School Boy Tours to the 1939 World's Fair was taken on James Street in front of the Y. (RHS.)

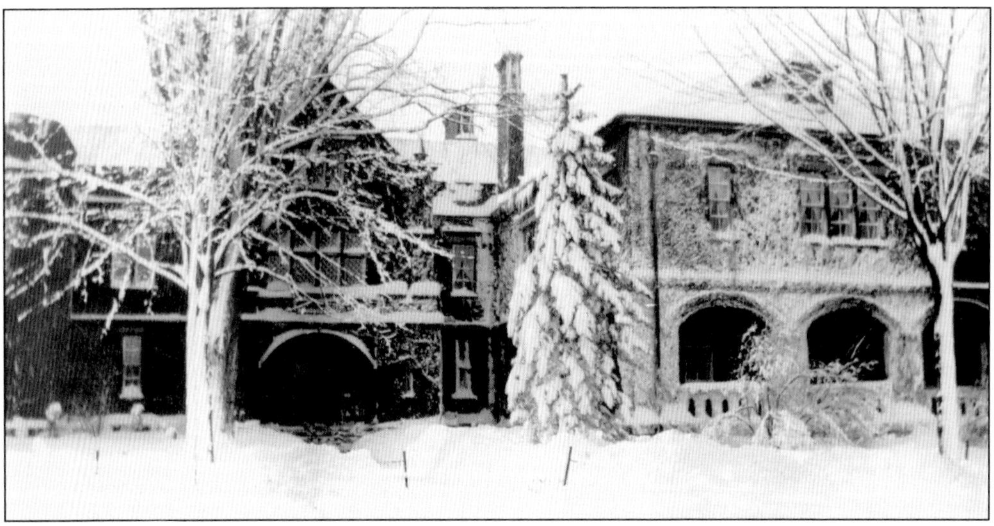

Originally an almshouse and then an asylum, the Rome State School assumed its name in 1919. A school for persons with developmental disabilities, the state school was at one time the area's largest employer. After several more name changes, the developmental center was phased out and eventually became the Oneida Correctional Facility. (RHS.)

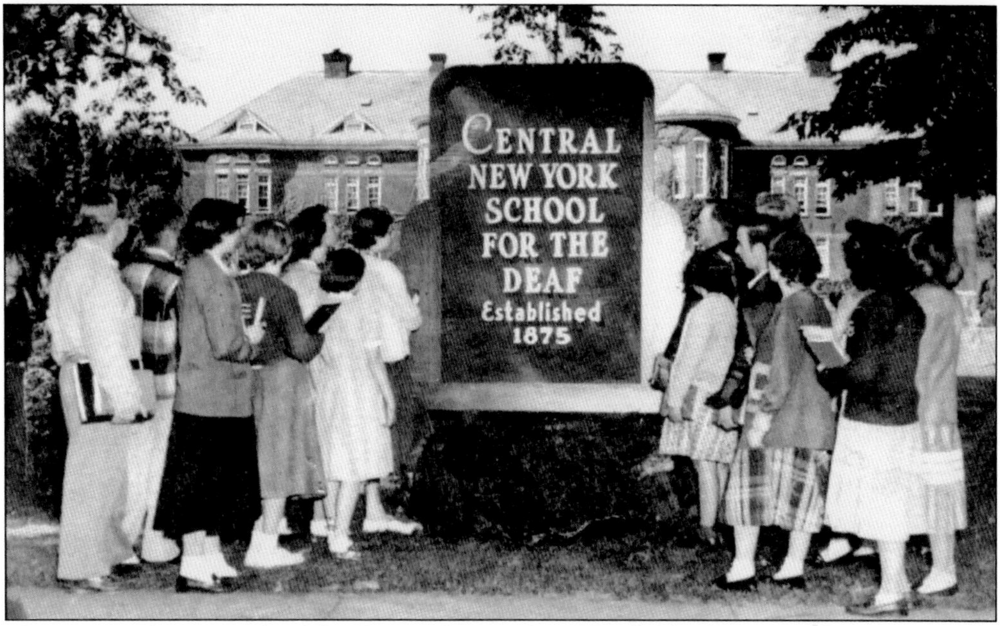

The New York State School for the Deaf opened on March 22, 1875, with four students. By 1878, enrollment of the school had reached nearly 100 students, resulting in the need for additional buildings. This photograph was probably taken *c.* 1931, when the name was changed to the Central New York State School for the Deaf. The "Central" part of the name was dropped in 1963, when the school became a state facility. (Richard Wilson.)

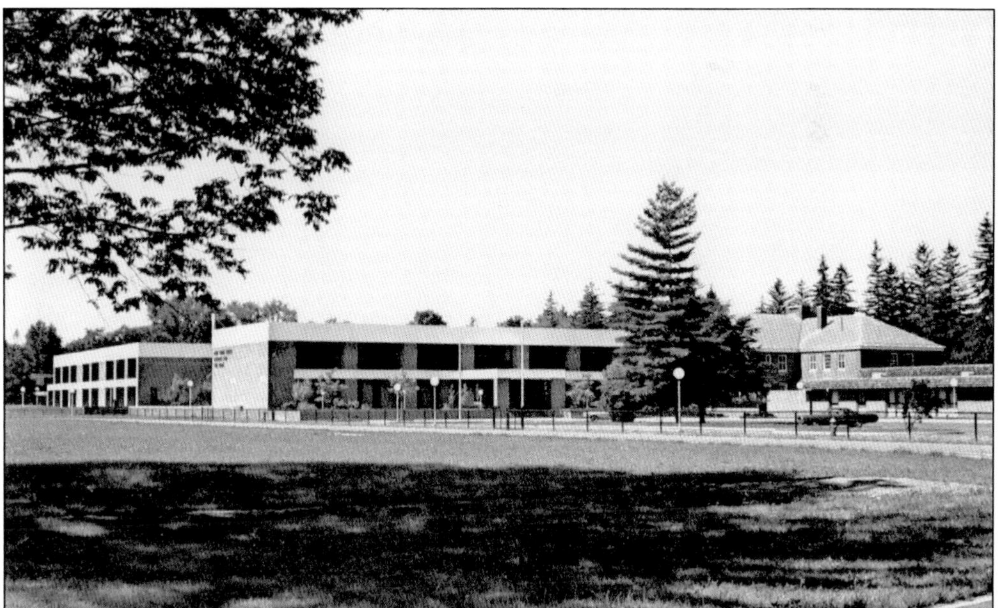
This is a view of the educational complex of the New York State School for the Deaf. In the foreground is the athletic field. (Margo Studio.)

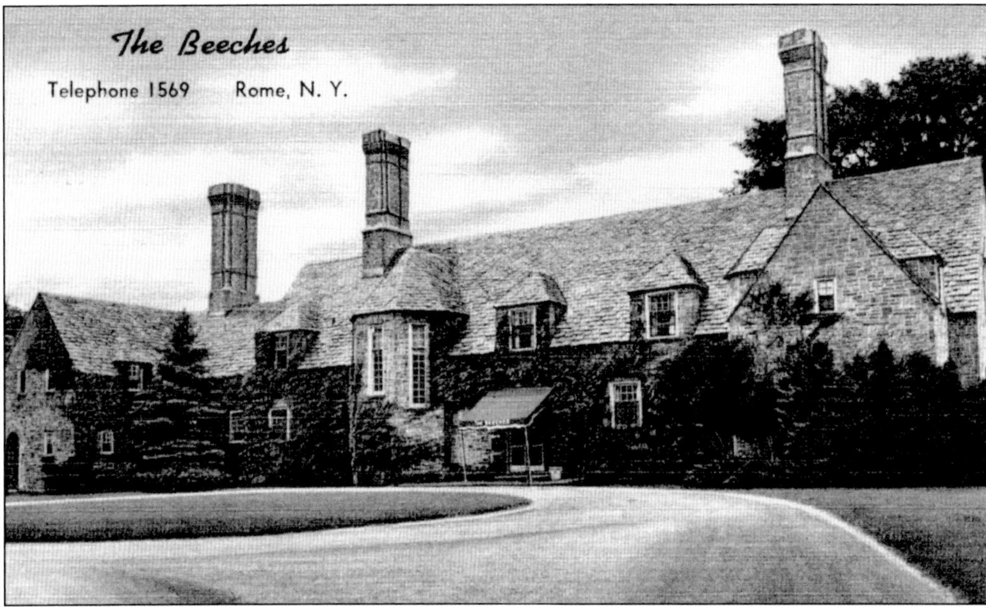

The Beeches Inn and Restaurant building is an example of English architecture. Owned by the Destito family, the establishment encompasses 52 acres of grounds. (Portia Vescio.)

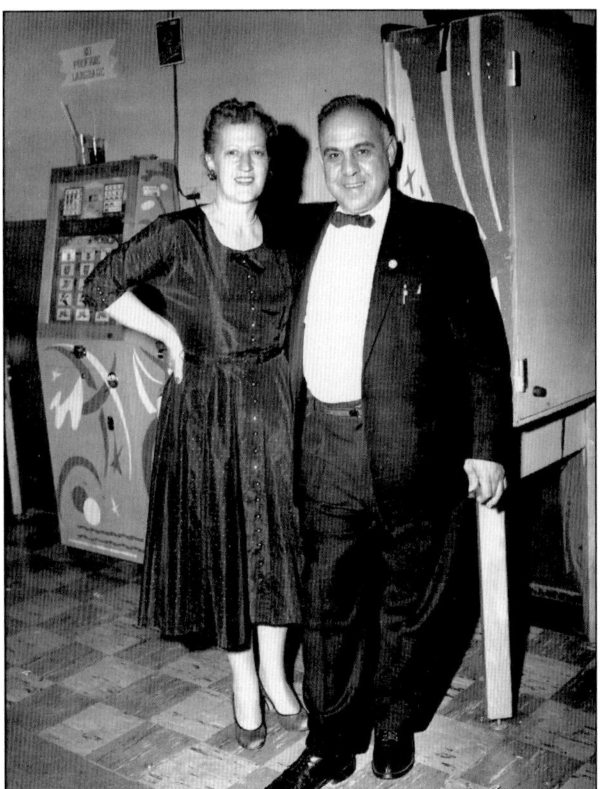

Carl and Minica Vescio are pictured at the St. Gregorio Club, on East Dominick Street, in 1957. The lottery machine in the background is called the Hunter. The sign above the machine reads, "No Profane Language." (Joseph Vescio.)

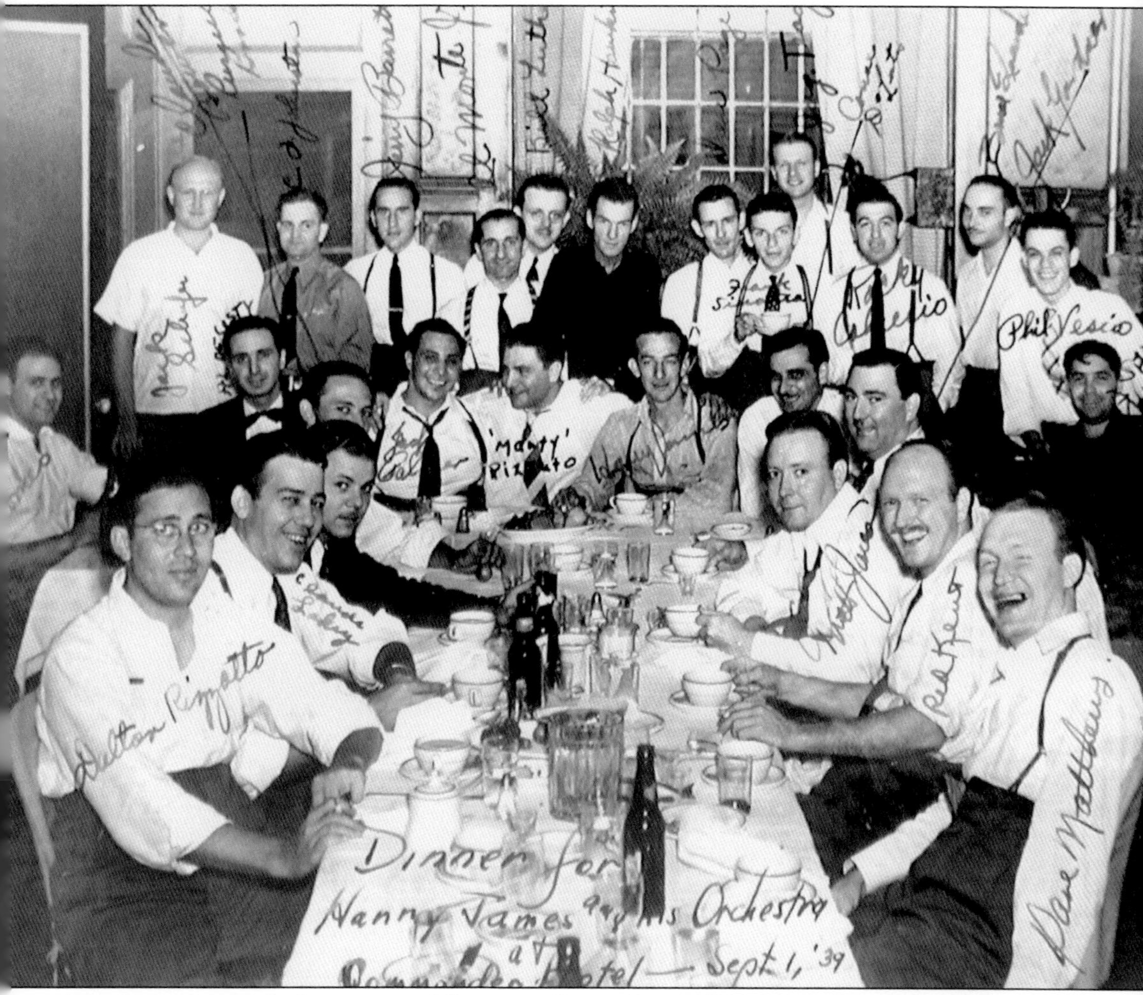

The Harry James Orchestra visited Rome on September 1, 1939. Harry James is seated at the far end of the table on the right side. Standing to the right behind Harry James is a very young Frank Sinatra, who once sang with the band. (Phil Vescio.)

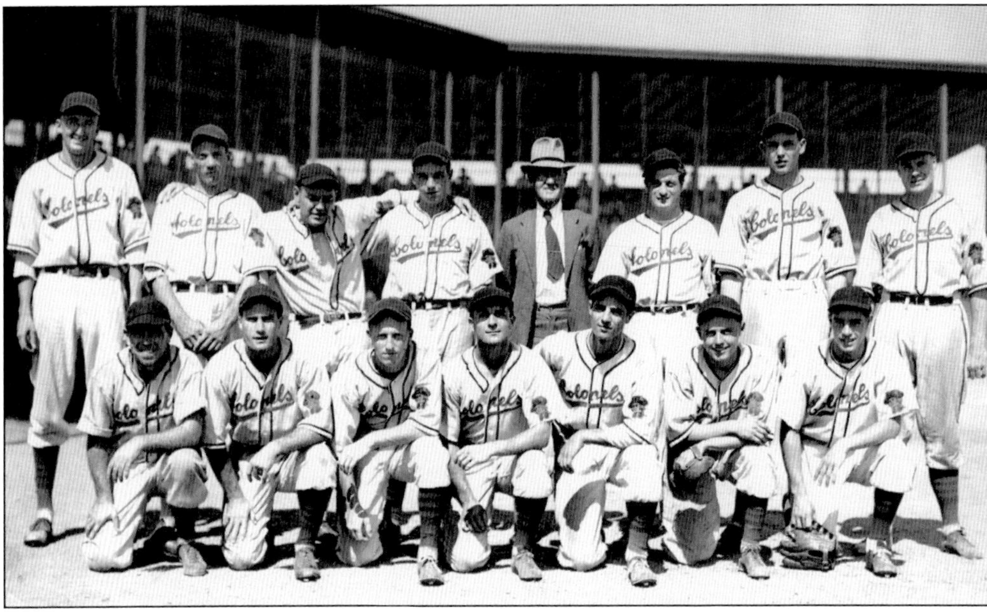

The Rome Colonels played in the Canadian-American Baseball League from 1931 to 1951 at Colonels Park, on Black River Boulevard. This is the 1938 team, with manager William J. Buckley in the center of the back row. (RHS.)

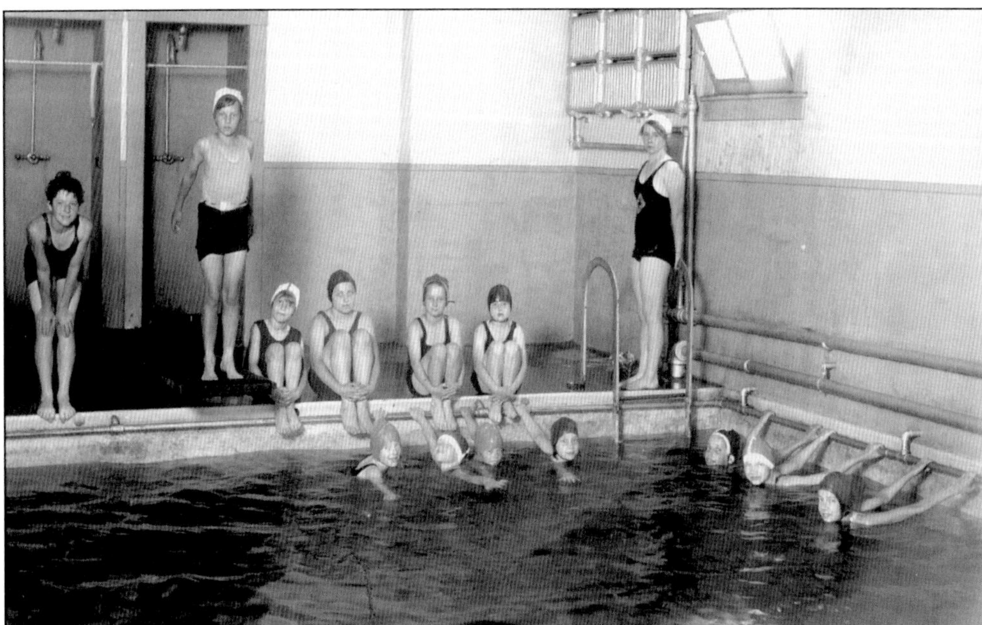

Women's groups were also active in sports. The Rome Sentinel Women's Club holds a swimming class on June 29, 1929. (RHS.)

Shown on the corner of West Thomas and Expense Streets is Helen Nittka of Helen's Home Bake Shop in 1940. (Melody Kiepert Milewski.)

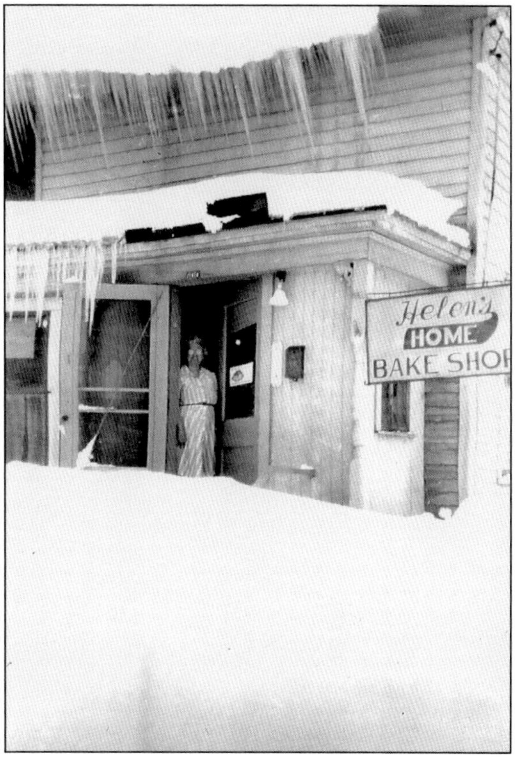

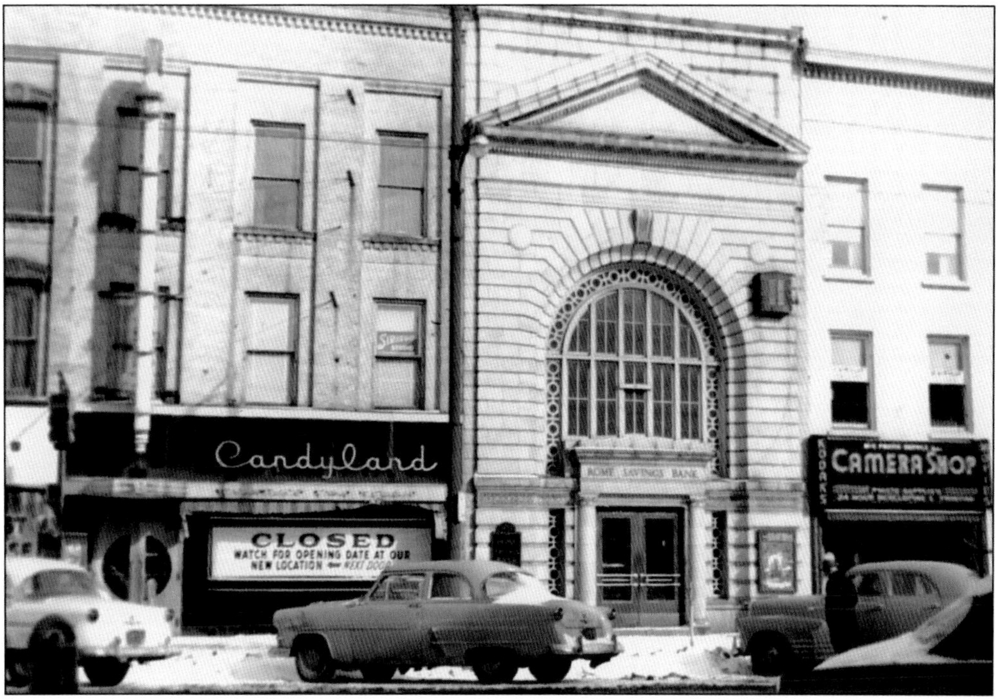

The Haritatos brothers started Candyland. They were well known locally for their chocolate candy Turkey Joints that they produced during Christmastime. Now produced year-round by Nora's Candy Shop, Turkey Joints are still popular. (RHS.)

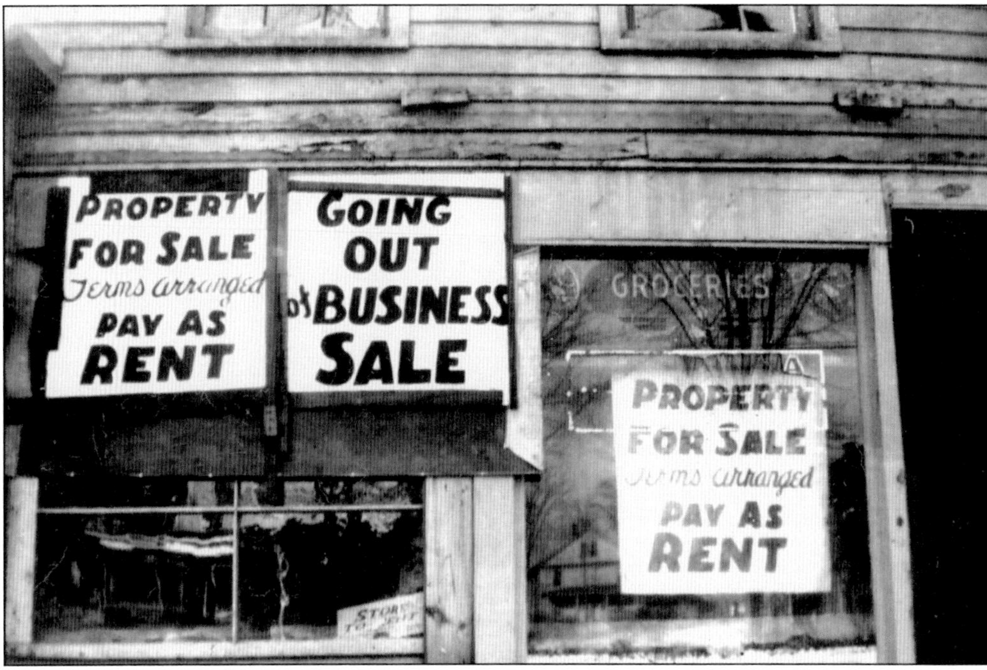

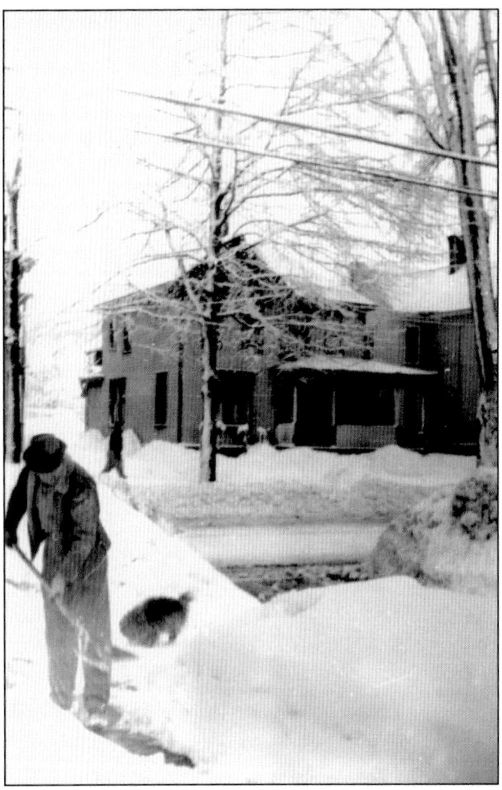

It was not unusual to see businesses and houses side by side in Rome. The top photograph shows the Colangelo Meat Market after a fire forced the store to go out of business in 1936. The store was located at 719 West Dominick Street. Next door at 717 West Dominick Street was a general store. To the left, Paul Nittka of 715 West Dominick Street clears the snow from his sidewalk after a storm in February 1940. (Melody Kiepert Milewski.)

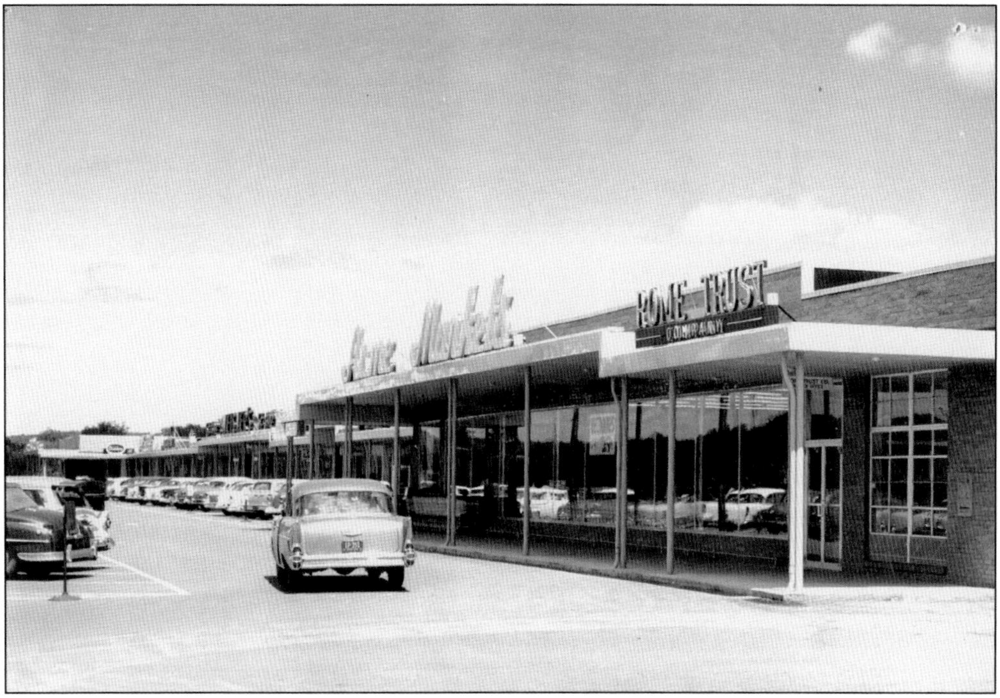

Due to Rome's economic and population growth in the 1950s and 1960s, a total of 20 stores opened at the Mohawk Acres Shopping Center. (RHS.)

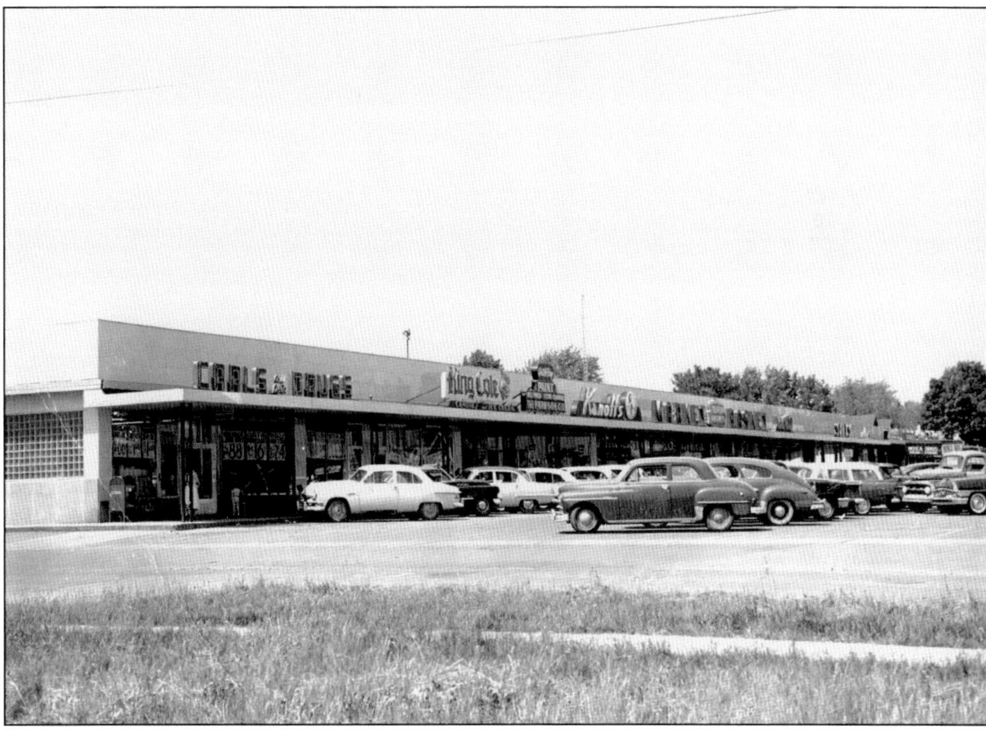

The Black River Boulevard Plaza was another popular shopping destination. The plaza is pictured in 1955. (RHS.)

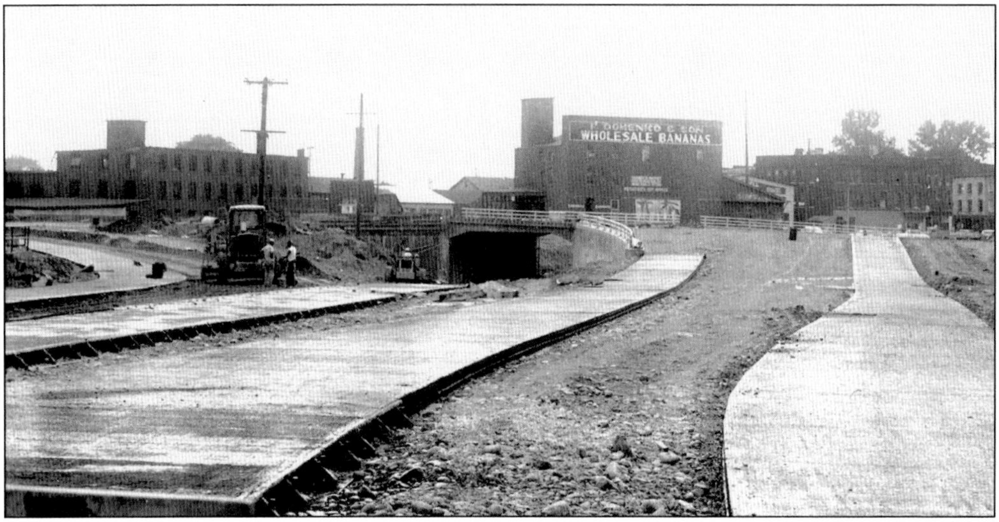

Erie Boulevard was built over the site of the Erie Canal. In 1958, with the beginning of the urban renewal project, work was done on Erie Boulevard West. Construction can be seen on the divided intersection and overhead crossing at Erie Boulevard. (RHS.)

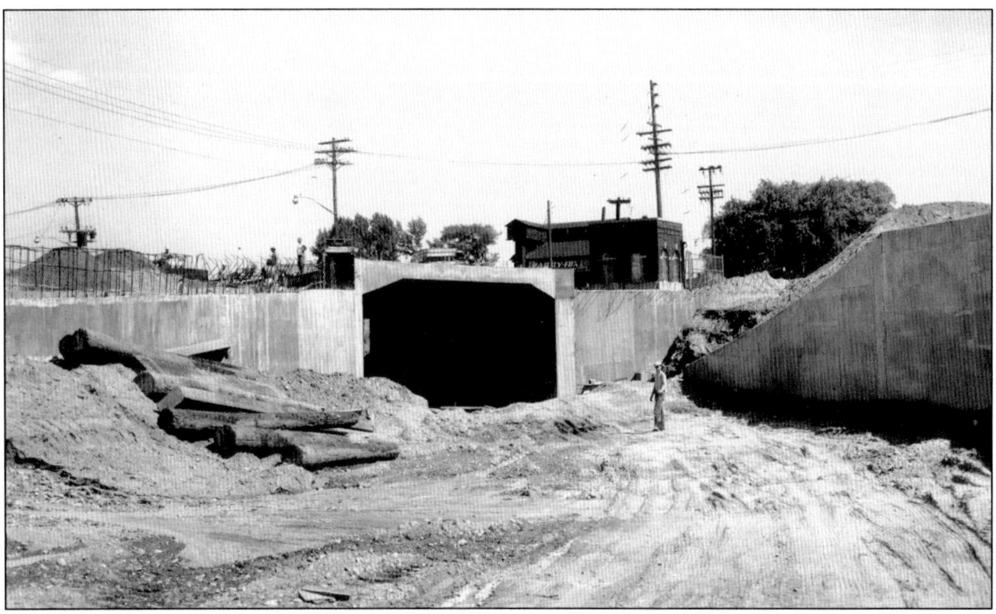

In 1960, Erie Boulevard was extended over the Barge Canal and the old New York Central Railroad tracks. (RHS.)

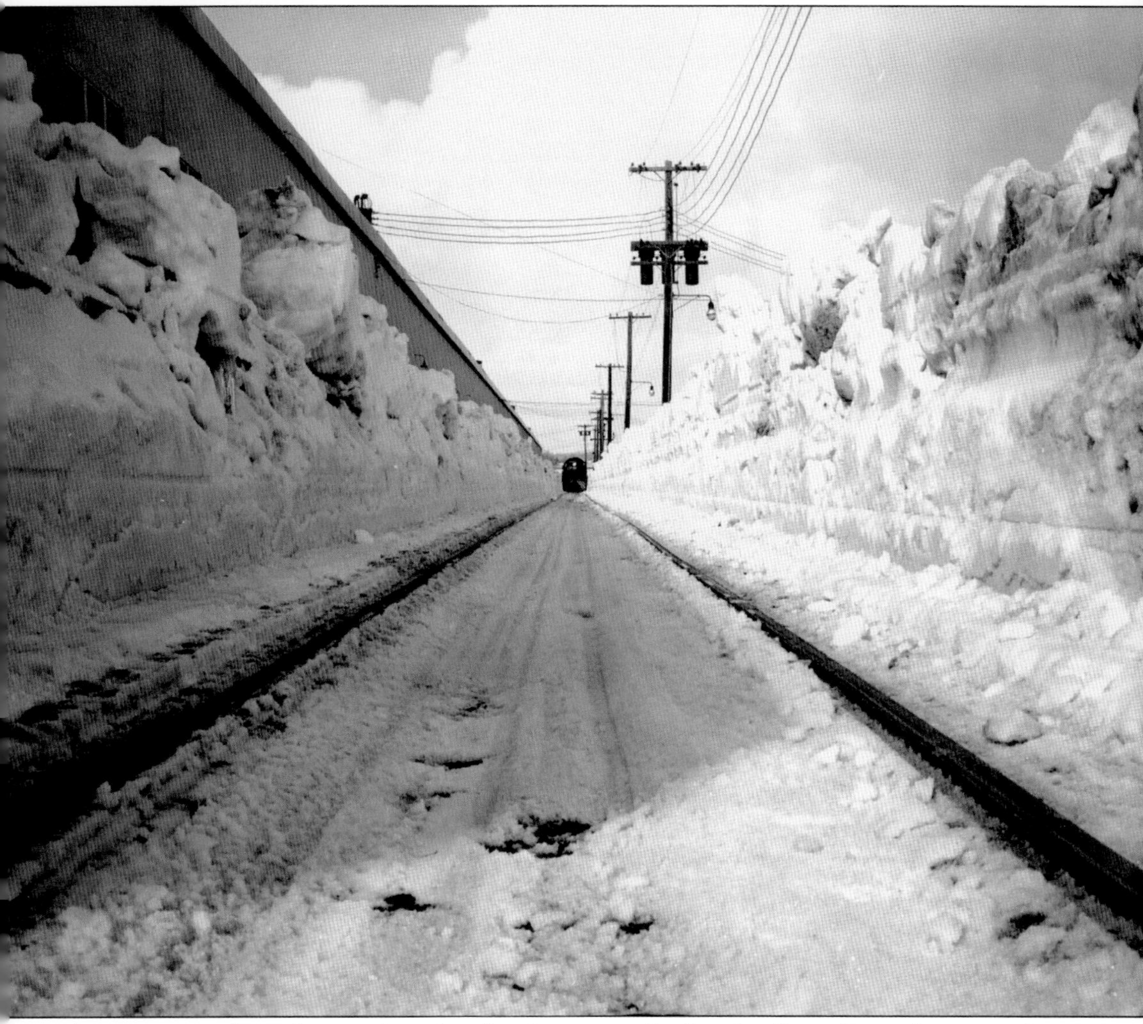

A train passes through tunnels and walls of snow on Griffiss Air Force Base after a two-day snowstorm on January 31 and February 1, 1966. (RHS.)

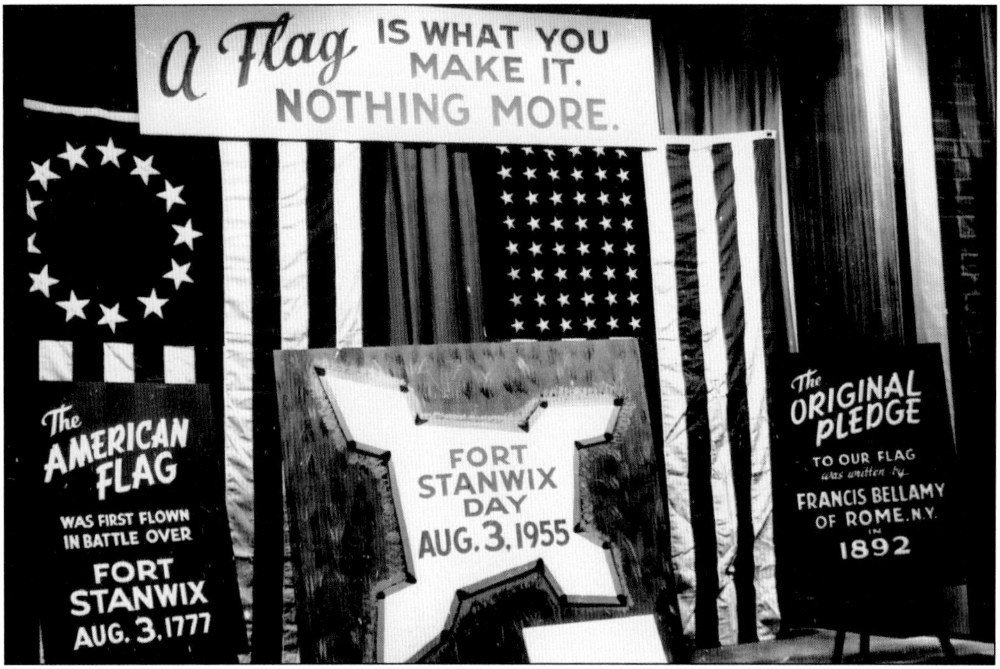

In 1955, Rome celebrated the anniversary of the siege of Fort Stanwix. Residents proudly displayed their two links to the American flag: it was first flown in battle at Fort Stanwix and Francis Bellamy's writing the Pledge of Allegiance. (RHS.)

CLASS OF SERVICE
This is a fast message unless its deferred character is indicated by the proper symbol.

WESTERN UNION
TELEGRAM

W. P. MARSHALL, PRESIDENT

1201

SYMBOLS
DL=Day Letter
NL=Night Letter
LT=International Letter Telegram

The filing time shown in the date line on domestic telegrams is STANDARD TIME at point of origin. Time of receipt is STANDARD TIME at point of destination

1956 AUG 1 AM 10 44

SYA043 301...(

SY WA181 GOVT PD=THE WHITE HOUSE WASHINGTON DC 1 1025AME=
JOHN H EIKENBERG, PRESIDENT ROME CHAMBER OF COMMERCE=
ROME NY=

I AM DELIGHTED TO SEND GREETINGS TO THE CITIZENS OF ROME, NEW YORK AND TO WISH THEM EVERY SUCCESS IN CELEBRATING THE ONE HUNDRED AND SEVENTY NINTH ANNIVERSARY OF THE BATTLE OF FORT STANWIX. OUTGUNNED AND OUTNUMBERED, THE MEN OF NEW YORK THERE DEMONSTRATED ON THE FIELD OF BATTLE THEIR DEVOTION TO LIBERTY, SETTING AN EXAMPLE OF SACRIFICE AND HEROISM FOR ALL WHO CHERISH HUMAN FREEDOM=

DWIGHT D EISENHOWER=(

Pres. Dwight D. Eisenhower sent a telegram to Rome congratulating the city on the 179th anniversary of the Battle of Fort Stanwix. It was Eisenhower, who on Flag Day, June 14, 1954, approved the addition of the words "under God" to the Pledge of Allegiance. (RHS.)

Four

LOOKING FORWARD, LOOKING BACK

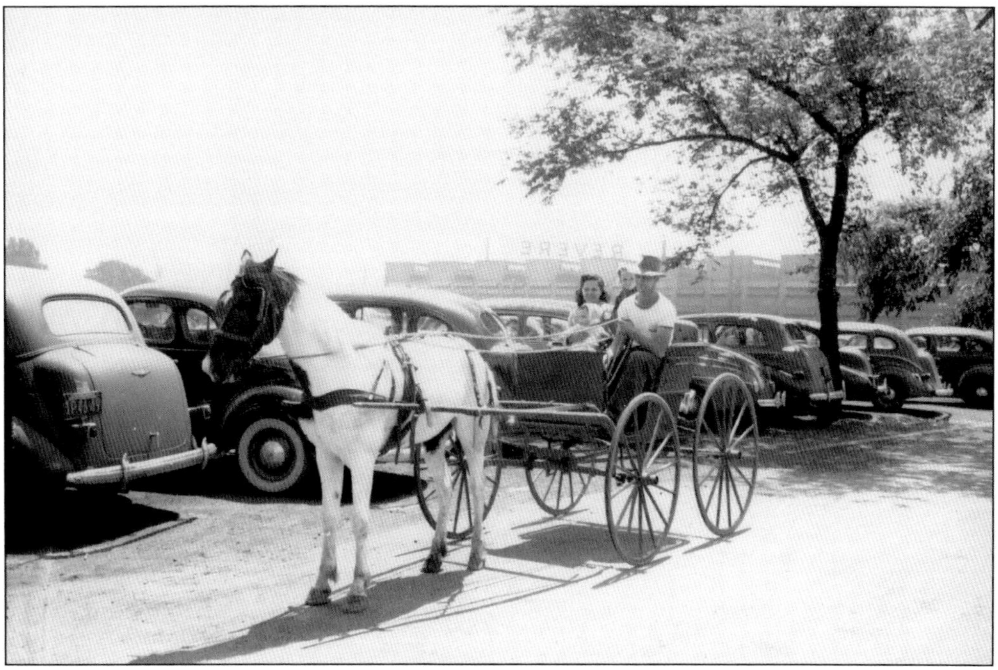

The old and new coexist in Rome. A man gives a couple a ride in a horse-drawn buggy, while Revere rises in the background. In the late 1960s, Rome began an urban renewal program, which destroyed many of the downtown buildings and greatly changed the face of the city. Rome was hit hard in 1995, when Griffiss Air Force Base was realigned, causing much of the city's population to depart. Today, Rome continues to keep its rich heritage alive with the Erie Canal Museum and the Fort Stanwix National Monument even as it strives to bring new industry to the community. (RHS.)

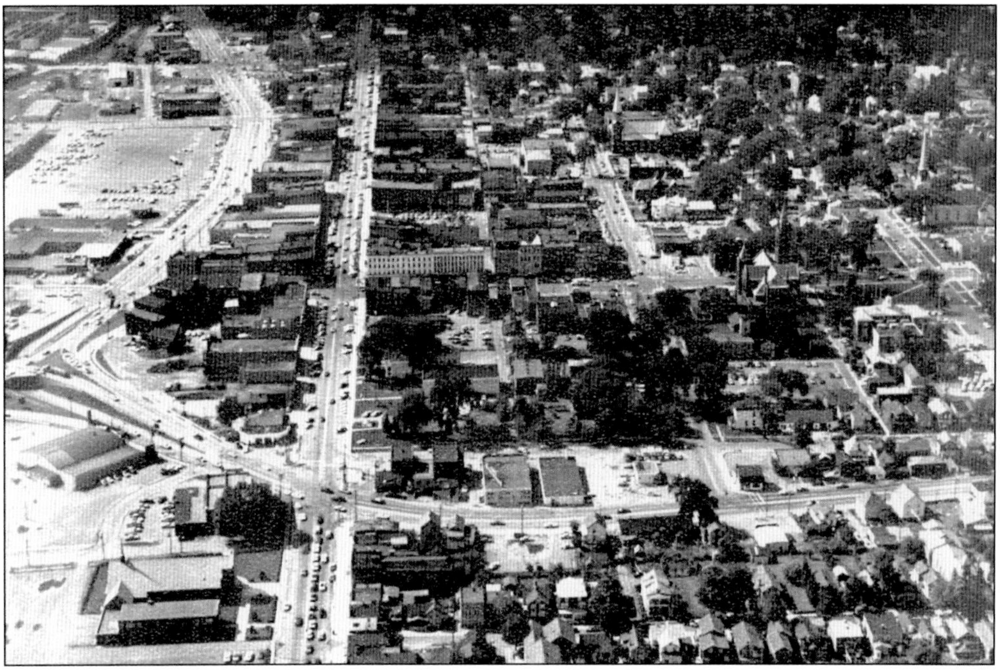

Some 14 acres of land in downtown Rome were cleared to make room for Fort Stanwix National Park, with the replica of Fort Stanwix in its original location. More than 30 buildings along Dominick Street were razed for the project. The photograph above shows an aerial view of downtown Rome in 1969, before much of the urban renewal program had taken place. The photograph below shows an aerial view of downtown Rome in 1976, after the construction of Fort Stanwix National Park. (RHS.)

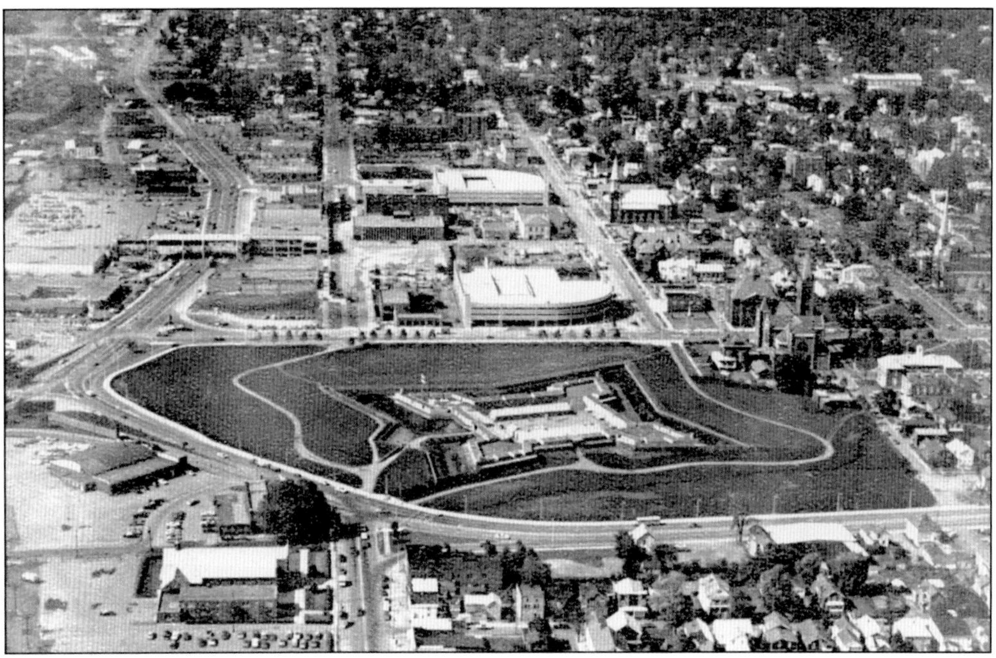

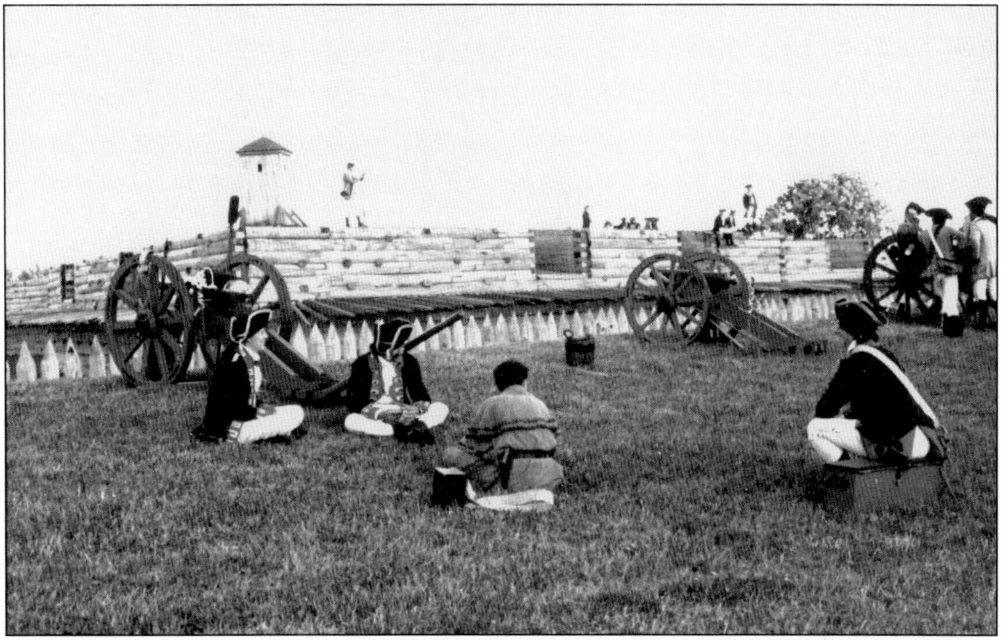

Part of the National Park Service, the Fort Stanwix National Monument gives visitors a chance to experience life as it was in the 18th century. Reenactors take a break and sit outside the fort during the summer months. (Rome Area Chamber of Commerce.)

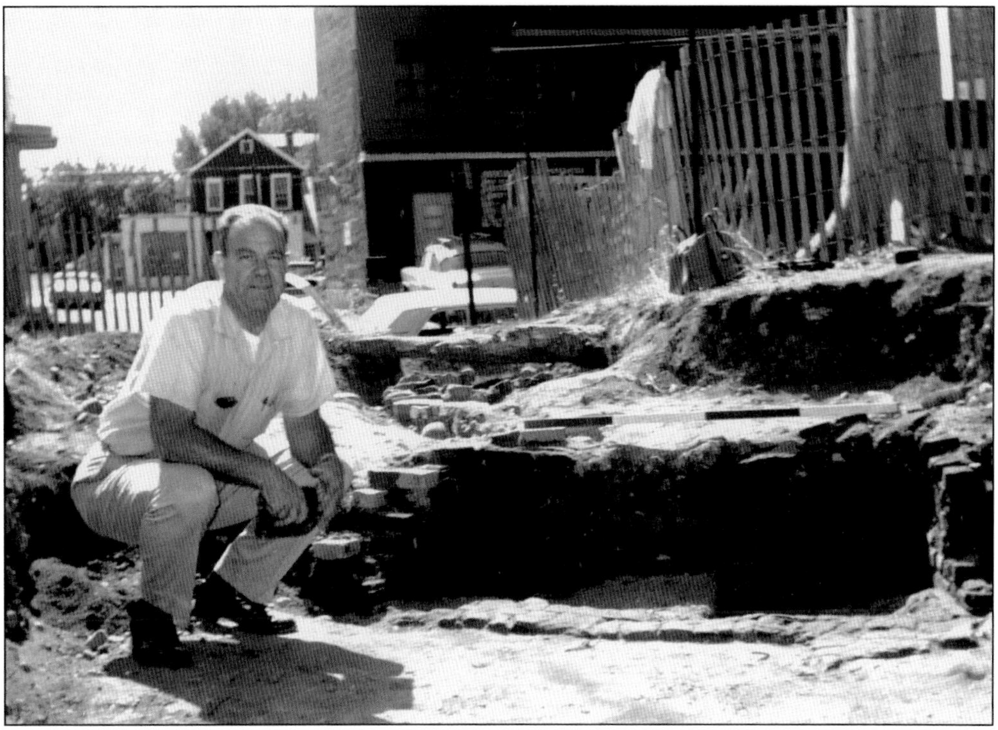

Archaeological excavations have been going on at the site of Fort Stanwix since the decision was made to rebuild the fort. (RHS.)

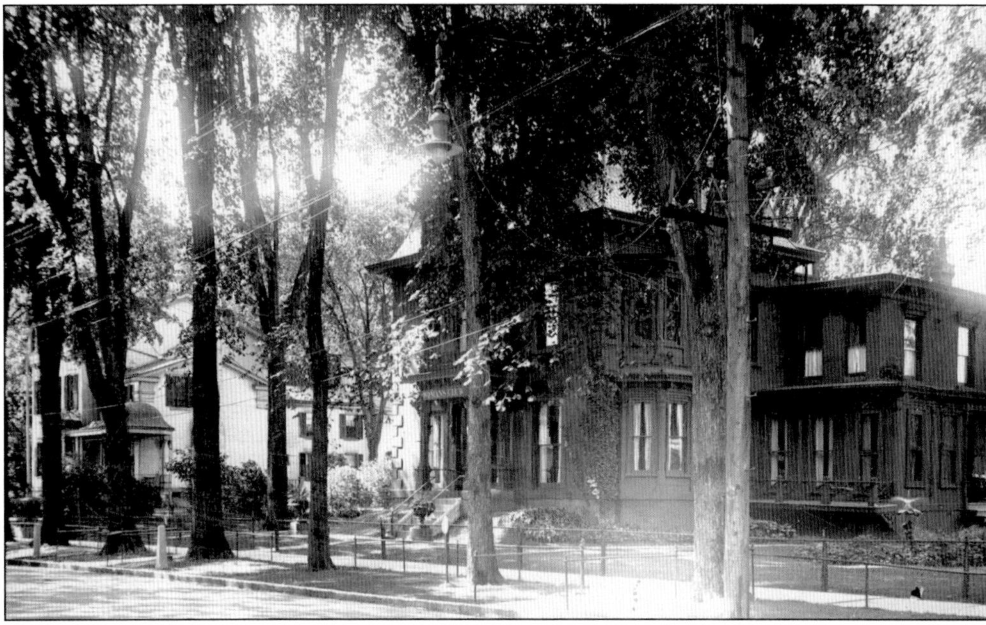

These four buildings are just a few examples of buildings torn down during the urban renewal project. The Cole-Kingsley house was built *c.* 1850 and eventually became the Woman's Club. This is what the building looked like in 1966, shortly before it was torn down. (RHS.)

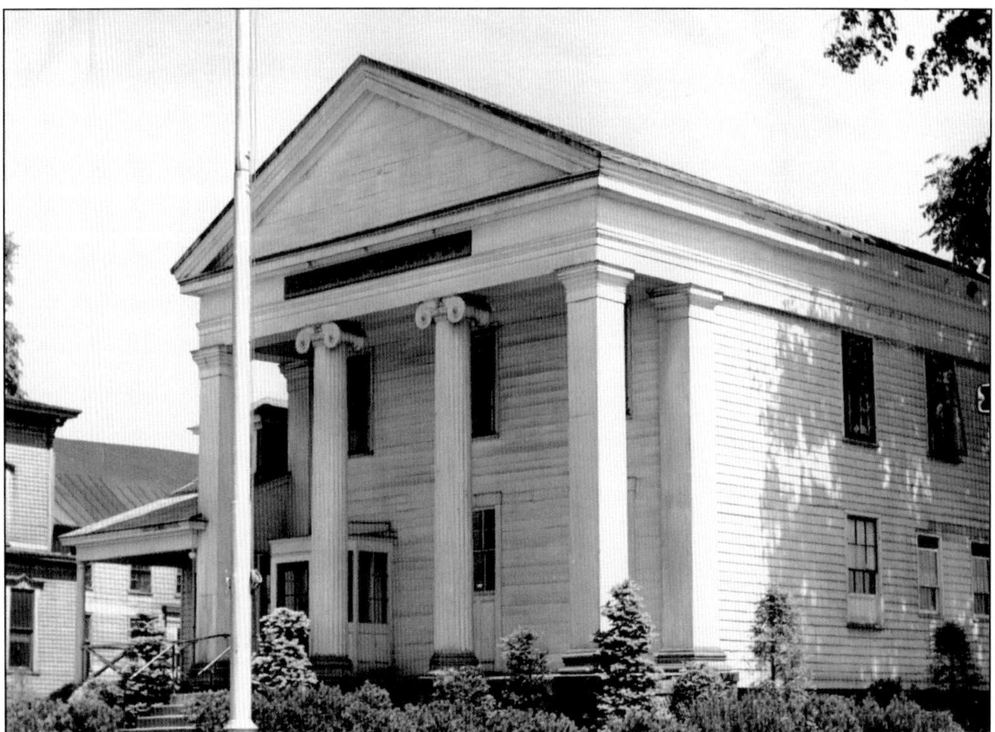

The American Legion, located on the corner of Dominick and Spring Streets, was also torn down. (RHS.)

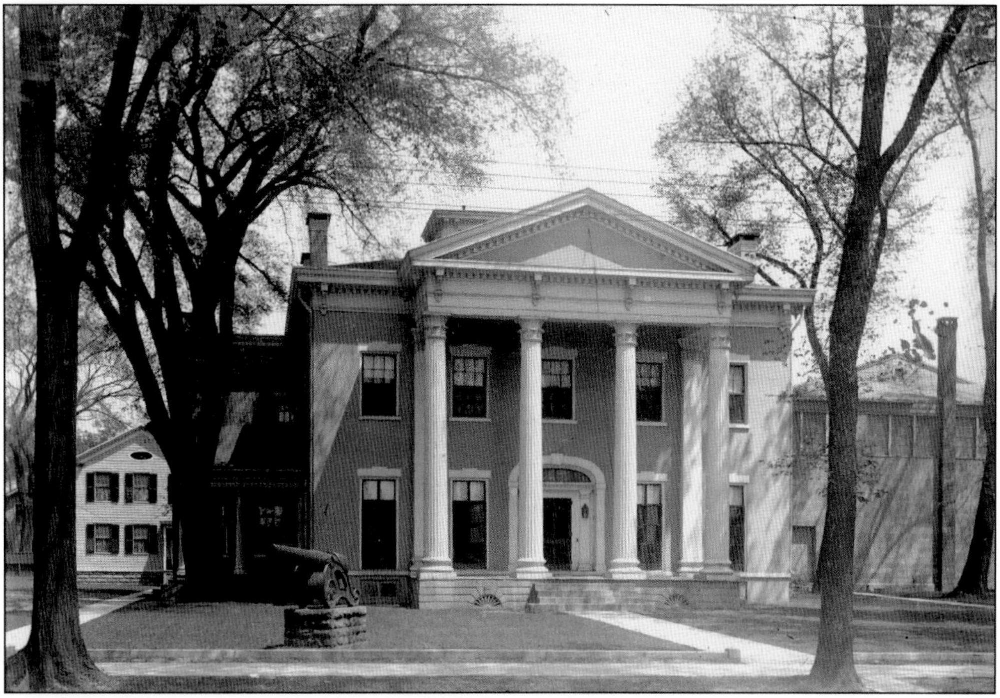

Located in the 100 block of East Dominick Street, the Rome Club was the former Barnes-Mudge house. The cannon was at the west bastion of the original Fort Stanwix. (RHS.)

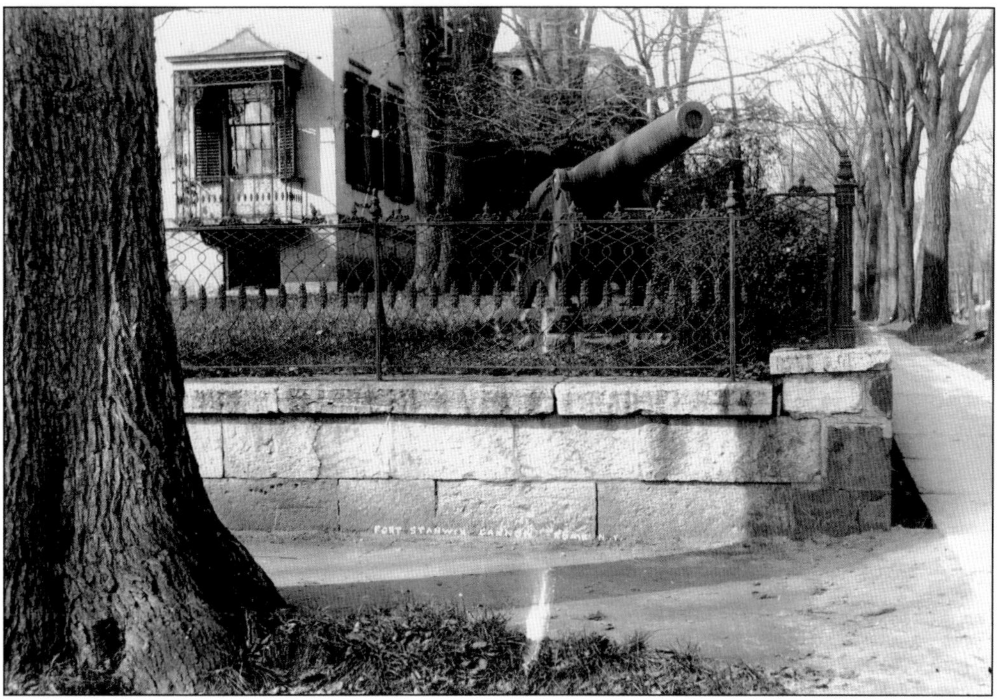

The Stryker house, on the corner of Spring Street and East Liberty Street, was located at the east bastion of Fort Stanwix. The cannon on the front lawn marked the original location of the bastion until the house was torn down and the replica fort constructed. (RHS.)

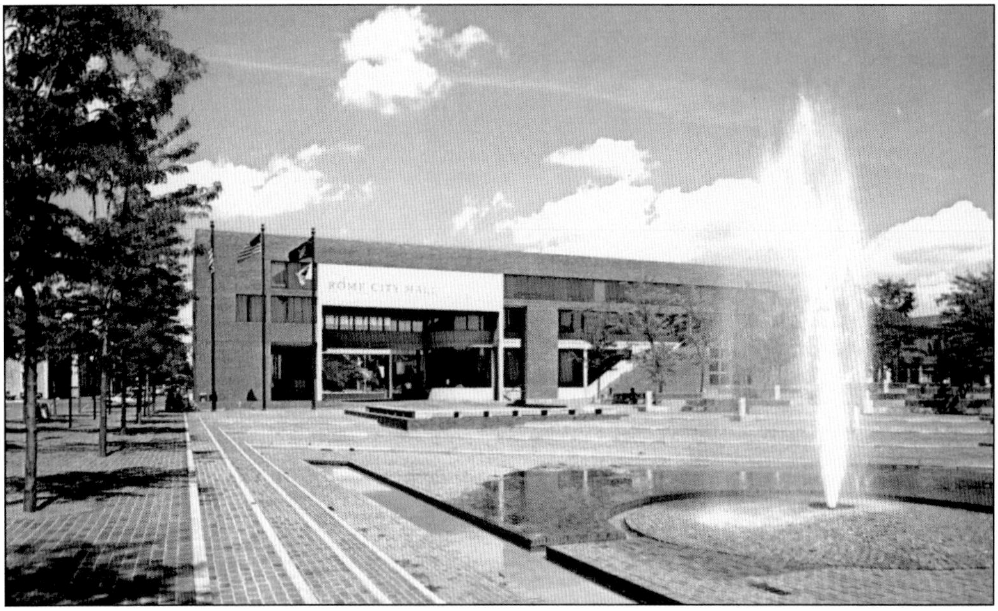

This is the new city hall, with a fountain on the Liberty Plaza. The Liberty Plaza was part of the revitalization program designed to create a new contemporary downtown. Also seen is the community bandstand. The revitalization project ended in 1979, the same year the new city hall opened. (Margo Studio.)

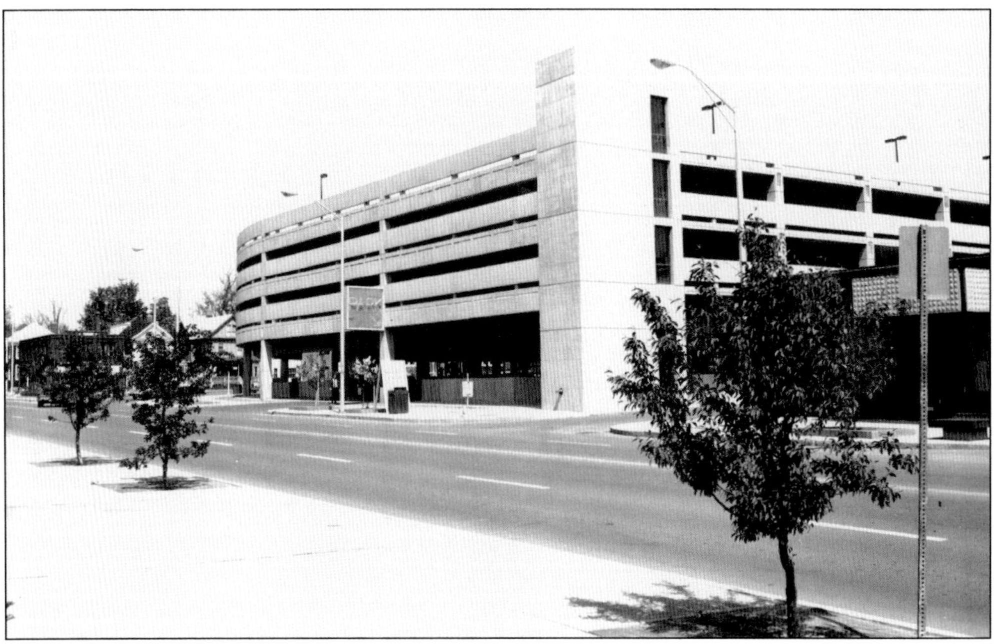

Also part of the new downtown was the Liberty-James parking garage, opened in 1976. (RHS.)

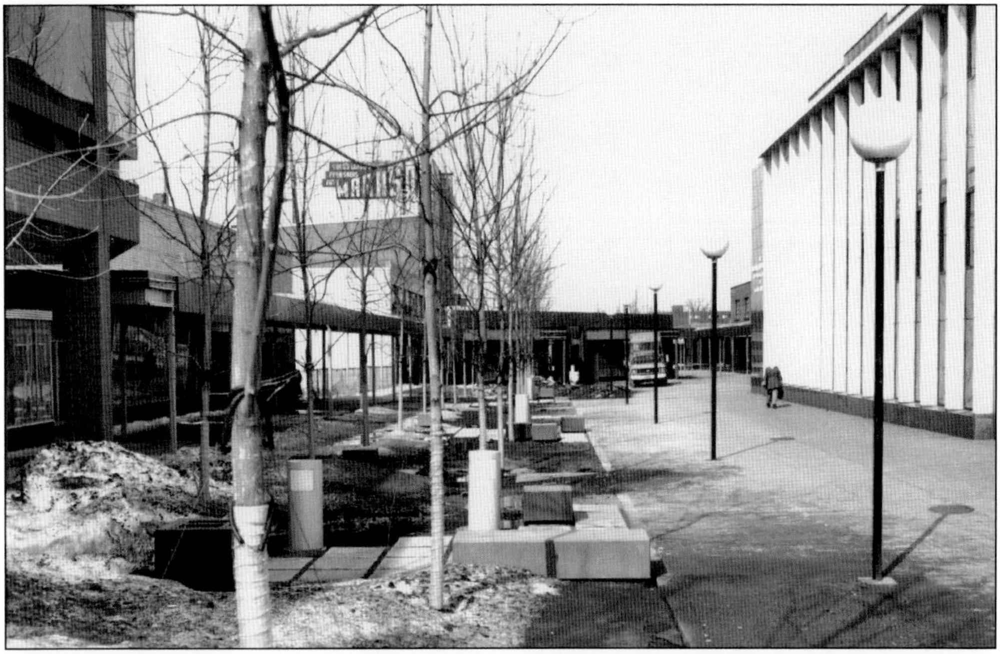

When urban renewal ended in 1979, there were three new bank buildings, several new stores with offices, new brick sidewalks, areas with benches, and a new downtown mall. (RHS.)

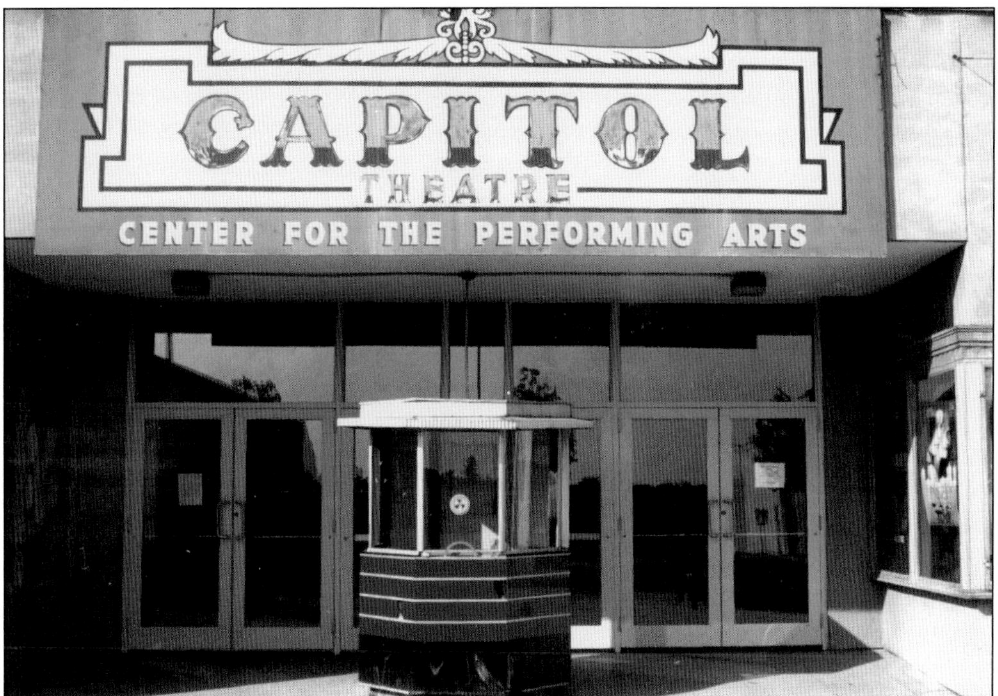

The Capitol Theatre is located in the downtown area. The 1,700-seat performing arts center provides a variety of plays and concerts for the entertainment of area residents. (RHS.)

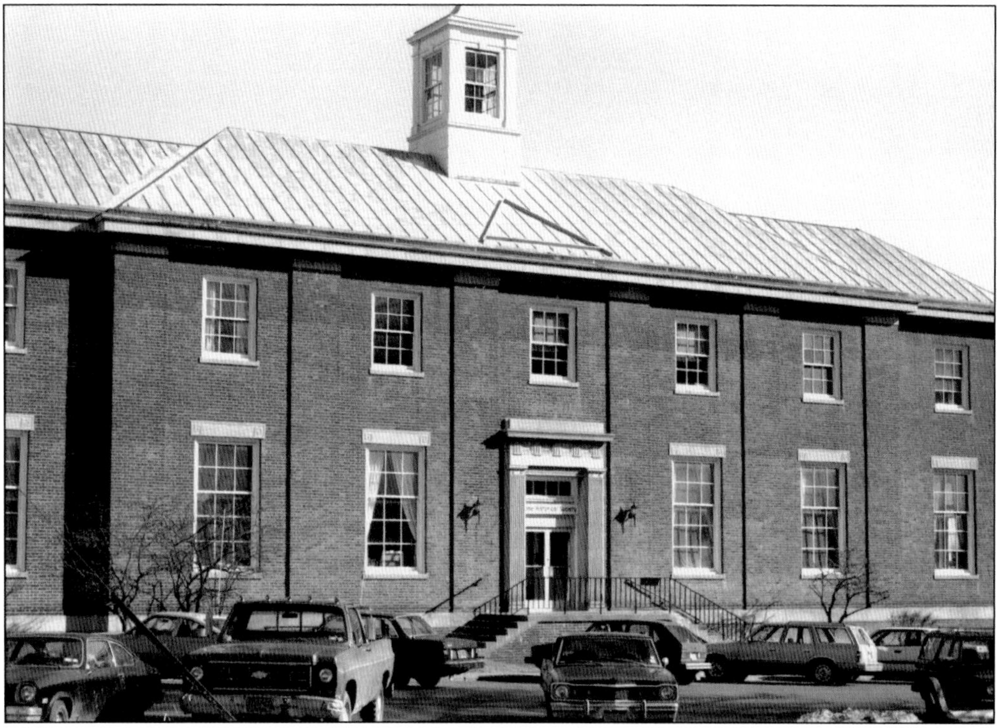

The Rome Historical Society, founded in 1936, moved into the former post office on Church Street in 1980. The society contains both a museum and a research library. Its goal is to preserve and promote Rome's rich history. (RHS.)

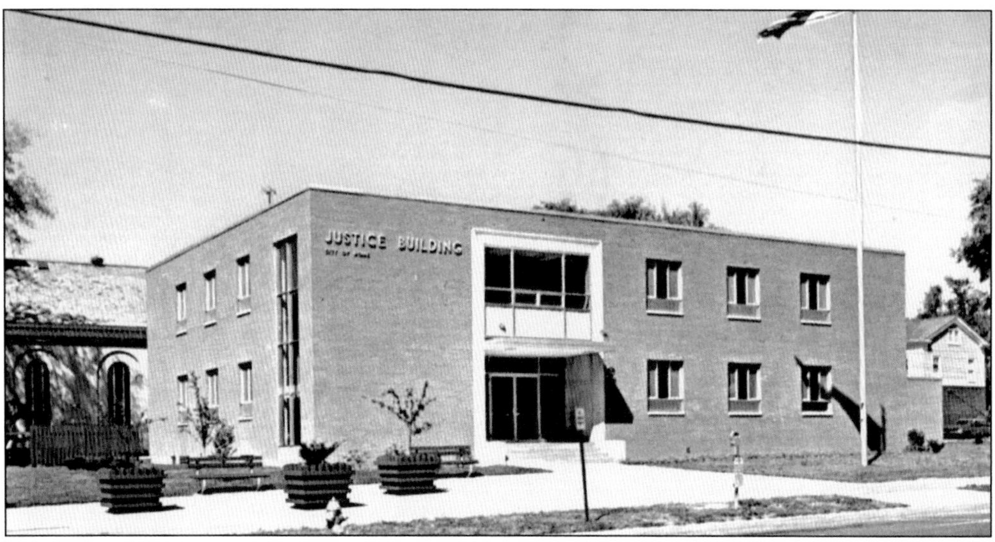

The Justice Building, erected in 1961, stands on the James Street site of the former Rome Free Academy. (Margo Studio.)

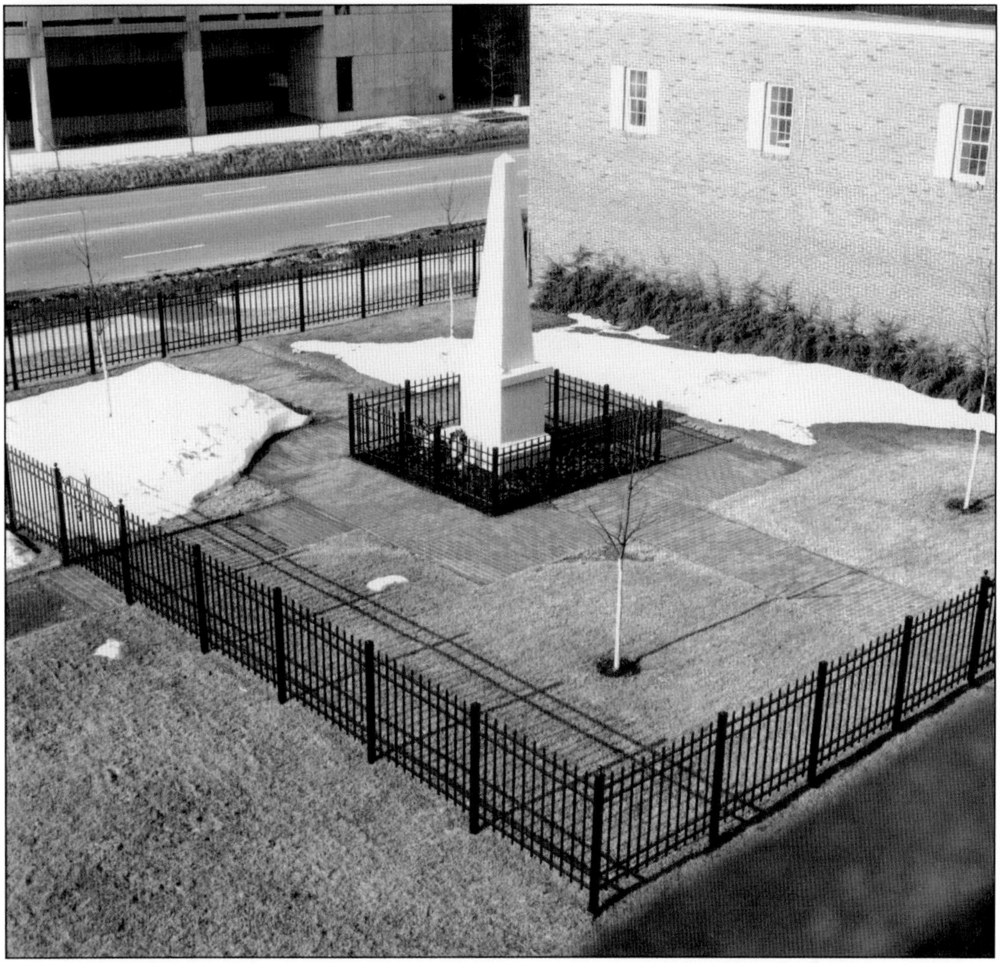

Lorimer Rich designed the Tomb of the Unknown Revolutionary Soldiers, which marks the remains of eight Revolutionary War soldiers entombed in a copper casket. The dedication ceremony took place on July 4, 1976, during the nation's bicentennial. (RHS.)

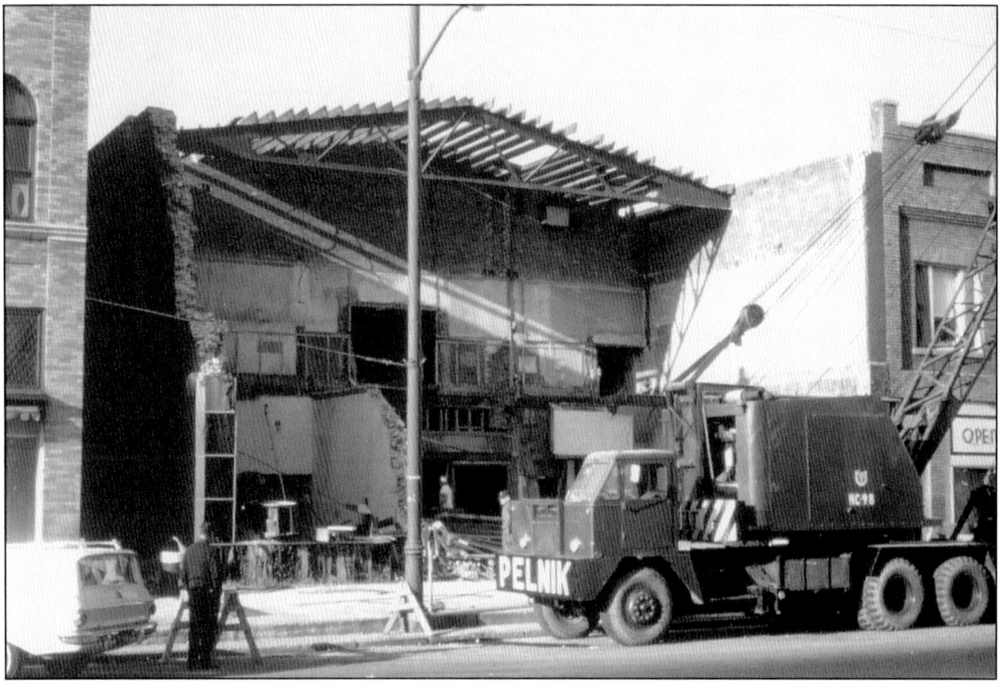

The mid-1960s were a time of great change in Rome. As some buildings were torn down, others were created. Above, the Strand Theater is torn down in September 1964. Below, a new senior citizens housing center is being built in August 1965. The center officially opened in 1966. (RHS.)

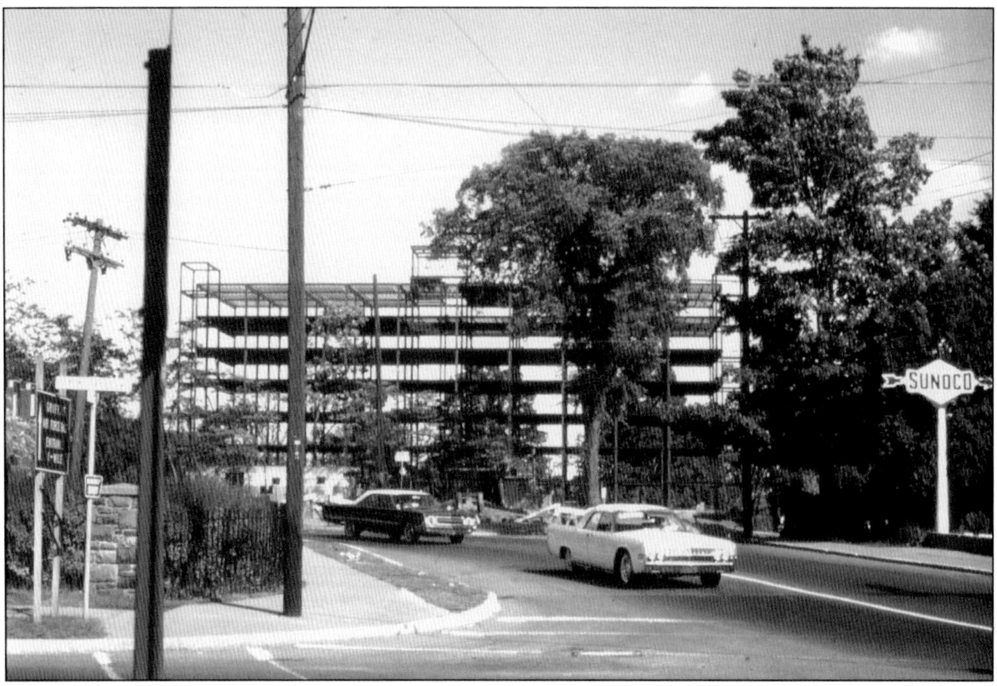

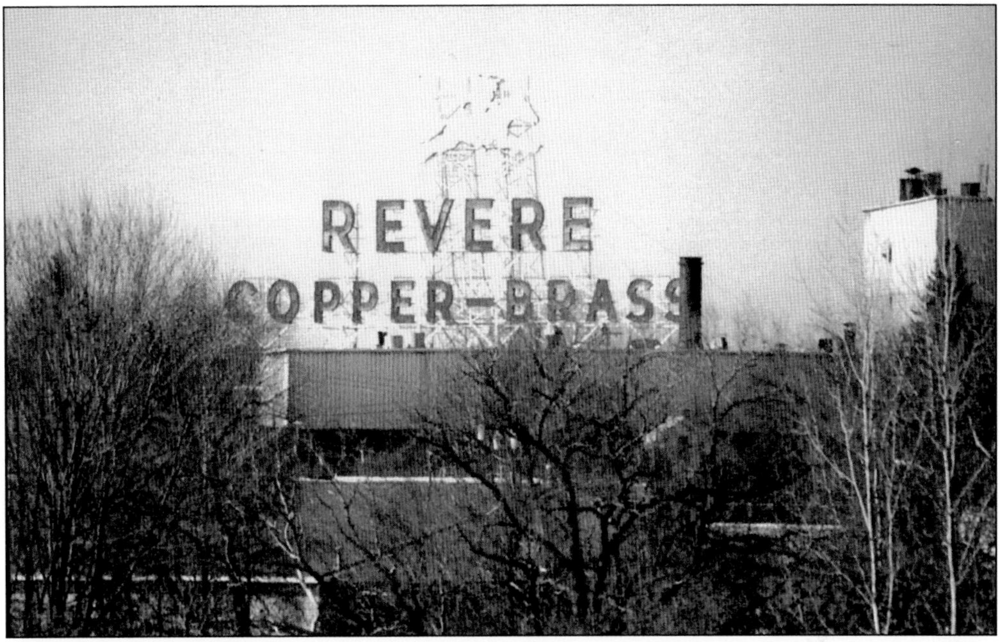

Revere Copper and Brass is one of the few industries remaining in Rome. A new rolling mill was constructed in Riverdale in the mid-1960s. The sign was erected in 1951 for the sesquicentennial of the founding of Paul Revere's original copper factory. Rome celebrated with an open house. (RHS/Kevin Kelley.)

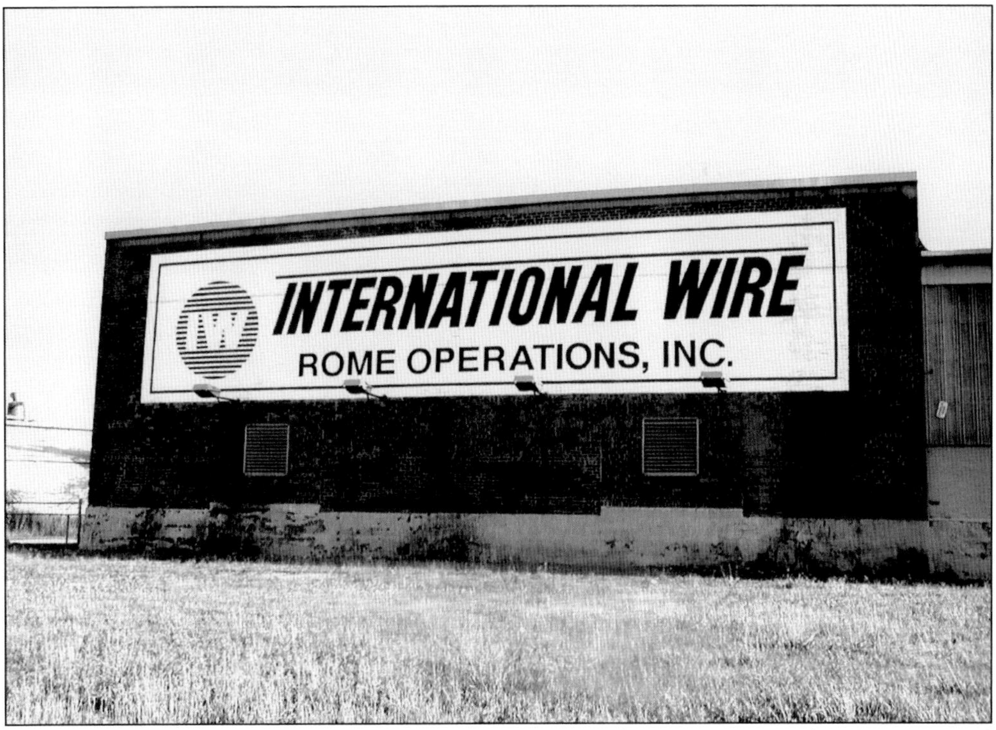

International Wire bought the Spargo Wire Company plant in 1998. Today, International continues the tradition of the wire industry in Rome. (Portia Vescio.)

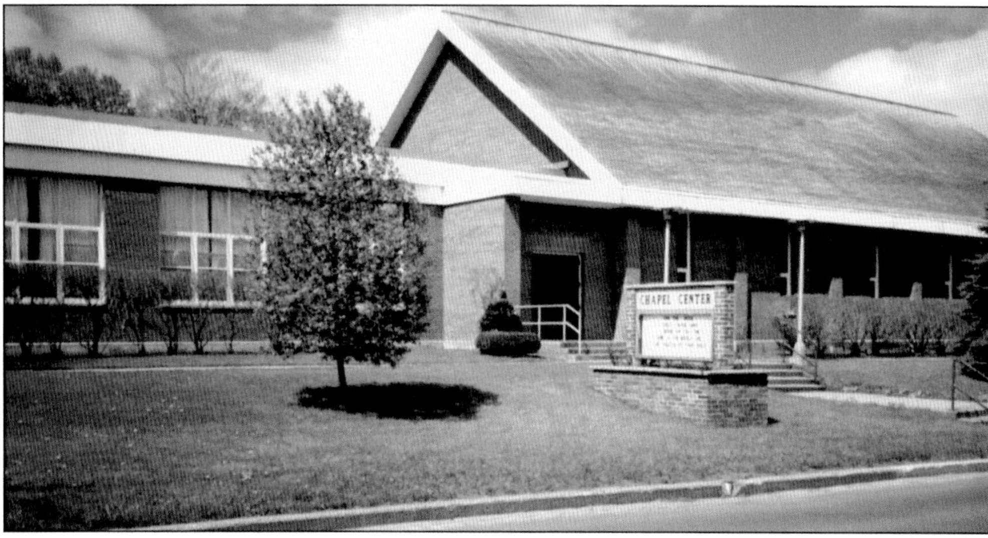

The Chapel Center was dedicated in May 1970, with 400 people in attendance. The nondenominational facility at Griffiss Air Force Base could seat more than 500 people. It was incorporated into the new high school after the base closed. (RHS.)

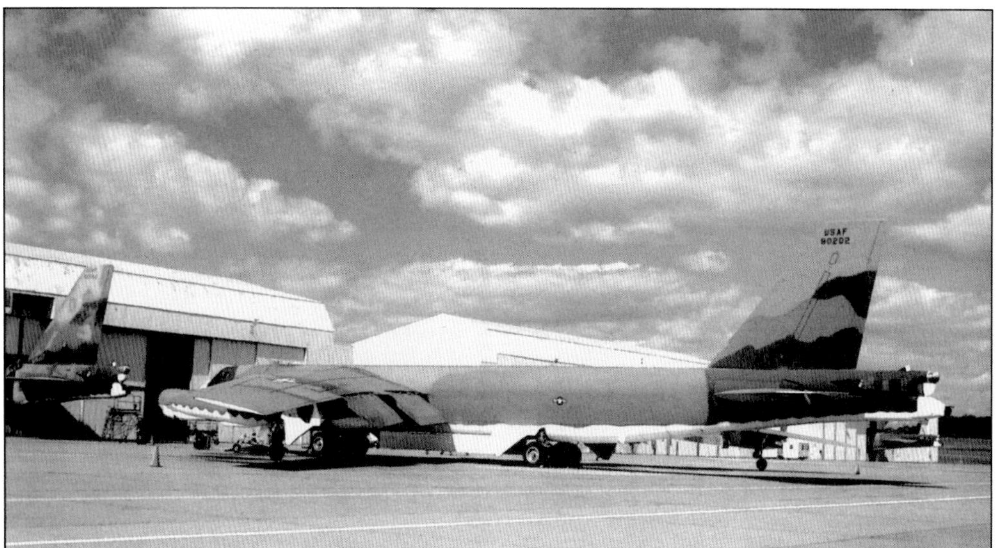

These camouflaged B-52 bombers, attached to the 416th Bombardment Wing at Griffiss Air Force Base, are shown at their maintenance hangar. The planes were on a continuous maintenance cycle to keep men and equipment mission-ready. (Margo Studio.)

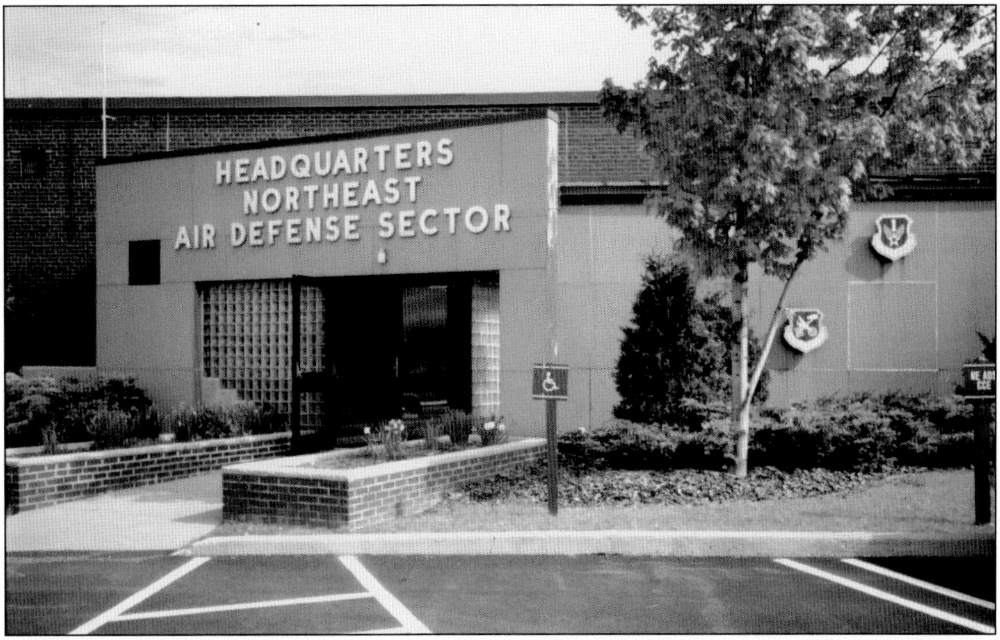

On July 1, 1987, the Northeast Air Defense Sector (NEADS) was activated at Griffiss Air Force Base. It is one of four air defense sectors in the country. In June 2003, reports indicated that it might merge with the Southeast Air Defense Sector to become the Eastern Air Defense Sector, monitoring everything east of the Mississippi River. (RHS/Kevin Kelley.)

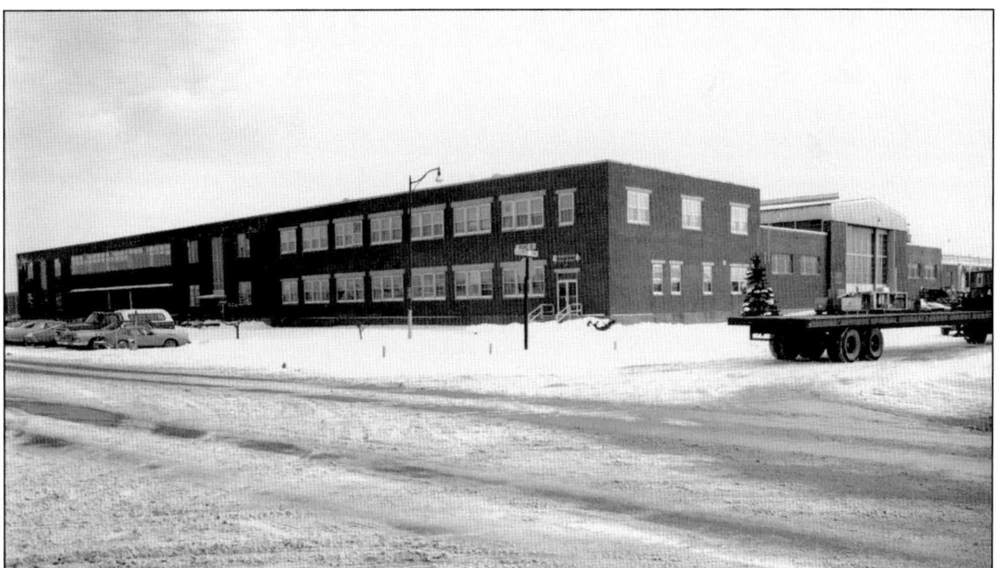

Watson Laboratory, later called Rome Laboratory, moved to the air base in 1948. This building, which once housed the Supply SQ and Transportation Offices, has housed Rome Laboratory since 1998. The research laboratory was not closed down when the rest of the base was realigned in 1995. (RHS/Kevin Kelley)

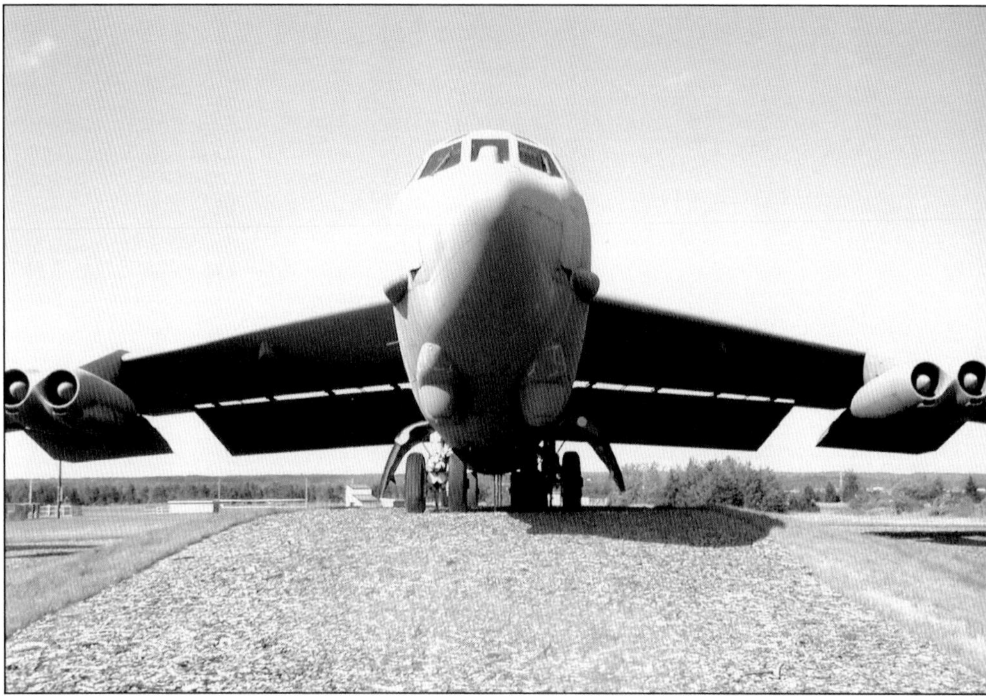

The *Mohawk Valley*, a G-Model B-52 bomber, first landed at Griffiss Air Force Base on January 12, 1960, just seven days after Boeing finished building it in Wichita, Kansas. Today, it sits on the land formerly occupied by the air base as a tribute to servicemen and women who dedicate their lives in defense of the nation. (Joseph Vescio.)

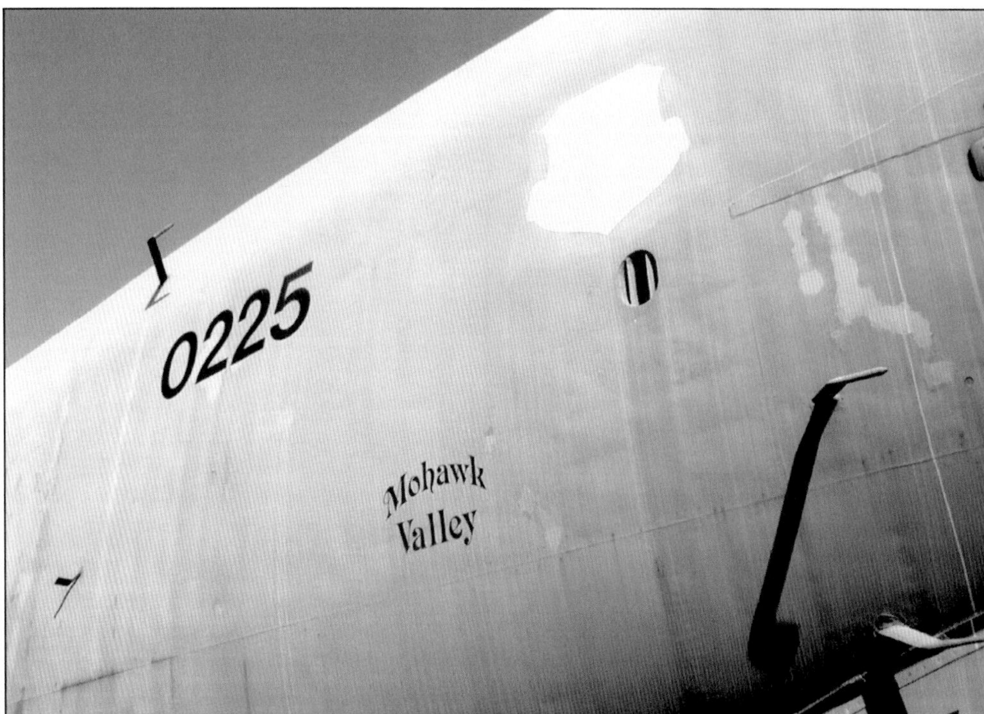

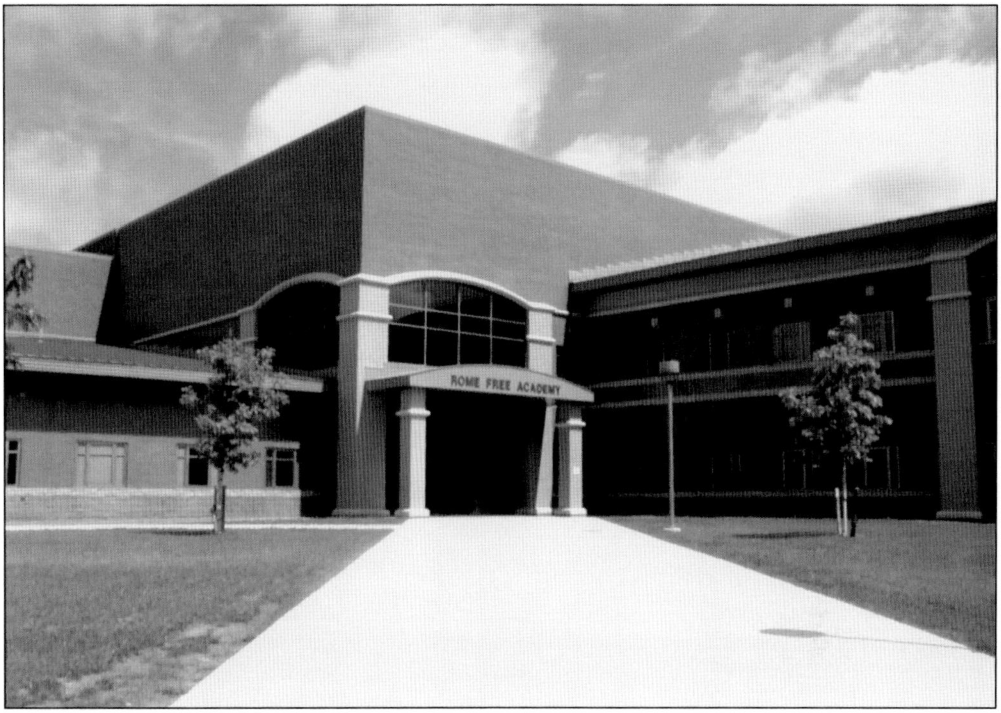

After the air base closed, new businesses moved onto the grounds. Among the new buildings on the former base site is the new Rome Free Academy, which first opened its doors to classes in September 2001. (Portia Vescio.)

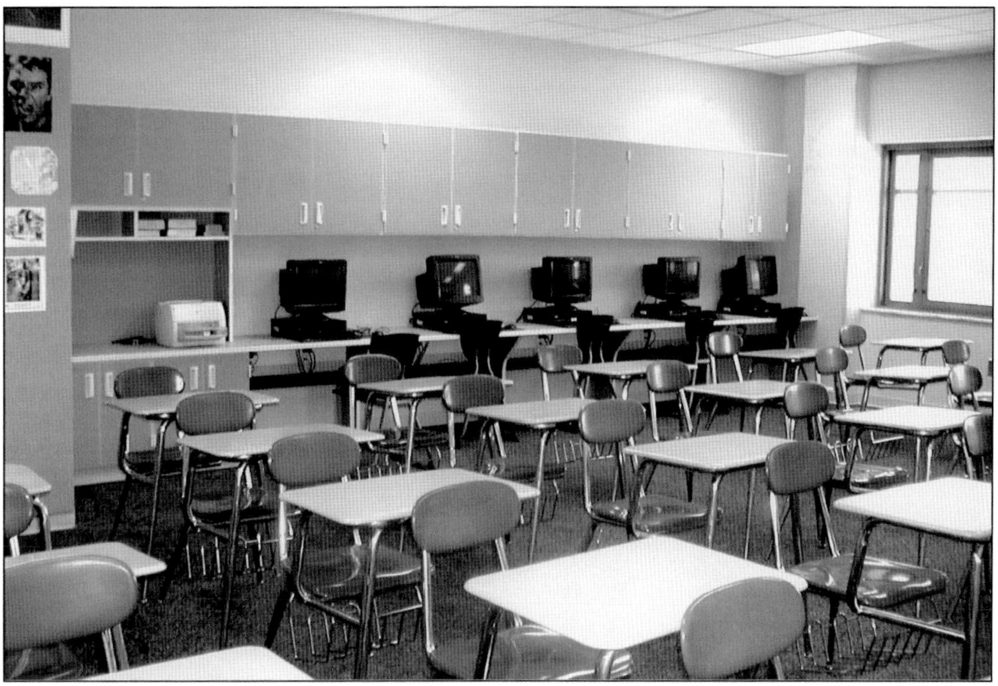

Each classroom is equipped with computers and wired with the latest technology. (Portia Vescio.)

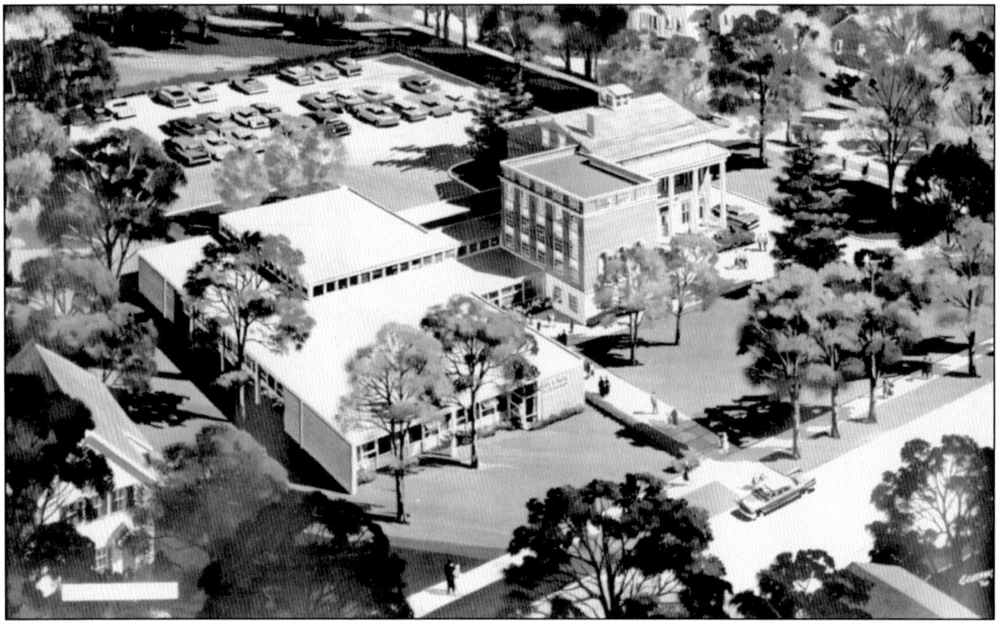

An aerial view of Jervis Library shows the additions over the years since John B. Jervis bequeathed the house for the library. (RHS/Margo Studio.)

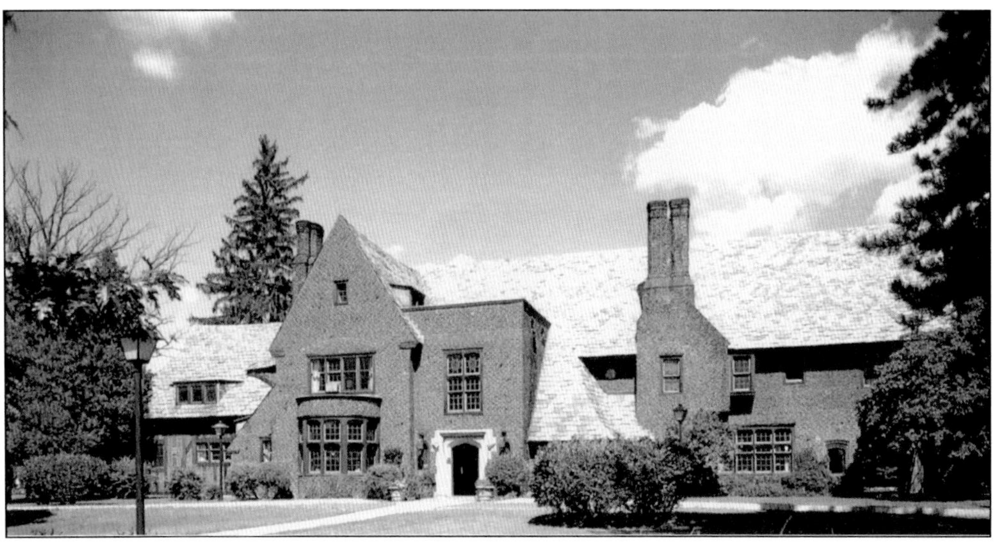

Built in 1923, this building was originally the Carpenter mansion. In 1968, the Rome Art and Community Center took over the West Bloomfield Street building. The center provides cultural programming to the community through art classes, concerts, poetry readings, and children's programs. (Margo Studio.)

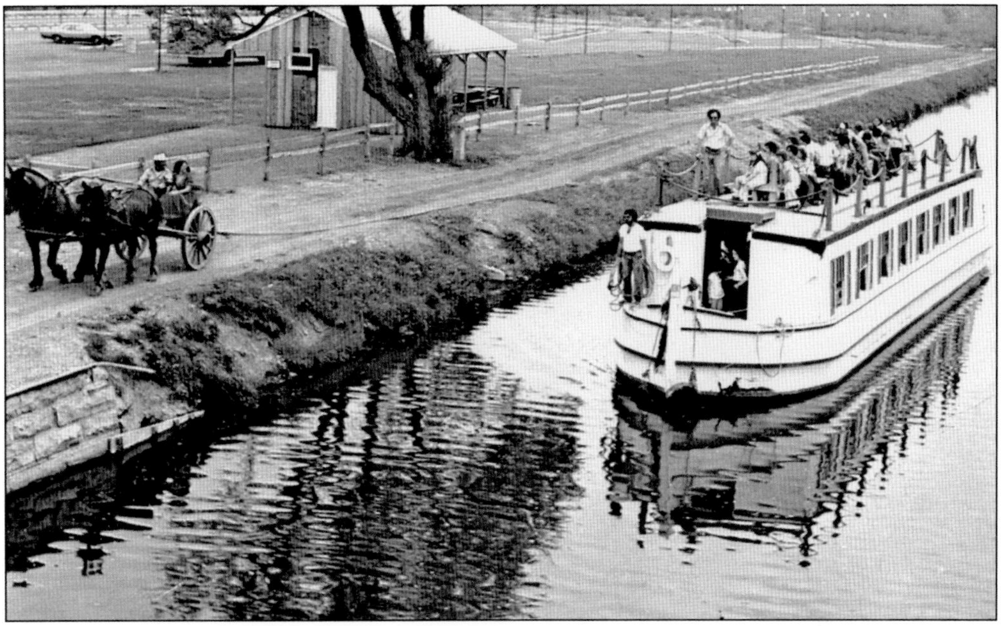

The recreation of the mule-drawn packet boat *Independence* was launched in 1973 at the Erie Canal Village. Although the *Independence* is no longer operational, visitors can still experience what it was like to ride on a packet or passenger boat by boarding the *Chief Engineer of Rome*. (Margo Studio.)

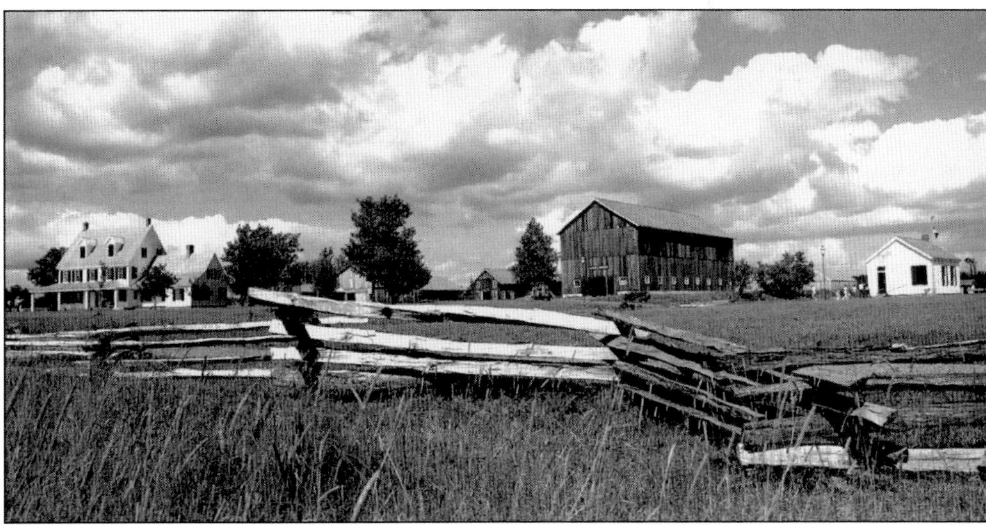

The Erie Canal Village is an outdoor living history museum, complete with blacksmith, tavern, and a train station. There are three museums within the village: the Erie Canal Museum, the Harden Museum, and the New York State Museum of Cheese. (Margo Studio.)

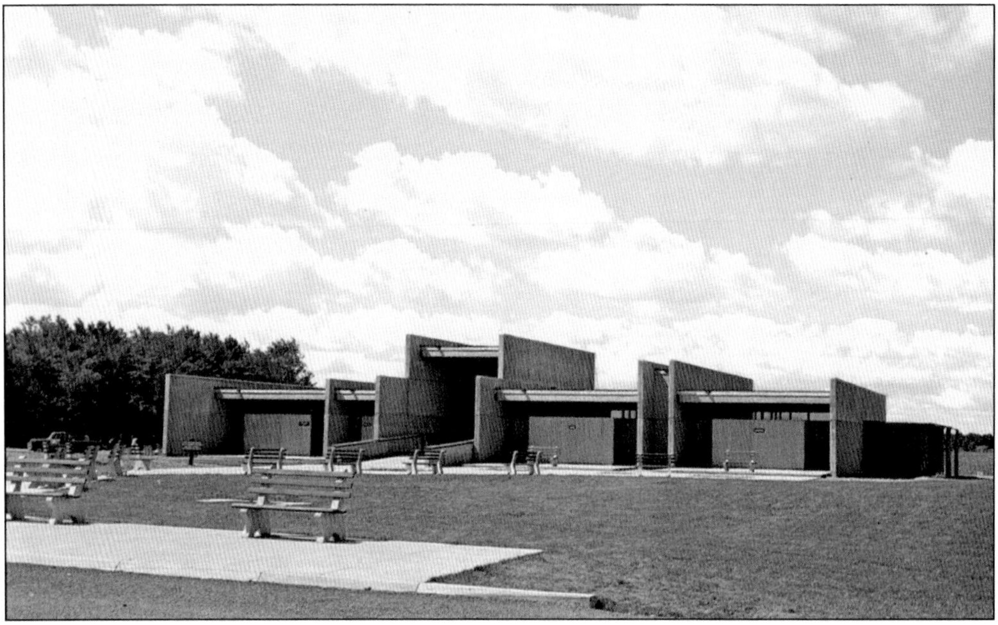

Delta Lake State Park is a fine recreational area that provides sites for picnicking, fishing, and swimming. (Margo Studio.)

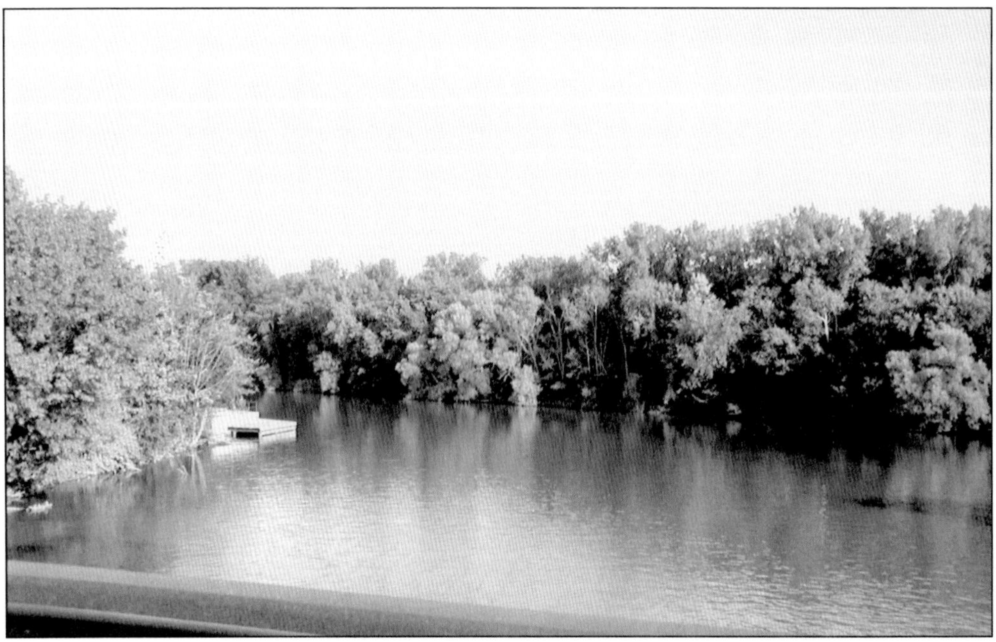

People who visit the newly created Bellamy Harbor Park on Race Street can watch the recreational boats pass by on the Barge Canal. (Joseph Vescio.)

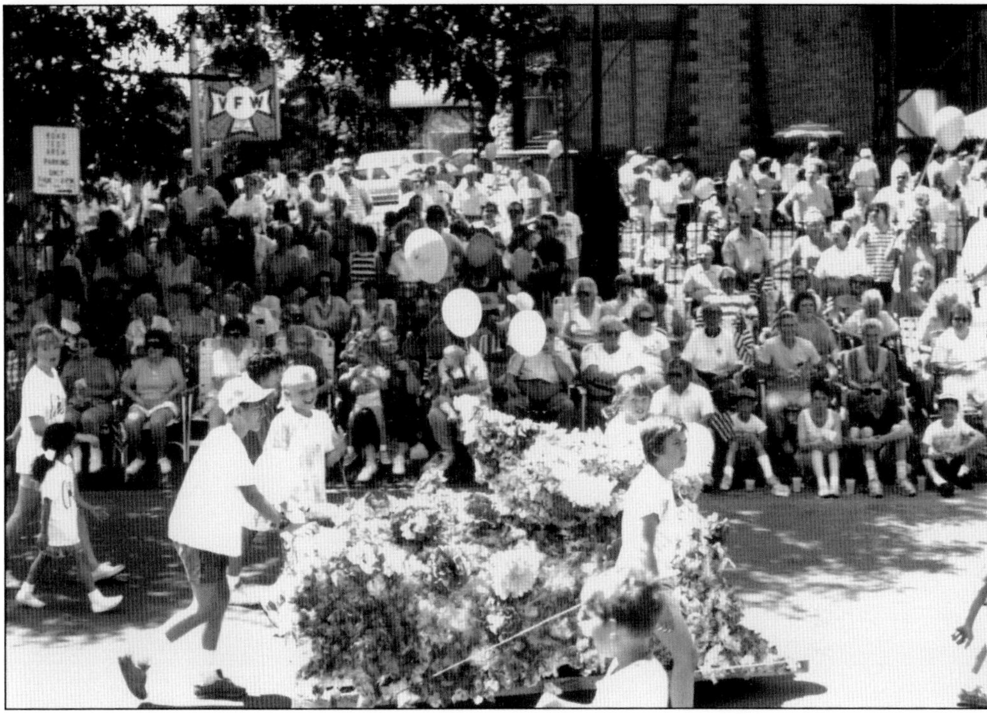

A summer parade goes past the Veterans of Foreign Wars building, which was once the Stevens house. (Rome Area Chamber of Commerce.)

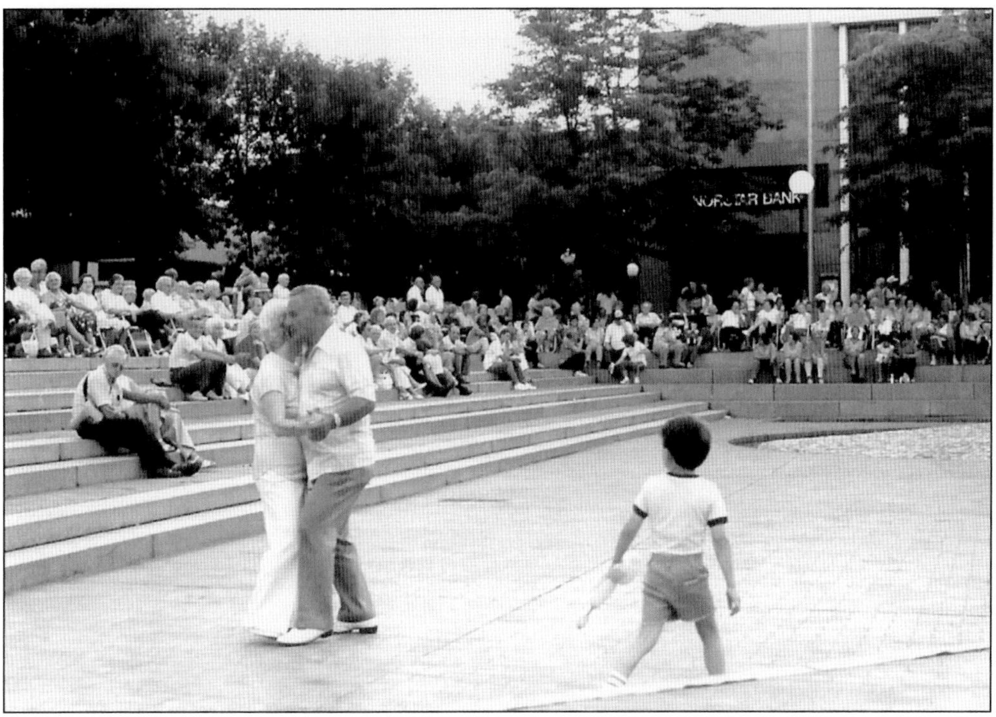

Folks gather for an evening concert and some dancing on the Liberty Plaza during the warm summer months. (Rome Area Chamber of Commerce.)

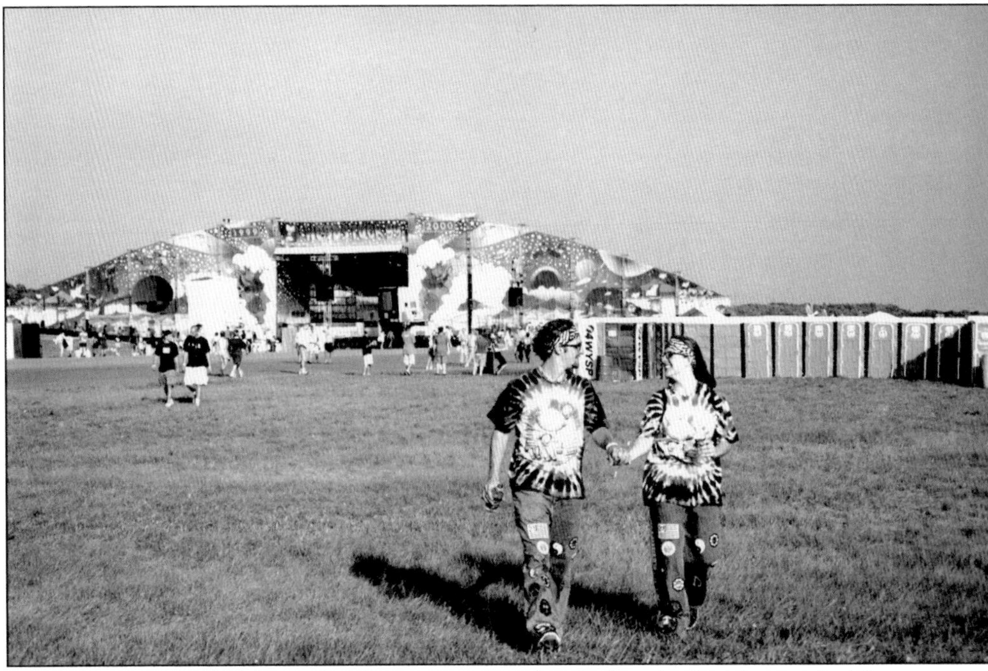

Woodstock '99 was held on July 23–24, 1999, on the Griffiss Air Field grounds. The east stage is decorated in 1960s psychedelic style. (RHS/Kevin Kelley.)

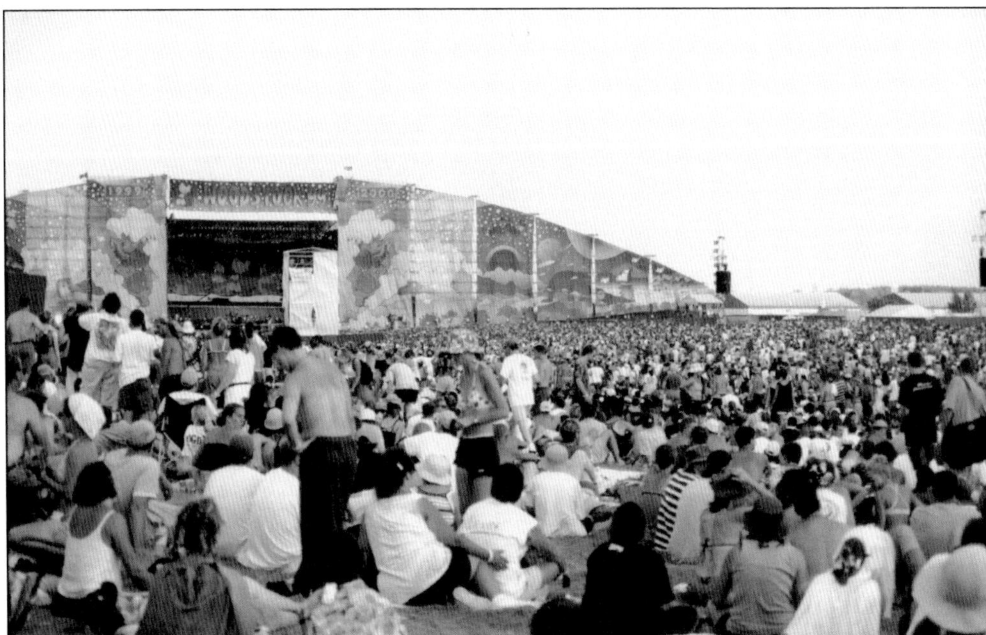

Like the original Woodstock, people came from all over the country to hear the concerts. More than 250,000 traveled to Rome for the event. The east stage area can be seen behind a large crowd of people. (RHS/Kevin Kelley.)

A peace sign drawn on the wall north of the west stage on the Griffiss Air Field during Woodstock '99 pays homage to the original Woodstock concert in 1969. (RHS/Kevin Kelley.)

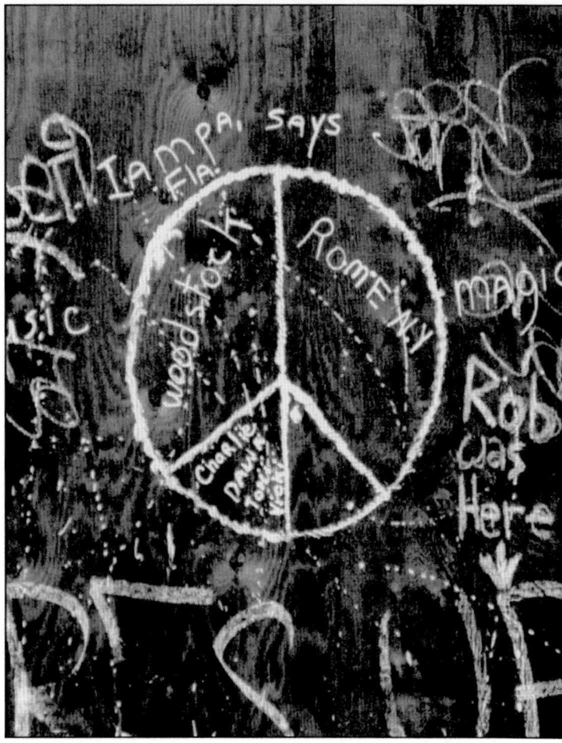

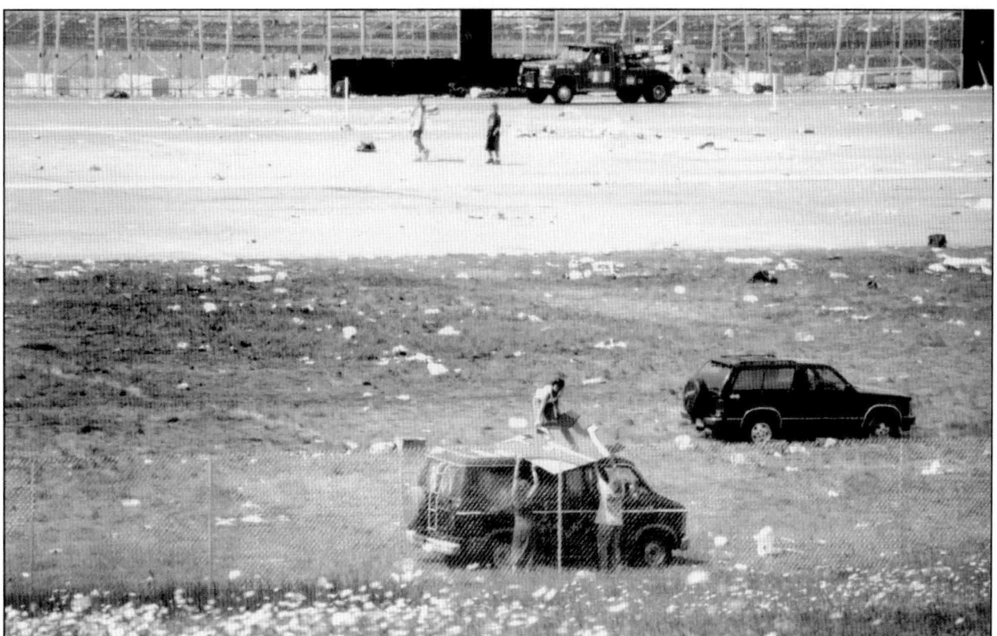

Not everything was peaceful during Woodstock '99. During the concert, 12 tractor-trailers and several vendor tents were set on fire. Here, people can be seen taking a piece of the stage as a souvenir amid a field of garbage. (RHS/Kevin Kelley.)

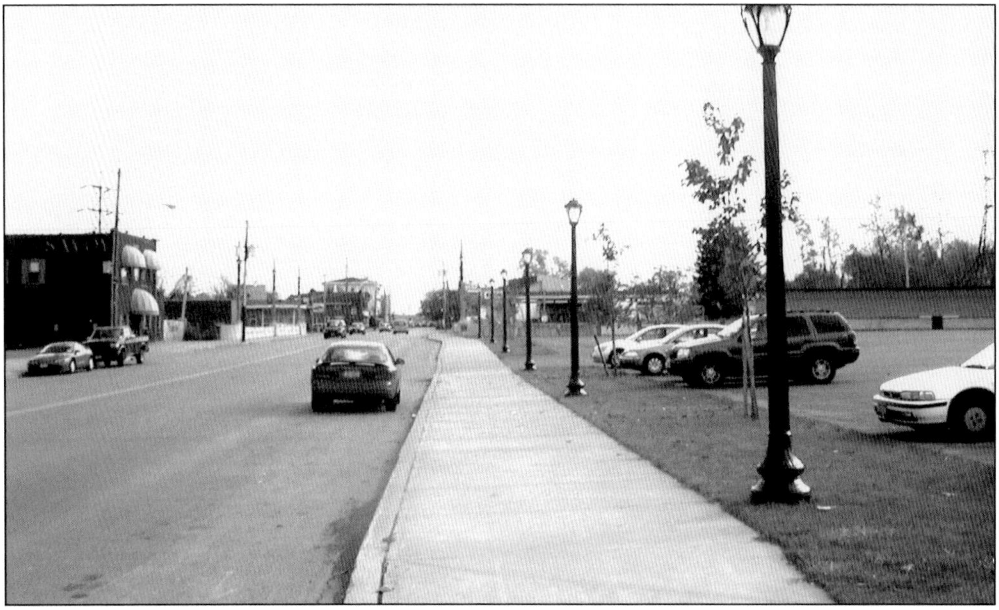

This is a view of the 100 block of East Dominick Street in 2003. The street lamps have been put in by the city, as have the grass and trees. The city of Rome, working in conjunction with the East Rome Merchant's Association, is trying to beautify the city's Dominick Street entrance. This work was paid for by community development and block grants funds from the federal government. (Joseph Vescio.)

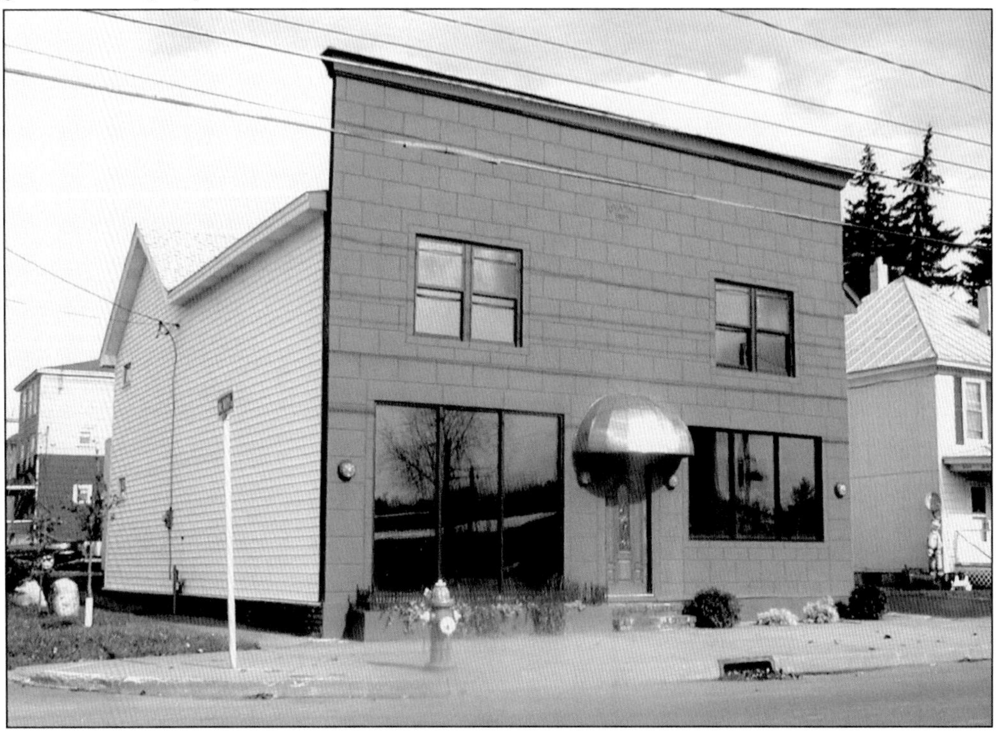

A new façade was put on this building through the city's façade program, which is trying to fix up storefronts on access streets. (Joseph Vescio.)

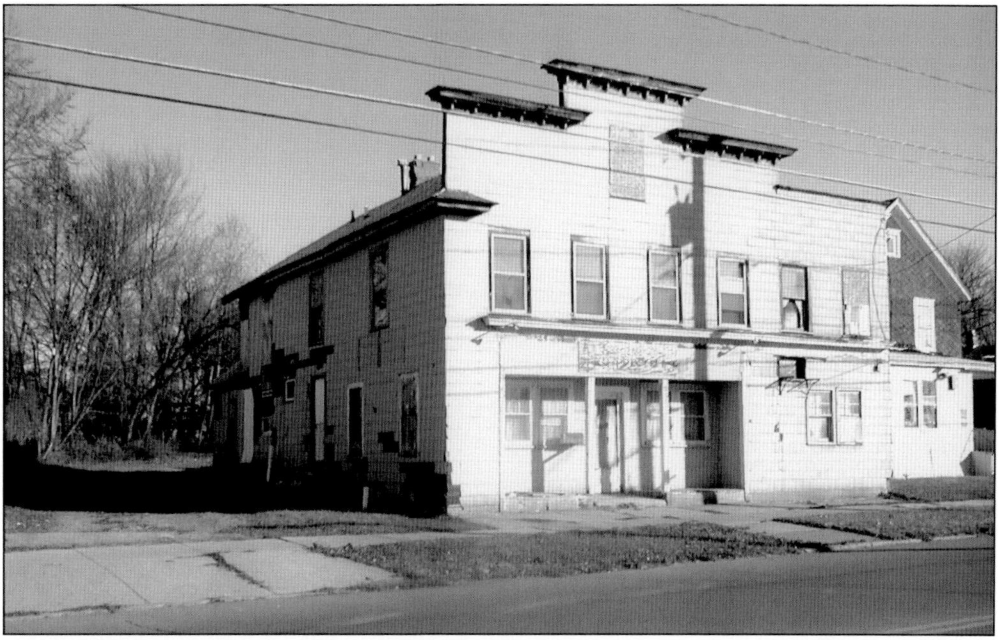

The East Rome Merchant's Association purchased this property in 2003 from the city for $1 in a tax sale. The association plans to rehabilitate the building and put on a new front in order to make the space more appealing to merchants. (Joseph Vescio.)

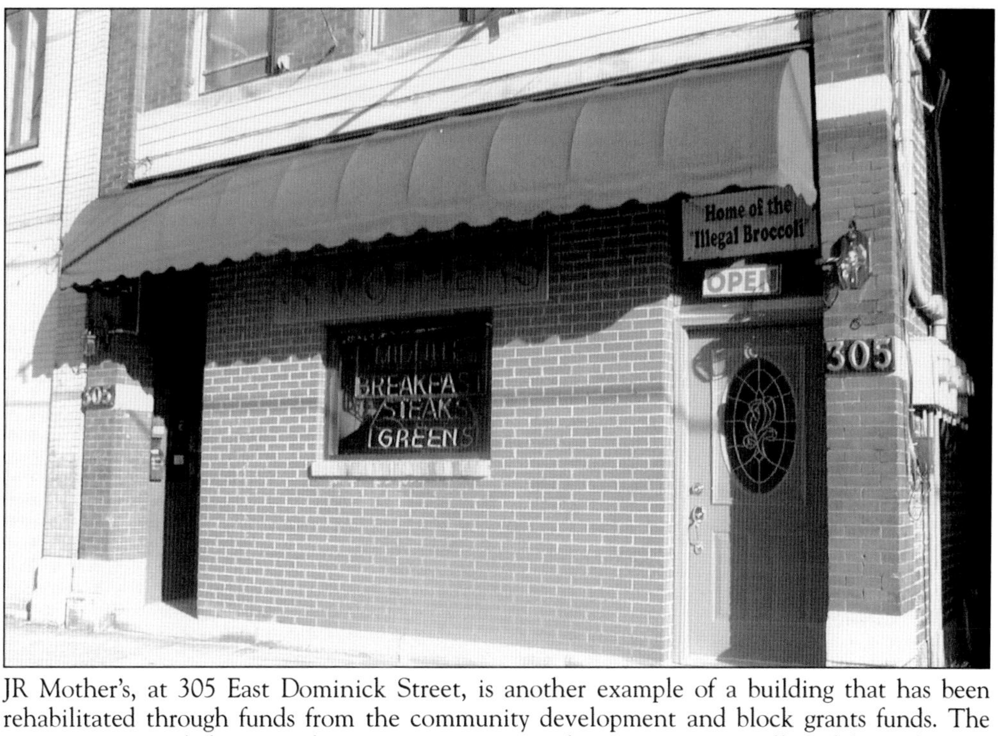

JR Mother's, at 305 East Dominick Street, is another example of a building that has been rehabilitated through funds from the community development and block grants funds. The awning, signage, lighting, and interior equipment and renovation were all paid for with grant funds. (Joseph Vescio.)

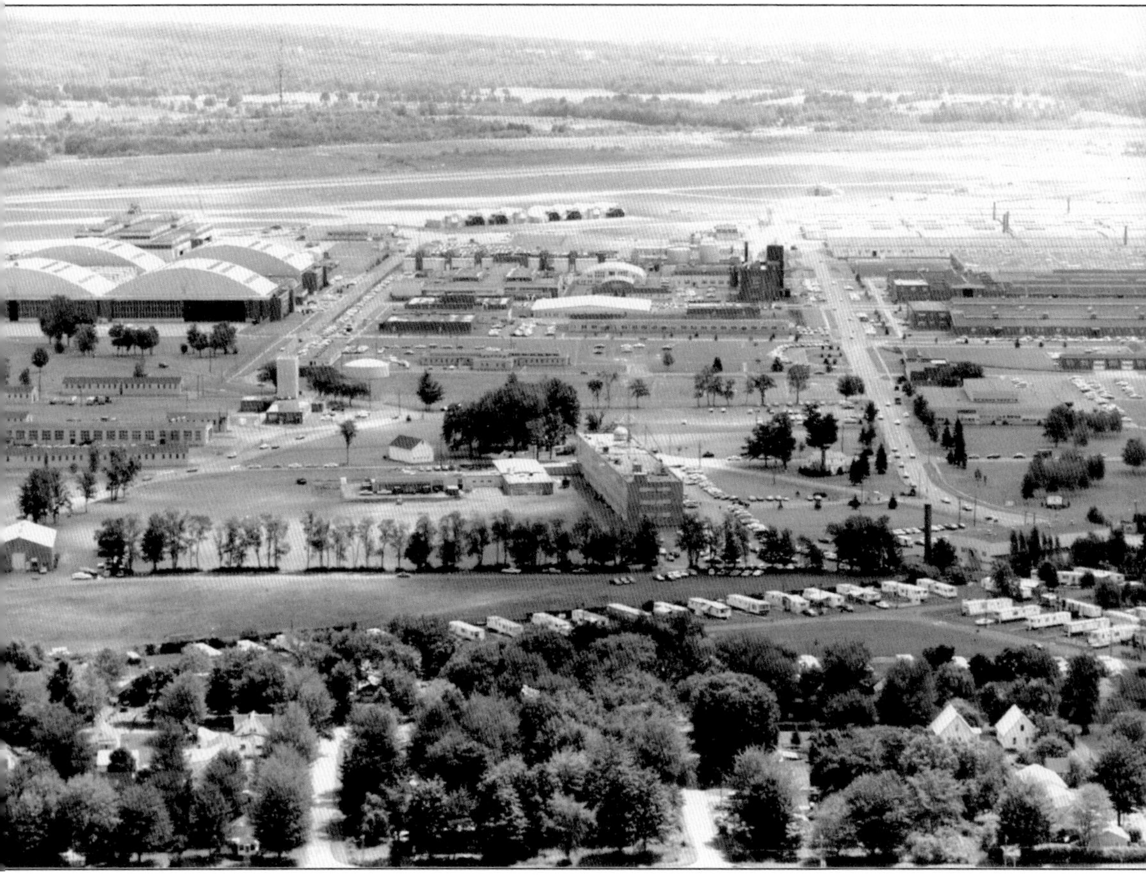

The Griffiss and Business Technology Park now stands on the 3,600 acres that was the Griffiss Air Force Base. Administered by the Griffiss Local Development Corporation, the technology park is bringing new kinds of industry to Rome. (RHS.)